Writing Ecofiction

Kevan Manwaring
Writing Ecofiction
Navigating the Challenges of Environmental Narrative

Kevan Manwaring
Graduate School
Arts University Bournemouth
Poole, UK

ISBN 978-3-031-55090-4   ISBN 978-3-031-55091-1 (eBook)
https://doi.org/10.1007/978-3-031-55091-1

© The Editor(s) (if applicable) and The Author(s), under exclusive license to Springer Nature Switzerland AG 2024

This work is subject to copyright. All rights are solely and exclusively licensed by the Publisher, whether the whole or part of the material is concerned, specifically the rights of translation, reprinting, reuse of illustrations, recitation, broadcasting, reproduction on microfilms or in any other physical way, and transmission or information storage and retrieval, electronic adaptation, computer software, or by similar or dissimilar methodology now known or hereafter developed.
The use of general descriptive names, registered names, trademarks, service marks, etc. in this publication does not imply, even in the absence of a specific statement, that such names are exempt from the relevant protective laws and regulations and therefore free for general use.
The publisher, the authors and the editors are safe to assume that the advice and information in this book are believed to be true and accurate at the date of publication. Neither the publisher nor the authors or the editors give a warranty, expressed or implied, with respect to the material contained herein or for any errors or omissions that may have been made. The publisher remains neutral with regard to jurisdictional claims in published maps and institutional affiliations.

Cover illustration: eStudio Calamar

This Palgrave Macmillan imprint is published by the registered company Springer Nature Switzerland AG
The registered company address is: Gewerbestrasse 11, 6330 Cham, Switzerland

If disposing of this product, please recycle the paper.

To all those using the arts to raise awareness about environmental issues.

Acknowledgements

Thank you to all the writers cited for their inspiration—especially those who generously responded to my questionnaire; and to all the students I have explored these issues, texts, and techniques with.

Contents

Part I   Taproots

1   Introduction   3
Identifying the Problem   3
Taproot Texts   6
Two Streams—The Novel and Nature Writing   12
New Nature Writing   14
Place Writing   16
Defining Ecofiction   16
Challenges and Limits   21
Using This Book   22
References   27

Part II   Branching Out

2   The Ground Beneath Your Feet   35
Starting From Where You Are   35
Acts of Perception   39
The Nature Table of the Notebook   44
Deep Mapping   47
The Weather in You   48
References   51

3 Going Beyond What You Know — 55
The Farthest Apple — 56
Ecology Without Theory — 58
Beyond Your Geography — 58
Beyond Your Temporality — 64
Beyond the White Picket Fence — 67
References — 72

4 Voices of the Global Majority — 75
Intersectionality — 79
Cultural Appropriation—The Lionel Shriver Position — 80
Approaching Writing the Other — 83
Let All Voices Be Heard — 84
Examples of the Global Majority in Ecofiction — 86
(Not) Another Brick in the Wall — 92
References — 94

5 Activism versus Art — 97
The Environmental Agenda — 99
The Agenda of Literature — 100
Some Examples — 103
Polonius Must Die: Practical Strategies — 115
Stealth Exposition — 116
The Democracy of Character — 118
(Don't) Bend the Plot — 119
Trust the Reader — 120
And Make the Reader Trust You — 121
Avoid Solutionism — 121
References — 124

6 Shaping a World in Flux — 129
Key Aspects of Form — 130
A River Runs Through It — 132
Making a Heap — 133
Intertextuality — 134
Archipelagic States — 135
Temporal Approaches — 136
Topographical Approaches — 142
Docemes — 143
Paratext — 144
Epistolary Devices — 145
New Media — 146

	The Non-linear and Biomimetic Structuring	146
	References	149
7	**One Man's Heaven**	153
	Utopias	153
	Dystopias	158
	Ustopias	159
	Thrutopias	163
	Solarpunk, Hopepunk, Green Stories	164
	Imagineering and Thinking Outside of the Box	167
	References	170
8	**The Rhizomatic Writer**	173
	Rhizomatic Thinking	174
	Emergent Forms	177
	Multimodality	178
	The Writer in the World	180
	A Potential Harvest	182
	References	184

Part III Interview

9	**Interviews**	189
	Adam Connor	189
	A. E. Copenhaver	192
	Ana Filomena Amaral	198
	Anna M. Holmes	200
	Anne Morddel	202
	Anthony Nanson	204
	April Doyle	206
	Austin Aslan	208
	David Barker	213
	Denise Baden	215
	Gill Lewis	220
	John Yunker	222
	Julie Carrick Dalton	224
	Lynn Buckle	227
	Manda Scott	230
	Mary Woodbury	232
	Michelle Cook	235

Midge Raymond	239
R.B. Kelly	243
Somto Ihezue	245
T.C. Boyle	247
Index	253

About the Author

Dr. Kevan Manwaring is Course Leader on the MA Creative Writing (online) and Senior Lecturer in Creative Writing at Arts University Bournemouth. He is the convenor of Writing the Earth—an annual programme of events for Earth Day. He is the author of *The Long Woman, Windsmith, The Well Under the Sea, The Burning Path, This Fearful Tempest, Lost Islands, Desiring Dragons*, contributor to *Storytelling for Nature Connection* (Hawthorn), *Coastal Environments in Popular Song* (Routledge Bioethics), and editor of *Heavy Weather: tempestuous tales of stranger climes* (The British Library). He has contributed articles to *Writing in Practice, New Writing, English Review,* and *Gothic Nature,* and *The New Nature Writing* editor for *Panorama: The Journal of Travel, Place, and Nature*. An academic consultant for BBC 4's *The Secret Life of Books*, and a contributor to BBC Radio 3's *Free Thinking*, he has much experience as a storyteller, poet, and guest speaker. He blogs as the Bardic Academic.

Part I

Taproots

1

Introduction

Identifying the Problem

In the opening scene of Jeff Nichols' climate apocalypse prepper movie, *Take Shelter* (2011), construction manager Curtis LaForche stands on his porch outside his house in Ohio staring at the sky on what appears to be a clear day—until we see his perspective: he watches a massive storm approach across the fields—a tornado-level vortex that looks strong enough to toss cars and cattle into the air, and turn homes to matchwood. No one else appears to be around; no one else seems to notice. Then it starts to rain: oil. It cuts to LaForche taking a shower, then quickly grabbing some breakfast, talking to his wife and signing to his deaf daughter, before heading out to work in his petrol-engine automobile—to his job in a large open cast mine. All seems normal (or rather petro-normative). LaForche's apocalyptic visions intensify, prompting him to renovate and extend the storm shelter in the family yard. He occasionally visits his dementia-suffering mother, and worries that he is rapidly heading the same way. Yet, Noah-like, he is convinced a meteorological armageddon is imminent, and prepares accordingly, his behaviour becoming more extreme. No one else notices the signs, such as birds falling dead from the sky. The film reaches a climax when LaForche locks his wife and child inside the shelter, apparently to protect them. In his psychosis has he become their captor? His wife begs him to unlock the hatch—but what will they find? Evidence of devastation, or of his madness? Until the final scene, Nichols' film cleverly sustains its ontological uncertainty—and thus affords intellectual room for different readings of the reality of Climate Change. Is LaForche just an unhinged 'prepper', or a man just trying to protect his family from a real threat? The drama allows a cross-section of perspectives about Climate Change to co-exist—from believer, to agnostic, to sceptic, to the atheistic (and the movie leans into the Biblical; although perhaps not as explicitly as Paul Schrader's 2018 film, *First Reformed*). This widens its potential audience and creates room for discussion. And it creates a strong visual metaphor for Climate Change—the reality of which back in 2011 was still up for heated debate (this continues today on extremist platforms, even though the evidence of it is before our eyes, and sometimes even on our doorstep). It is a Mortonesque 'hyper-object' (2013) that only some can perceive, suggests Nichols. This steers into the skid of the Climate denier's common spurious argument: the misunderstanding between weather and climate. Just because the *local weather* is fine, that doesn't mean the *seasons* are not being affected, and the *global climate* is not awry (as charts showing the unprecedented spike in carbon dioxide in the atmosphere prove; alongside many other scientifically-verifiable indicators).

As Fox Mulder's poster declaimed in *The X-Files*, 'The Truth Is Out There', although ironically it is the conspiracy theorist and oil-industry funded lobbyist who choose to deny it.

The United Nations has called Climate Change 'the defining crisis of our time' (UN 2019). But what exactly is the nature of this crisis? One only needs to scroll news platforms to see examples: an increasing frequency of extreme weather events; floods; deadly heat waves; tornadoes; wildfires; pandemics; retreat of glaciers and collapse of ice-sheets; lung and skin conditions; species extinction; habitat loss; acidification of the ocean; the ubiquity of plastics in the food chain and in ecosystems; decreasing yields; deforestation; thawing of the permafrost. The litany is long and chilling. There is a scientific consensus that Climate Change is a reality, as the Assessment Reports by the Intergovernmental Panel on Climate Change (1992–2022) has evidenced with increasing severity and urgency. Deniers and conspiracy theorists—funded by the oil lobby or fuelled by the extremist echo-chamber of social media—exist, but their viewpoints should not be taken seriously or given the oxygen of publicity, so I will not dwell upon them here beyond to acknowledge that any novel addressing the Climate Crisis in a contemporary setting should accept that a continuum of stances exists and these need to be factored into any dramatisation.

Whatever the hot air of Climate Deniers, many of whom are voluble and popular (Alt-Right influencers and demagogues have found it to be a winning formula—a consoling fiction that allows their followers to continue with their destructive, indulgent, and irresponsible lifestyles), the bedrock of evidence is literally to be found beneath our feet. The impact of anthropogenic Climate Change will be preserved in the fossil record, which is why the International Commission on Stratigraphy have decided that the world has entered a new epoch: the Anthropocene. The Cambridge Dictionary defines the Anthropocene as: 'the most recent period in the earth's history, when human activities have a very important effect on the earth's environment and climate (= weather conditions)'. The term is contentious and has been critiqued at length elsewhere—(Bould, 2021; MacFarlane, 2019; Oziewicz, et al, 2022; Parham, 2021) yet it has proven a useful 'umbrella term' and focus for discourse. After much debate it was decided that this new geological epoch began on 1945 with the explosion of atomic weapons in Hiroshima and Nagasaki. There was impact before this, as noted as early as the Eighteenth Century by John Ruskin, but the radioactive fallout of these explosions provides a clear marker point. More recently and tangibly, there have been repeated 'hottest year on record'. For millions, especially in the so-called Global South—another problematic term that risks totalising the broad spectrum of ethnicities, cultures, levels of development, disparities of wealth, etc., and one we shall interrogate more fully later—Climate Change has become a daily reality.

Despite various agreements and targets (from the Earth Summit in Rio 1992, onwards), including business-orientated concepts such as 'Sustainable Development' and 'Net Zero', which suggest eco-fixes with a Capitalist paradigm—some of which seem little more than greenwash—the overwhelming scientific consensus (Harvey 2022) is we will rapidly exceed the 1.5 degree Celsius 'Tipping Point', beyond which the impacts of Climate Change will accelerate exponentially. Indeed, as Rupert Read has pointed out (2022) we need to accept the impossibility of keeping levels below this much-cited IPCC target—the 'cruel optimism' of that particular 'climate story'—and accelerate any ameliorating endeavours accordingly.

And so is any endeavour too little, too late?

Arguably, perhaps, but human imagination and ingenuity is fathomless, and we have long narrativised uncertainty as a way of navigating it. Storytelling, in spoken, written and emergent forms, is one of the most effective tools for raising awareness, motivating, inspiring, and strengthening communities (Gersie et al. 2014; Nanson 2021).

It is only one of a raft of solutions and measures needed, but as Ben Okri (2021), Rob Hopkins (2019), Roman Krznaric (2020), George Monbiot (2019), Jonathan Porrit (2013), Rebecca Solnit (2023), and others have argued, imagination and creativity are essential tools.

Solnit argues: 'What the climate crisis is, what we can do about it, and what kind of a world we can have is all about what stories we tell and whose stories are heard' (2023).

Writer and Barrister, Charles Foster, commenting on his book, *Cry of the Wild* (2023), which focuses on eight species (orca, fox, otter, rabbit, gannet, eel, mayfly, and human) and how they co-exist, observed how it is the smaller stories that affect us: 'We can't bring ourselves to care sufficiently about climate change, mass extinction etc. It all seems too abstract and too remote. We're only moved and convinced by little, local, personal stories because we are little, local personal people' (2023).

And so let us now turn to early examples of these stories, going back to some of the earliest in recorded civilisation.

Taproot Texts

Writers have been exploring ecological concerns for centuries, even millennia—from the anonymous authors of 'Gilgamesh' and 'Gawain and the Green Knight', to Mary Shelley, John Ruskin, Margaret Attwood, Barbara Kingsolver, Richard Flanagan, Jennette Winterson, and Richard Powers—but it is in recent years that such writing has gained increasing poignancy and urgency.

In 1999, John Clute defined his term, 'Taproot Texts': 'Only in the last decades of the Eighteenth Century, when (at least in the West) a HORIZON OF EXPECTATIONS emerged among writers and readers did a delimitable genre now called FANTASY appear. Before that there were writing which included the FANTASTIC—and such works can be described as taproot texts' (1999: 921). Clute deploys Hans Robert Jauss' term, and elsewhere defines this as 'the context within which a given generation of readers will understand a work' (1999: 478). In terms of ecofiction, this horizon is Climate Change, or awareness of it, and so earlier works are unlikely to demonstrate this explicitly. They may contain proto-ecological aspects, but may not be considered bona fide 'ecofiction', but nevertheless remain seminal in some way. And that is where the notion of the 'taproot text' becomes useful. In this chapter, we'll extend this organic metaphor to include the critical discourses and wider reading that inform the ideation of 'Ecofiction'. But, to begin with, let us conduct a brief survey of some key taproot texts.

The earliest recorded narratives show elements of 'ecofiction'. In myths and legends, such as Creation Myths, and Flood Myths, there are discernible environmental aspects. It could be argued that the first stories emerged to narrativize the precarity of humanity in the face of powerful, and sometimes catastrophic, environmental factors: inundation, drought, violent storms, tsunamis, earthquakes, wildfires caused by lightning strikes and heatwaves, blizzards, and so forth. Karen Armstrong argues that the Palaeolithic hunter developed myth, 'to reconcile himself to the tragic facts of life that threatened to overwhelm him, and prevent him from acting effectively' (2005: 32). This could be a definition of ecofiction: narratives that help avoid nihilism and paralysis by narrativising both the challenges we face and, *critically,* a way through. Hence the inherent usefulness of myth, and all of its branches on the tree of story—legend, folk tale, fairy tale, and fiction. It is a map of metaphors, not a dogma—at best, a 'guide to behaviour' (ibid. 2005: 22). Evolving from 'profound anxiety about essentially practical problems which cannot be assuaged by purely logical arguments', (ibid.: 30) '[m]ythology is the discourse we need in extremity' (ibid.: 35).

Myths, legends, folk tales, and fairy tales often have a moral element, conveying ethical codes, and salutary warnings about what happens when these codes are transgressed (Bettelheim 1976 [1991]; Zipes 1983; Warner 1995). The breaking of taboos, especially around the perceived natural order, and the sanctity of certain places (trees, rocks, springs, caves) and animals, is often the narrative catalyst—so many cautionary tales, many of which have an ecological subtext. Let us look at some specific examples to illustrate this point.

In the Persian Creation Myth, as recorded by the Iranian poet Firdausi in the epic poem, *Shah-Nāma,* the King-Book, a Manichean cosmology is set out: Omuzd creating all that is good and light in the world; against Ahrimān, who is the personification of darkness and evil. While Ormuzd is for life, peace, truth, and plenty; Ahrimān is for death, war, lies, and destruction. They are locked in eternal enmity. Next, we are told of the first king, Keyumars, who ruled over the whole world. A mountain-dweller, he wore the skins of leopards, and was just and wise. His people lived on the wild fruits and roots which they gathered, and wore clothes of leaves, and seemed to exist in prelapsarian bliss at one with nature. But there was an enemy of happiness, Ahrimān, the 'father of all ill', who sent the Black Demon to make war upon Keyumans and his people. The King's son, Siyāmek, went into battle but was slain. The King was heartbroken, but with the aid of Husheng, his grandson, rallied. Keyumans called forth not only his people, but all the wild animals, to fight against Ahrimān. Leopards, lions, tigers, the ox, the ass, and the horse, and all the birds of the air came forth to help. The King put Husheng in charge of this army of the wild, which clashes with the agents of Ahrimān in a mighty battle. Husheng smote down the Black Demon and struck off its head. The death of his son avenged, Keyumans died, passing on his crown and realm to Husheng. In Husheng's reign, humankind developed agriculture: learning to irrigate the land to grow crops, so they were no longer reliant upon the vicissitudes of hunting and gathering. Iron ore was discovered, and tools were forged to till the soil. And the secret of fire was discovered.

And so we can see in this Persian Creation Myth how humankind developed from a hunter-gatherer society into an agrarian one, and how the first kingdoms prospered because the people learned to live in harmony with the land and all that lived upon it. Of course, the discovery of iron, agriculture, and fire ultimately leads to the Industrial Revolution, and the Climate Crisis of the Anthropocene. But it is clear in this one example how intrinsic environmental factors were in these founding myths. The destiny of the land and its people were one: a critical reciprocity is personified by conflict between cosmological forces, but is ultimately played out on terra firma. When a ruler is just and wise, the land prospers and the people reap the benefits. This sets up the archetypal motif of the health of the land and its ruler being intrinsically entwined—a motif that eventually found its way to Western Europe and the figure of the Fisher King in Arthurian Tradition (Clarke 2001). And yet this sense of personal accountability is there in the earliest myths.

In the *Epic of Gilgamesh,* recorded on a series of clay tablets from Ancient Mesopotamia—fragile, shattered fragments discovered in the Nineteenth Century by archaeologists digging in what is now modern-day Iraq—we have perhaps the first depiction of *ecocide*, the concept of making corporations and governments accountable for intentional environmental destruction, which the late English lawyer Polly Higgins campaigned to have enshrined in international law (Higgins 2010). Gilgamesh is a Sumerian king proudly ruling over the proto-city of Babylon. He befriends a wild man called Enkidu—who enjoys all the freedom that the king, burdened with responsibility, can no longer enjoy. Together, they fight the demon Humbaba, who is set on destroying the city. They slay the demon and cut down the sacred cedar wood where it lived. In the fight Enkidu is fatally wounded, and Gilgamesh, stricken with grief, journeys to the Underworld to try to restore his friend to life, but fails: the Flower of Life which he retrieves after great effort and hardship, is eaten by a snake as the hero sleeps, exhausted from his ordeal. The King returns to his city, a chastened man. It is surprisingly melancholic cautionary tale about the 'cost' of civilisation: one risks not only forsaking the wild part of oneself, but also the connection to the inherent sacredness of nature. A fallen world, thinned out by disenchantment and grief, is the result. Sometimes referred to as the 'first novel', *The Epic of Gilgamesh*, could be arguably the first ecofiction too. It has cast a long shadow, manifesting in various adaptations, but also perhaps foreshadowing elements of *Beowulf, Sir Gawain and the Green Knight, Robin Hood, La Morte D'arthur*, and other classics.

In the 2020–2021 lockdowns in the UK, the writer Robert Macfarlane and singer-songwriter Johnny Flynn collaborated on a song-cycle based upon the epic, *Lost in the Cedar Wood* (2021). As a creative response to the bewilderment and rewilding of that period, Macfarlane and Flynn said: 'We began just wanting to make music together in response to (defence against) those dangerous, disorientating spring days, when birdsong was brighter—and the sense of bewilderment more powerful—than any of us had known before' (sleeve notes). The opening words on the first of the twelve clay tablets (originally translated, in part, by working-class autodidact George Smith, who taught himself Assyrian), reads: He Who Looked Into The Abyss. Macfarlane and Flynn said, '*Gilgamesh* seized both our imaginations at a time when we were all looking 'into the abyss". This shows how myths can speak to us across the millennia, and how narrative can help us navigate uncertain, challenging times.

Creation Myths often give significant roles to women—renowned as the creators of life in many cultures, but often subsumed within a hegemonic patriarchy. In the *Divine Feminine* exhibition at the British Museum in 2021, a formidable array of Creatrixes were on display:

Shintoism (The Way of the Spirits) is based on the relationship between people and the natural world. Izanami-no-mikoto (She Who Beckons) is a Shinto creator spirit, who alongside her sometimes lover, Izanagi-no-mikoto (He Who Beckons), brought forth the archipelago of Japan and the numerous spirits of Shinto cosmology. Izanami-no-mikoto dies in childbirth, and descends to the Underworld. When Izanagi journeys there to retrieve her and is confronted by her putrefying body, he has second thoughts and flees. She chases, but is finally escaped. The myth seems to suggest there are consequences to creation. The shadow side of the feminine is symbolic of the 'shadow' of nature: we cannot have fertility without decay, life without death.

Staying on the Pacific Rim, and travelling south to Aotearoa/New Zealand, we find an Earth Mother figure, Papatūānuku, the Maori creatrix alongside the sky father, Ranginui. She embodies *mana wahine*—female power and potency, which for some men is as terrifying as Izanami-no-mikoto. Another strong female deity is Pele, the Hawaiian goddess of volcanoes, who is also known by the epithet: Eater of the Land. With her flaming red hair and fierce temper, she can take the form of all-consuming lava. And yet volcanic eruptions can create new land and new life, as the recently emerged Surtsey

Island, part of the Vestmannaeyjar island group off Iceland, has shown. Only appearing in 1964, it has been carefully preserved and monitored as a living laboratory revealing how life first emerged on land.

In the Arctic and Sub-Arctic, the Inuit people venerate Sedna, the Mistress of the Sea, who offers up her bounty to those who take care of her. If her children are disrespected through exploitation and disregard of sacred hunting rites, she hides them in her hair, causing hunts to fail and hunger to ensue. A contemporary, Secondary World variant of this can be seen in James Cameron's mega-budget sequel to his *Avatar* (2009)—the most successful film of all time, grossing nearly three billion dollars—*Avatar: The Way of Water* (2022), where the 'Sky People'(rapacious, vengeful human colonizers) hunt Tulkuns, massive cetacean-like creatures prized for their valuable oil, only for the indigenous Metkayina to be radicalised into becoming agents of ecological resistance. Despite the weakness of characterisation, dialogue, and plot, the ecologically-flavoured mythopoeia (a Gaia-like planetary-wide consciousness; the complex biodiversity of rainforests and reefs; catastrophic destruction of nature and indigenous tribal hunting grounds, including 'sacred' trees straight out of the *Gilgamesh* playbook) of Cameron's vast canvas is inculcating an environmental awareness into its audience of millions.

Other creator goddesses include Laksmi, the Hindu goddess of abundance; Oshun, the Yoruba *orisha* ('forces governing all aspects of the natural world and human experience') of water and life; and Mami Wata, a single or collective spirit of water and wealth worshipped across Africa, South America, and the Caribbean.

Tales of the creation, destruction, and rebirth of the Earth and all living things are found all over the world, from the stories of the Aboriginal Dreamtime describing how the windings of the Rainbow Serpent created the world; to Ragnarok as described in the Poetic Edda of the Norse Tradition—where a giant serpent, Nidhug, gnaws at the based on the World Tree, Yggdrasil; and Thor wrestles with Jörmungandr, the World Serpent who encircles Midgard, biting its own tail. When the death of Baldur triggers a calamitous series of events resulting in the Twilight of the Gods, the world is beset by the ferocious Fimbulwinter, Fenris the Wolf eats the sun, and all life is destroyed except for Ask and Edda, Adam and Eve figures who emerge in the aftermath of this apocalypse to repeople the Earth.

Myths of inundation are perhaps the most ubiquitous of taproot texts—from Utnapishtim, a Noah-like figure, in *The Epic of Gilgamesh,* to Noah himself. The fortunate, devout, or simply prepared—depending on your perspective—are saved from the Great Deluge, given a second chance to amend for the errors of humanity and live a better life: the ultimate 'redraft'.

A key element of Creation Myths that is rarely acknowledged is that someone created them. The exact process of authorship is often very obscure, except in more recent attempts at mythopoeia (e.g. the Finnish national epic, the Kalevala, which was largely the work of Elias Lönnrot). Creation Myths are often co-authored texts created orally over a long period of time in an organic folk process, as in the Aboriginal Dreamtime stories, or the Tibetan epic, The Gesar of Ling. Of course, when these are written down a more conventional orthography can be gleaned. Yet it is interesting to note that Creation Myths inevitably feature creator gods and goddesses (such as their sine qua non) who bring the world into being in the ultimate act of 'authorship'. And this is mirrored, in microcosm, by the teller of these tales (often a highly ritualised act to emphasise the 'sacred' nature of the material) with their speech acts. In the beginning was the Word, according to the Christian tradition, and the Word has to manifest to have effectiveness. As Karen Armstrong iterates, a myth is only a stepping stone: 'Its truth will only be revealed if it is put into practice—ritually or ethically' (ibid. 1995: 22). However obscure some may seem to us today, from this end of history, it is good to remember that myths spoke in the language of metaphors, of symbolism, *familiar to the intended audience*. This can still be experienced in recitals of The Book of Genesis: a highly stylised, archaic, eccentric, and scientifically inaccurate version of the creation of the world, but one that is comprehensible to most modern congregations, because the symbolism is so familiar: it has become hardwired into Western cultural DNA after two millennia of dissemination. A myth is a transmission whose effectiveness is contingent upon the quality of its receiver. This is another cornerstone principle that can be applied to ecofiction, which first and foremost needs to communicate effectively. The ideas and solutions are available, but as Solnit argues, we need new narratives to help raise awareness about them and to shift popular misconceptions about what difference we can make on an individual, community, and governmental level: a 'literature of hope'. Bleak dystopias, which once provided salutary warnings about worst-case scenarios but which now suffer from a surfeit, foreclose on the future and encourage doomism:

> There are so many doom-soaked stories out there – about how civilisation, humanity, even life itself, are scheduled to die out. This apocalyptic thinking is due to another narrative failure: the inability to imagine a world different than the one we currently inhabit. (Solnit 2023)

We need to imagine the world differently, but that begins with imagining new narratives—ones that resist the formulaic. Innovation occurs when two or more disparate influences converge, and that is the case with (the best of) ecofiction.

Two Streams—The Novel and Nature Writing

Ecofiction has emerged out of the conjoining of two distinct strands—the novel, and nature writing. In terms of the novel, it is in the Medieval form of the Romance that one finds the strongest influence. The term derives from the Old French, *roman,* (still used for the modern idea of a novel in France), courtly stories in verse about the adventures of King Arthur, Charlemagne, or classical heroes like Alexander the Great. These emerged in the Middle Ages and were very popular. By the Thirteenth Century they were being translated into Early English, and included *Sir Orfeo, King Horn,* and *Havelok.* One of the most famous, drawing upon this tradition but situating it within a distinctive landscape (another key aspect of ecofiction) was composed by an anonymous poet from the north of England in the Fourteenth Century: *Sir Gawain and the Green Knight.* One Christmas into Arthur's court appears the Green Knight, who challenges those gathered to the Beheading Game: he will take one blow, but whoever deals the blow will have to receive one in exchange a year hence, if he survives. Arthur's bold young nephew, Gawain, volunteers, and strikes off the Green Knight's head. However, to the young knight's horror, the beheaded figure gets up, picks up his head, and, reminding Gawain of his obligation, rides off. Gawain has a whole year to dwell on his fate, before he sets off into the wild fastnesses of the north to find the Green Chapel. After an arduous journey, he finds shelter and hospitality at the home of Sir Bertilak, a merry huntsman, and his wife. There the virtuous young knight is tested. Each day the lady tempts him with kisses, and the lord asks for what he has 'won'. On the final day, the lady gives him a green garter to protect him. Gawain sets off to the Green Chapel nearby. Here he receives the blow, but survives—shamed by the protection of the green garter. Returning to Court, this becomes a badge of honour and is adopted by Arthur, who forms the Order of the Green Garter.

The Green Knight is the very personification of untamed nature. His arrival brings the wild, and the more-than-human, into the civilised space of the Court. Something vital is at risk of being forgotten, even in Camelot. As with Gilgamesh and Humbaba, Hrothgar and Grendel, this is ecological karma at work. A rewilding, metaphoric or literal, needs to take place. The protagonist is forced out of their comfort zone into the wilderness, where they are tested. The sense of place, of the untamed spaces beyond the purview of civilisation, is vividly evoked by the Gawain poet. The 'hunting game' played inadvertently with Lord and Lady Bertilak, where the bloody spoils of the hunt are exchanged for kisses won within comfortable chambers—the entwined forces of thanatos and eros—are symbolic of the ecological cost of human society, but also a kind of ecosystem in itself: reciprocal, but not in a quid pro quo way. The 'green fuse', as Dylan Thomas puts it, is circulated about. The Green Chapel is the epitome of the inherent sanctity of nature. The Green Knight is its personification. The fate facing Gawain one that humanity faces in the Anthropocene: it is time to face the consequences of an unsustainable carbon-dependent lifestyle. It a scene of ultimate eco-justice—terrifyingly harsh, but if survived, one that can be chastening and galvanising. Humankind could adopt the 'green garter' to symbolise its commitment to the planet—the various Climate Agreements are a version of this, although they mean nothing unless honoured by all.

Yet, we can see in the *Gawain* poem how all the most positive and powerful elements of ecofiction are there in embryo. Margaret Drabble sums up the Romance by emphasising its ethicality: 'Defining them by theme is very difficult; they usually involve the suspension of the circumstances normally attendant on human actions (often through magic) in order to illustrate a moral point' (1985: 842).

The other main influence on the evolution of ecofiction is to be found in Nature Writing. Acknowledging that this is a much-contested term that has been discussed at length elsewhere (Prentiss and Wilkins 2016; Lilley 2017; Smith 2018) I just want to acknowledge some of the key texts that have helped shape this tradition, e.g. *A Natural History of Selborne* (1789); *Journals of Dorothy Wordsworth* (1897); *Walden, or A Life in the Woods* (1854); *South Country* (1909); *My First Summer in the Sierra* (1911), *Pilgrim at Tinker Creek* (1974); and *The Living Mountain* (1977), to name a few.

Critiques of nature writing include that it has been (until relatively recently) Anglocentric and western-focused; white; male-dominated; neo-colonialist; and that it perpetuates other hegemonic discourses. Recent critiques have included Charles Foster, who has written 'Against Nature Writing' (Emergence Magazine 2021); and Richard Smyth's article, 'Nature writing's fascist roots' (The New Statesman 2019). Foster himself is a nature writer, barrister, and Fellow of Green Templeton College, University of Oxford, and it seems very exclusionary and elitist of him to slam the gates shut when so many much-needed non-white, non-male, non-binary perspectives are starting to see print. Smyth's critique hinges upon only three writers:

Henry Williamson, TH White, and Paul Kingsnorth—I think it unreasonable to condemn a whole tradition because of three writers with problematic views: they are not representative of anything other than themselves. There are many other voices and perspectives out there, and many of these are part of a 'second wave', evolving Nature Writing into the Twenty-first Century: New Nature Writing.

New Nature Writing

In 2008 *Granta* editor Jason Cowley posited a 'new nature writing', with his selection of creative non-fiction pieces covering travel, place, and nature writing, but move those respective traditions forward via a heightened sensitivity to the complicity and precarity of humans as an apex species, works that 'share a sense that we are devouring our world, that there is simply no longer any natural landscape or ecosystem that is unchanged by humans' (Cowley 2008). Acknowledging a tendency for previous writers to lapse into reverie and romanticisation, Cowley argues that this new wave 'don't simply want to walk into the wild, to rhapsodize and commune: they aspire to see with a scientific eye and write with literary effect' (ibid.).

Lilley, in her critical survey and of New Nature Writing suggests its distinguishing feature: 'Here, ecological crisis is framed not simply as the provocation for these new writings about nature, but also as a provocation that demands new ways of writing about nature' (Lilley 2017). Eschewing the 'scientific eye' and 'rhapsodizing' poles of earlier nature writing, Lilley argues that this emerging form is less empirical and omniscient ('made more urgent, and less certain by ecological crisis'), with a sharp awareness, at best, of any kind of privilege in its gaze. Indeed, the critical gaze is turned inward, not outward, as Macfarlane acknowledges in his own survey serialised in *The Guardian*, 'Only Connect': 'the real subject of landscape writing is not landscape, but a restructuring of the human attitude towards nature' (2005). The directionality of this new nature writing helps it to avoid the well-trodden paths of previous generations—as Kathleen Jamie suggests in her own writing, it is writing 'towards', not 'about' the natural world (2016).

Identifying traits in New Nature Writing include: 'a pervasive current of self consciousness' (Lilley 2017); 'constant culpability' (Jamie 2011); writing that demonstrates an awareness of the Climate Emergency; an emphasis on the subjective experience; a distinct situatedness; intersectionality; criticality of hegemonic discourses and traditions; experimentation; hybrid forms (often a combination of travel-writing, nature writing, and memoir).

New Nature Writing is proving to be a popular form, and often dominates the front of bookshops (in Britain and Ireland). It works best when it is focused on a single, embodied experience—scenes of visceral immediacy interwoven with personal reflections and associations. It is distinguished by writing that looks inward as well as outward, acknowledging the fallacy of omniscience, the fallibility of the author, and the bittersweet imperfections that entangle the epiphanies. Grounded in place as much as grounded in a sense of self, New Nature Writing welcomes in the marginalised and intersectional—giving voice to those who have not been traditionally represented in the so-called canon.

Without limiting its wide-ranging possibilities, good examples include *Arctic Dreams* (Lopez 1986); *Waterlog* (Deakin 1999); *The Wild Places* (Macfarlane 2017); *Soil and Soul* (McIntosh 2004); *The Salt Path* (Wynn 2019); *Wild* (Strayed 2015); *Wild: an element journey* (Griffiths 2008); *A Walk in the Woods* (Bryson 1998); *Crow Country* (Cocker 2008); *The Summer Isles* (Marsden 2020); *The Snow Geese* (Fiennes 2002); *H is for Hawk* (Macdonald 2014); *Deep Country: five years in the Welsh hills* (Ansell 2011); *The Outrun* (Liptrott 2016); *Findings*, and *Surfacing* (Jamie 2005, 2020); *I Belong Here* (Sethi 2021), *The Grassling* (Burnett 2020); *The Book of Trespass* (Hayes 2021); *Thin Places* (Dochartaigh 2022); *Diary of a Young Naturalist* (McNulty 2020); *Where the Wild Winds Are* (Hunt 2018); *The January Man* (Somerville 2017); *Silence: in the age of noise* (Kagge 2017); *Ghost Land: in search of a haunted country* (Parnell 2020); *The Wood: the life and times of Cockshutt Wood* (Lewis-Stempel 2018); *Heavy Light* (Clare 2022); *Underland: a Deep Time journey* (Macfarlane 2019); and *On Gallows Down* (Chester 2022). An eclectic, ever-expanding list, but one that illustrates a shift in scale, urgency, gaze, and voice, as Lilley emphasizes: 'The new British nature writing is new because the scale of the environmental harm is new, and because British authors have written in distinctly new ways in response' (2017). Of course, many works that could be loosely defined as new nature writing as being published across the world (Robin Wall Kimmerer's 2015 *Braiding Sweetgrass* is just one example), but perhaps Britain can be taken as a key trailblazer because of its long tradition, and because of its overwhelming need to challenge that—to exorcise its own colonial ghosts.

Every year dozens of new titles emerge, and the form is being actively encouraged in Britain by the Wainwright Prize for UK Nature and Conservation, and The Richard Jefferies Award, publications such as *Panorama: the journal of travel, place, and nature,* and by the range of undergraduate and postgraduate degrees being offered at universities across the world, which explore nature writing in various ways. Thanks to these efforts—by publishers, booksellers, libraries, HEIs, and literary prizes—New Nature Writing is in rude health.

Place Writing

Place Writing intersects with both nature writing and ecofiction, with the caveat that place writing is primarily creative non-fiction. Certainly, ecofiction may well have strong elements of place writing, for, as Robert Macfarlane acknowledges: 'Placeless events are inconceivable, in that everything that happens must happen somewhere, and so history issues from geography in the same way that water issues from a spring: unpredictably but site-specifically' (Macfarlane 2007: 113). Place writing is an elusive term, a 'fuzzy set', but Cooper and Lichtenstein do well to delineate it: 'Place writing, as showcased by Evans and Robson, is characterised by an attentiveness to the textural particularities of specific sites: an attentiveness that is often generated through the embodied experience of walking through-place. By extension, place writing invites readers to find ways of (re)connecting with the material landscape' (What is Place Writing? David Cooper and Rachel Lichtenstein 2020). So, Place Writing, if not just a subset of Nature Writing, could be added to the Venn diagram of ecofiction.

Successful elements of all of these forms—nature writing/place writing/ecofiction—include: adopting a personal perspective; going for a niche angle; embodied; embedded; a hybrid approach—e.g. nature/memoir/travel; a strong sense of place; placiality and specificity; the avoidance of romanticisation, nostalgia, and valorisation (Jamie's 'lone, enraptured male'); eschewing any false claims to omniscience by acknowledging fallibility; celebrating the commonplace; honouring the marginalised.

And so, by listing such criteria, we are drawing close to a definition via a convergence of streams. Let us now attempt to pin this down.

Defining Ecofiction

As I have charted above, ecofiction—in its broadest sense as nature-predicated narratives—has deep taproots and has existed in various, embryonic forms for centuries if not millennia, but as a term, it first emerged in the Twentieth

Century amid the Counterculture of the Sixties and Seventies, when environmentalism became part of the growing antihegemonic lexicon of rebellion. It is defined in *The Cambridge History of the American Novel* (2011), as follows:

> Ecofiction is an elastic term, capacious enough to accommodate a variety of fictional works that address the relationship between natural settings and the human communities that dwell within them. The term emerged soon after ecology took hold as a popular scientific paradigm and a broad cultural attitude in the 1960s and 1970s.

The authors cite Rachel Carson's *Silent Spring* (1962) as a seminal text in this shift of awareness. They also acknowledge the influence of the developing field of ecology, which gave scientists a deeper awareness of the interconnectedness of biota and habitats within the biosphere. First formatted by the discoveries in evolutionary theory during the Nineteenth Century, ecology became 'the default framework through which many people would view the natural world' (ibid.). As this ecosystem of consciousness and reciprocity gained traction within the scientific community, so did it start to gain credence and kudos in the Counterculture, manifesting in popular culture: in movies, marches, campaign groups, exhibitions, albums, wholefood shops, and 'back to the land' initiatives, as exemplified by the *Whole Earth Catalog* (1968–1971), which could be seen as an alternative ur-text.

Providing food for thought and helping to fuel this paradigm shift was fiction—often within the spectrum of Fantasy, Speculative Fiction, and Science Fiction—which dramatised this eco-consciousness. John Stadler's anthology of environmental sci-fi, *Eco-fiction* (Washington Press 1971), which featured a cross-section of classic and contemporary authors from Isaac Asimov to Kurt Vonnegut Jr, Daphne du Maurier to JG Ballard, pioneered the ideation of the form, although it had less impact than standalone titles such as Aldous Huxley's *Island* (1960) or Frank Herbert's *Dune* (1965).

If Stadler's anthology can be thought of an Anthropocene-like marker in the literary strata, with everything preceding it being 'Early Period' ecofiction, then one influential example of the form in its 'Middle Period' (which arguably ended in 1992 with the Earth Summit in Rio) is Ernest Callenbach's *Ecotopia*, which first appeared in the *Oregon Times* between October and November 1975. Told from the initially sceptical viewpoint of Weston, a reporter who is sent on assignment to investigate the titular nation state (formed when Northern California, Oregon, and Washington seceded from the Union), it describes the environmental solutions the citizens have adopted to address the multiple challenges of an impactful, developed country from energy, education, entertainment, and employment, to ethics and sexual politics. Although a product of its time in its depiction of a liberal, communitarian, free love society at 'one with the land', if published now, *Ecotopia* would be categorised as Solarpunk—environmentally-conscious speculative fiction that seeks to dramatise positive visions of the future, in contrast to the ubiquity of dystopian near future scenarios that have increasingly saturated fiction and film since the late Sixties (*The Planet of the Apes* (1968); *Silent Running* (1972); *Blade Runner* (1982) *Terminator 2: Judgement Day* (1991); *The Day After Tomorrow* (2004); *The Road* (2009); *The Quiet Place* (2018), being just a cross-section of examples).

Ecofiction has become an increasingly tangible marketing category, with a spate of articles identify texts—from classics to recent publications. Each of these articles (e.g. Christie 2020; Munteanu 2021) offers a variation on the basic definition—novels that foreground environmental issues. Jim Dwyer, in *Where the Wild Books Are: A Field Guide to Eco-Fiction* (2010) draws upon Lawrence Buell's criteria to chart the burgeoning field:

- The non-human environment is present not merely as a framing device but as a presence that begins to suggest that human history is implicated in natural history.
- The human history is not understood to be the only legitimate interest.
- Human accountability to the environment is part of the text's ethical orientation.
- Some sense of the environment as a process rather than as a constant or a given is at least implicit in the text. (1995: 6)

An alternative, more recent, term for ecofiction is 'Climate Fiction' or 'Cli-Fi'—writing that takes climate change and global warming as its inspiration, foregrounding the environmental crisis through a fictional lens. Cli-Fi is indistinguishable from ecofiction, except for it being more commonly used in the marketing copy of recent titles than the earlier term, and in magazines and blogs such as 'So You Want to Read Cli-Fi?'.

The Climate Fiction Writers League founded by former physicist Lauren James (author of the 2021 YA ecofiction, *Green Rising*, and others) eschew a precise definition of 'Climate Fiction', but emphasise the need to create positive, empowering narratives to inspire readers:

> The climate debate needs to move beyond fear at rising sea levels and pollution towards a more solutions-based view on climate change. I feel strongly that we should not be telling a generation of children that their future is unavoidably broken. Change is possible. The climate crisis is an urgent, yet utterly solvable issue. Our fiction should reflect that.

How does ecofiction differ, if at all, from New Nature Writing?

Well, the essential difference is in the form—the former is fiction, the latter is creative non-fiction. Key concepts that help to define modern ecofiction in its 'Late Period' (1992–) include: placiality (Casey 1998); planetarity (Spivak 2017); autogeography (Steinberg 1976); placelessness (Massey 1995); and transgeographical identity (Fermour 1977).

Firstly, let us look at 'Placiality'. Casey emphasises the fundamental importance of place: 'we are implaced beings to begin with, that place is an a priori of our existence on earth' (1998: x). Resisting the colonising of 'place' by 'space', which Casey memorably describes as 'a cosmic and extracosmic Moloch that consumes every corpuscle of place to be found within its greedy reach' (ibid.). This absorption into the wider term has resulted in 'place' being relegated to mere 'location'. Casey takes a phenomenological approach in his reclamation of the term. Stephen Hardy, in his analysis of Casey's concept, carefully parses the concepts of 'space' and 'place'—acknowledging that, although the latter could be considered a subcategory of the former, our relationship with it is qualitatively different. As Casey himself puts it: 'Place is a part of space which a body takes up' (1998: 150). Following in the footsteps of Husserl, Heidegger, Merleau-Ponty, and Deleuze, Casey sees place as something that is experienced in a proprioceptive, multi-layered way: what could be called the 'affect'. Hardy, Stephen Paul. 'Placiality: The renewal of the significance of place in modern cultural theory' (2001: 85–100).

Philosopher David Kolb summarises Casey's ideation effectively: 'Casey's overall idea is that place is not simple location in uniform geometrical space, but concrete bodily locatedness. Place is qualitative, relational and textured, enclosing and defining. The opening of place happens in the intertwining of nature and the lived body'.

Scaling up placiality, we arrive at Spivak's planetarity.

Spivak outlined her ideation of Planetarity, as cited below. Spivak is at pains to disassociate this from globalisation, which she critiques as 'the imposition of the same system of exchange everywhere'. In direct resistance to this default capitalist discourse, she sums up Planetarity as 'socialism at its best': it is communality on a planet-wide scale. Yet, beyond the Marxism, such a concept offers a sympathetic frame for alterity: for a world where we can hear the 'subaltern' speak.

> The planet is in the species of alterity, belonging to another system; and yet we inhabit it, on loan. It is not really amenable to a neat contrast with the globe. I cannot say 'the planet, on the other hand.' When I invoke the planet, I think of the effort required to figure the (im)possibility of this underived intuition…. Planet-thought opens up to embrace an inexhaustible taxonomy

of such names, including but not identical with the whole range of human universals.... If we imagine ourselves as planetary creatures rather than global entities, alterity remains underived from us; it is not our dialectical negation, it contains us as much as it flings us away. (Spivak, cited by Majumder 2017)

Another increasingly important concept in a world where enforced migration—due to conflict, ecological disaster, economic factors, religious persecution has created millions of refugees and asylum seekers—is 'placelessness'. On a very real human level, this is literally being without a home—a country, but beyond these humanitarian concerns (and Human Rights), there is another valuation of the term, which sees it as a positive, not a negative status. It is a more porous sense of place. Massey articulates this:

> It is a sense of place, an understanding of its 'character', which can only be constructed by linking that place to places beyond. A progressive sense of place would recognize that, without being threatened by it. What we need, it seems to me, is a global sense of the local, a global sense of place.' (Massey 1994: 177)

This is best expressed as transgeographical identity, something which certain writers have felt, in particular Patrick Leigh Fermour, who has something of an epiphany on his famous walk from Rotterdam to Istanbul, which he recorded in his journal at the time, and later refined for *A Time of Gifts* (1977):

> The notion that I had walked twelve hundred miles since Rotterdam filled me with a legitimate feeling of something achieved. But why should the thought that nobody knew where I was, as though I were in flight from bloodhounds or from worshipping corybants bent on dismemberment, generate such a feeling of triumph? It always did.

The opposite of this could be seen as 'autogeography'—a deep sense of situatedness within a particular landscape. Steinberg, Saul, in his: 'View of the World from 9th Avenue & Steinbergian Cartography' (1976) depicted a very subjectivised 'map' of the world, as viewed from his New York apartment.

> Over a plain meanders the river of Steinberg's life, weaving among dozens of place names sized and sited according to the vagaries of fond or bitter memory: Râmnicu Sărat ('a place invented for me to be born in'); Tashkent and Tuba City ('where I bought a hat'), Riverhead and Calcutta, Milan and New York. Here, as so often in a career spanning six decades, Steinberg used a language of his own devising to recreate the world in his own image.

This personal Mappa Mundi was featured on the cover of *The New Yorker* (1976) and epitomises a personal approach to cartography—a grassroots, ground zero viewpoint which emphasises the fact we are emplaced beings.

All of these qualities—placiality; planetarity; autogeography; placelessness; and transgeographical identity—can be applied to New Nature Writing as much as ecofiction, but in the latter case, the author fictionalizes, taking the raw material of news footage and field research, and the research of conference papers, articles, documentaries, and non-fiction and transforming it into the (hopeful) coherence of long-form narrative.

Challenges and Limits

Kathleen Jamie, in her typically excoriating critique of early nature writing, compares Rachel Carson's seminal environmental classic, *Silent Spring* (1962) and J.A. Baker's *The Peregrine* (1967) to Gavin Maxwell's *Ring of Bright Water* (1960), and declares, 'whatever nature writing is now, its [sic] not "an otter asleep upon its back among the cushions on the sofa, forepaws in the air"' (2011). This echoes Terry Gifford's parsing of 'statistics' from the 'seduction' of nature writing (2007), and yet the jettisoning of both a scientific foundation for any dramatisation, *and* the aesthetic and emotional 'pull' that nature offers risks throwing the baby out with the bathwater. New nature writing may wish to avoid anthropomorphic sentimentality, but fiction revels in such effects: perhaps not full *Watership Down* (1972), but certainly a strong use of imagery, and a focusing on the intimate interstices and little epiphanies, which create impact in the novel-reader and can thus win over hearts and mind.

The power of fiction aside for a moment, it is acknowledged that there are challenges and limits to *any* attempt at demarcating a category of artistic endeavour, which, by its nature, should be exploratory, experimental, and continually disrupting its own borders. But to make such a book practical let us focus on the parameters established above, with all the caveats and without wishing to identify a canon. The most exciting work is usually at the edges of a tradition or movement, under the radar, and just breaking through. With that acknowledged, this book includes in its purview environmental writing in prose fiction, creative non-fiction, *and* emergent forms—offering readers a broad spectrum of creative responses, for as we have seen they overlap in ways which are often fecund and cross-fertilising. This acknowledges the nature of influence, which is never just linear or discreet. Ecofiction is a slippery, trans-species form of literature: the returning salmon feeds the bear, and if it survives, spawns and dies, its body enriching the mother forest—providing nutrients that help the sylvan and riparine ecosystems.

Diverse voices will be considered from around the world. A desire to represent a wider spectrum (e.g. from the 'Global South') struggles against a 'tradition' which is only now being challenged with a concerted effort in publishing to represent BAME, LGBTQI+, and working-class writers. Nevertheless, a lot of excellent work is now emerging, which healthily challenges the hegemonies and shibboleths.

While not strictly fiction—which is itself a fuzzy set, with autofiction blurring the boundaries between non/fictional categories—important associated examples (from the broader church of New Nature Writing) include Anita Sethi's *I Belong Here* (2021) and *Wanderland* (Reddy 2021). Initiatives like Muslims Hike, and the work of Professor Corinne Fowler on bringing to light the legacy of slavery in the British countryside (*Unpleasant Land: creative responses to rural England's colonial connections* 2020), which seek to decolonise and reclaim the countryside for *all*. Addressing the biases of class, race, gender, and sexuality, new anthologies are emerging with promising frequency, e.g. *Antlers of Water* (Jamie 2020), *Gifts of Gravity and Light* (Roy and Marland 2021), and *Gathering* (Durre and Nasia 2024). The ongoing work of decolonising the curriculum continues—a vital way of dismantling colonial hegemonies and repositioning marginal voices, as Waidner highlights:

> In a 'post-truth' sociopolitical context where powerful narratives and metaphors shape public opinion and influence electoral results, fictions and literary imaginaries must aim to advance a more progressive politics within marginalised communities and beyond, and to act as a mode of cultural resistance. (2018: 10)

Ecofiction offers one such mode, although one with its own fault-lines and blindspots, and so it is critical that writers of such works remain vigilant.

While racism, sexism, classism, climate injustice, and inequality of any kind remain the work goes on, and the conscious lecturer, writer, agent, editor, publisher, reviewer, bookseller, and librarian must remain awake.

Using This Book

The way we frame things is indicative of our values, the locus of our intention. It shows what we consider significant, and influences how we see the world. Adopting an 'ecosophic' frame (Arne Naess's term, cited in Stibbe

2021) in this book unashamedly emphasises this valuative paradigm, but as with much bio-mimicry, it is actually the most effective and elegant solution too. In Part I we consider **Taproots**—seminal texts and epistemological preliminaries. In Part II, **Branching Out**, we consider new voices and emergent forms. Each subsequent chapter includes a themed essay followed by **Mycelia** (interdisciplinarity and other connections) and **Spores** (writing activities), grounding each section in useful follow-up resources, real-world links, and practical activities—extending the discussion out into the world. Part III, **INTERVIEWS**, features conversations with 21 practitioners of ecofiction to provide a contemporary cross-section of approaches, texts, and perspectives.

Each chapter claims to be not exhaustively comprehensive, but a border oak indicating the riches beyond, enticing you to explore further, to delve deeper.

In terms of the individual chapters, we start with a consideration of Chapter 2, '**The Ground Beneath Your Feet**'. In this chapter, we shall consider the importance of 'starting from where you are', and how so much good Ecofiction comes from close, long-term observation of the local (what has been called 'deep mapping'; or 'deep place'). Starting with the body, we'll slowly extend our focus to one's immediate locality, from the doorstep to the nearest park. There will be close attention given to the senses, and to the act of perception. The notebook will be our primary tool. Through words we'll seek to capture 'qualia', (from 'quale', C.S. Peirce's 1866 term for 'phenomenal character', extrapolated on by Lodge 2003) and start to intimately, incrementally create a subjective 'map' of one's local universe—one echoed in the counter-mapping projects of indigenous peoples (e.g. The Zuni Map Art Project), and in the new 'situated' fiction emerging from writers like Rebecca Roanhorse (*Black Sun* 2021); and Silvia Moreno-Garcia (*Mexican Gothic* 2020).

In Chapter 3, '**Going Beyond What You Know**', we consider the benefits of going *beyond* the local, looking at classic and contemporary examples of writers who have transcended their locality. How to chart the unfamiliar? How to make the most of going beyond comfort zones? What are the risks, and the advantages of adapting this approach? We'll consider different kinds of research: virtual; archival; experiential; interviews.

In Chapter 4, '**Voices of the Global Majority**', we'll look at new voices since the millennium, in particular what is called Ecofiction, or 'Cli-Fi': voices which destabilise existing power structures, and offer a spectrum of diverse voices from across the globe. Also, this chapter considers an essential area that all writers of conscience must engage with: the ethics of representation.

Every writer must consider their position regarding 'cultural appropriation'. What could be called 'The Lionel Shriver position' will be considered alongside more sensitive ones. With nods to Spivak and Said we'll consider the importance empowering marginalised voices, representing indigenous rights, and post-colonial considerations—perspectives that have problematized the Anthropocene. How can approaches that eschew the heteronormative, neuronormal, and the spectre of 'white privilege' help to defamiliarize nature writing?

In Chapter 5, '**Activism versus Art**', we consider the problem of didacticism, drawing upon John Fowles' belief that 'When literature serves dogma, it ceases to be literature'. How to avoid the 'wagging finger', as well fatalistic nihilism, exploitation, romanticisation, assumptions of privilege, and cultural myopia. The spectre of didacticism can be banished via a number of strategies, including the representation of a cross-section of voices: the advocates; dissenters; heretics, etc. We will consider hybrid forms, and key voices engaged in the field today, such as Rebecca Solnit, who eloquently and intelligently treads the line between the two. Recent initiatives such as 'Climate Declares Emergency' (the artistic wing of 'Extinction Rebellion'), #XRWritersRebel, and Emergence Magazine will be considered, alongside earlier ones such as 'The Dark Mountain Project' (although founder Paul Kingsnorth's later stance is challenged).

In Chapter 6, '**Shaping a World in Flux**', we consider the challenges of shaping your material. How to find the form? We'll look at the fundamentals of structure and plotting, with an especial emphasis on 'found structure' and bio-mimicry—finding inherent forms in nature, thereby creating a marriage of form and content. How can we use different kinds of text—a heteroglossic approach comprising text messages; news reports; tweets; adverts; AI, etc.—to provide 'texture' and a healthy range of voices?

In Chapter 7, we consider '**One Man's Heaven**'. In this chapter, we'll look at the tropes and pitfalls of writing utopian and dystopian fiction, and consider the blended approach of Margaret Atwood: 'ustopia' and Rupert Read's 'thrutopia'. We consider critical perspectives of Charles Fourier, China Miéville, and others. The value of offering more positive visions of the future—new 'myths to live by'—has been posited by the likes of Ben Okri, Roman Krznaric, Kim Stanley Robinson, and Rob Hopkins. The use of creativity can be a valuable tool for imagining other modalities.

Chapter 8, '**The Rhizomatic Writer**'—explores the cross-fertilisation of creative collaboration and the benefits of interdisciplinarity. We look at emergent forms, which can be used to reach out to new audiences and raise awareness about the Climate Crisis: 'transmedia storytelling' (Henry Jenkins);

interactive fiction; audio drama; digital writing: apps; online role-playing games; site-specific commissions. These forms often have an ergodic (Aarseth 1997) quality which pushes the reader/player beyond the passive. We'll look at ecoliteracy community projects; writing residencies; commissions; performance; and other multi-modal approaches. Drawing upon Deleuze and Guattari, we'll consider the idea of being a 'rhizomatic writer'—developing an organic creative practice, and mutually supportive ecosystems.

* * *

Having looked at the context of Climate Change, the seminal texts that have fed into the evolving forms of nature writing, place writing, and ecofiction, and what defines the latter in particular, along with the challenges and limits of any such category, we shall now turn to the more practical side of things, starting from the ground beneath your feet.

Mycelia: Connections to Other Writers, Texts, and Resources
- Aalto, Kathryn. 2020. *Writing Wild: Women Poets, Ramblers, and Mavericks Who Shape How We See the Natural World.* Portland, OR: Timber Press.
- Bal, P. Matthijs, and Martijn Veltkamp. 2013. How does Fiction Reading Influence Empathy? An Experimental Investigation on the Role of Emotional Transportation. *PloS ONE* 8 (1): e55341. https://doi.org/10.1371/journal.pone.0055341.
- BBC. Skellig Michael: 'I like the solitude and peace of the island'. 13 August 2022. https://www.bbc.com/news/world-europe-62280677 (Accessed 12 July 2023).
- Climate Fiction (ecofiction database). https://climate-fiction.org/.
- Cooper, David, and Rachel Lichtenstein. 2020. What is Place Writing? https://www.mmu.ac.uk/media/mmuacuk/content/documents/english/What-is-Place-Writing-June-2020.pdf (Accessed 13 January 2023).
- Cresswell, Tim. 2013. *Place: An Introduction.* Hoboken, NJ: Wily-Blackwell.
- Dragonfly (ecofiction database). https://dragonfly.eco/title-author-publication-date-search/.
- Edensor, T. et al., eds. 2020. *The Routledge Handbook of Place.* London: Routledge.
- Evans, Gareth, and Di Robson. 2010. *Towards Re-Enchantment: Place and Its Meanings: A Collection of New Writing.* n.p.: Artevents.
- Free Thinking: Nature Writing. BBC Radio 3, 15 July 2020: https://www.bbc.co.uk/programmes/m000ktf4 (Accessed 12 July 2023).

- Hudston, Sara. 2022, February 11. Tigers at the Gates of Dawn. *Times Literary Supplement*. https://www.thetls.co.uk/articles/nature-writing-book-review-sara-hudston/ (Accessed 12 July 2023).
- Jamie, Kathleen, ed. 2020. *Antlers of Water: Writing on the Nature and Environment of Scotland*. Edinburgh: Canongate.
- Lease, Joseph R., ed. 2022. *Climate Consciousness and Environmental Activism in Composition: Writing to Save the World (Ecocritical Theory and Practice)*. Blue Ridge Summit, PA: Lexington Books.
- Massey, D. 1994. *Space, Place and Gender*. Cambridge: Polity Press.
- Murray, John A. 2003. *Writing About Nature: A Creative Guide*. Albuquerque, NM: University of New Mexico Press.
- Prentiss, Sean & Joe Wilkins. 2016. *Environmental and Nature Writing: A Writer's Guide and Anthology*. London: Bloomsbury.
- Roy, Anita, and Pippa Marland. 2021. *Gifts of Gravity and Light: A Nature Almanac for the 21st Century*. London: Hodder & Stoughton.
- Sedgwick, Marcus. 2020, December 8. 'But We All Know this Stuff. Don't We?' Climate Fiction Writers' League. https://climatefictionwritersleague.substack.com/p/but-we-all-know-this-stuff-dont-we (Accessed 12 July 2023).
- Shahwar, Durre, & Sarwar-Skuse, Nasia. 2024. *Gathering: women of colour on nature*. Edinburgh: 404 Ink.
- Smith, Jos. 2018. *The New Nature Writing: Rethinking the Literature of Place (Environmental Cultures)*. London: Bloomsbury.

Spores: Writing Activities

- What does 'nature' mean to you? Is it in the hedgerows? Is it in remote wilderness? Is it in the city? Is it in your body? Where does one end and the other begin? Spend a few minutes freewriting on the theme of nature—letting your words stray from the path and become 'wilder' as you do so. Write fast, in an unselfconscious, stream-of-consciousness way. How 'feral' can you get?
- Have a notebook with you whenever you go for a walk. Record sensory impressions; capture 'qualia'—sensory phenomena—perhaps in a synaesthetic way, e.g. draw sounds; create onomatopoeia neologisms; include 'feral pages' when you doodle, daydream, write wild, or 'blind' (with eyes closed) at different angles across the page, in spirals and sine waves, and other organic forms.
- Start to notice the telling details of the turning seasons: perhaps adopting a multi-modal 'nature journalling' approach—botanical observation in text and image combined with meta-data such as weather, location, time of day, etc.

- Read nature writing in any form—weekly 'nature diaries' in newspapers, podcasts, audio books, hardbacks, essays and chapters, anthologies, etc.
- Pick one aspect of the natural world that particularly intrigues you, e.g. a certain type of tree, seahorses, orchids, moss, etc. Research it and write about it in a free-range way.

References

Aarseth, Espen. 1997. *Cybertext: Perspectives on Ergodic Literature*. Baltimore and London: The John Hopkins University Press.
Adams, Richard. 1972. *Watership Down*. London: Rex Collings.
Ansell, Neil. 2011. *Deep Country: Five Years in the Welsh Hills*. London: Penguin.
Armstrong, Karen. 2005. *A Short History of Myth*. Edinburgh: Canongate.
Baker, J.A. 1967. *The Peregrine*. London: Harper Collins.
Bettelheim, Bruno. 1991 [1976]. *The Uses of Enchantment: The Meaning and Importance of Fairy Tales*. London: Penguin.
Bould, Mark. 2021. *The Anthropocene Unconscious: Climate Catastrophe Culture*. New York: Verso
Bryson, Bill. 1998. *A Walk in the Woods: Rediscovering America on the Appalachian Trial*. New York: Broadway Books.
Buell, Lawrence. 1995. *The Environmental Imagination: Thoreau, Nature Writing, and the Formation of American Culture*. Cambridge, MA: Harvard University Press.
Burnett, Elizabeth-Jane. 2020. *The Grassling: A Geological Memoir*. London: Penguin.
Carson, Rachel. 2000 [1962]. *Silent Spring*. London: Penguin Classics.
Casey, Edward. 1998. *The Fate of Place: A Philosophical History*. Berkeley: University of California Press.
Chester, Nicola. 2022. *On Gallows Down: Place, Protest, and Belonging*. London: Chelsea Green Publishing.
Christie, Michael. 2020, February 12. Top 10 Books of Eco-fiction. *Guardian*. https://www.theguardian.com/books/2020/feb/12/top-10-books-of-eco-fiction (Accessed 27 May 2023).
Clare, Horatio. 2022. *Heavy Light: A Journey Through Madness, Mania, and Healing*. London: Vintage.
Clarke, Lindsay. 2001. *Parzival and the Stone from Heaven*. London: Voyager.
Cooper, David, and Rachel Lichtenstein. 2021. "What is Place Writing?." *Centre for Place Writing, Manchester Metropolitan University*. Accessed April 12.
Clute, John, and John Grant. 1999. *The Encyclopedia of Fantasy*. London: Orbit.
Cocker, Mark. 2008. *Crow Country*. London: Vintage.
Cowley, Jason, ed. 2008. *Granta 102: The New Nature Writing*. Cambridge: Granta.

Deakin, Roger. 1999. *Waterlog: A Swimmers Journey Through Britain*. London: Vintage.
Dochartaigh, Kerri ní. 2022. *Thin Places*. Edinburgh: Canongate.
Drabble, Margaret. 1985. *The Oxford Companion to English Literature*. London: Guild Publishing.
Dwyer, Jim. 2010. *Where the Wild Books Are: A Field Guide to Ecofiction*. Reno, NV: University of Nevada Press.
Fermour, Patrick Leigh. 1977. *A Time of Gifts*. London: John Murray.
Fiennes, William. 2002. *The Snow Geese*. London: Picador.
Flynn, Johnny, and Robert Macfarlane. 2021. *Lost in a Cedar Wood*. London: Transgressive.
Foster, Charles. 2023. *Cry of the Wild: Eight Animals Under Siege*. London: Penguin.
Fowler, Corinne. 2020. *Green Unpleasant Land: Creative Responses to Rural England's Colonial Connections*. Leeds: Peepal Tree Press.
Gersie, Alida, Edward Schieffelin, and Anthony Nanson. 2014. *Storytelling for a Greener World: environment, community and story-based learning*. Stroud: Hawthorn Press.
Gifford, Terry. 2007, July 30. Engagement with the Natural World. Letters, *The Guardian*. https://www.theguardian.com/uk/2007/jul/31/ruralaffairs.leadersandreply (Accessed 18 July 2023).
Griffiths, Jay. 2008. *Wild: An Element Journey*. London: Penguin.
Hardy, Stephen Paul. 2001 "Placiality: The renewal of the significance of place in modern cultural theory." *Brno studies in English* 26, no. 1 (2001): 85–100.
Harvey, Chelsea. 2022, November 11. The World Will Likely Miss 1.5 Degrees C—Why Isn't Anyone Saying So? *Scientific American*. https://www.scientificamerican.com/article/the-world-will-likely-miss-1-5-degrees-c-why-isnt-anyone-saying-so/ (Accessed 27 May 2023).
Hayes, Nick. 2021. *The Book of Trespass: Crossing the Lines that Divide Us*. London: Bloomsbury.
Higgins, Polly. 2010. *Eradicating Ecocide: Laws and Governance to Stop the Destruction of the Planet*. London: Shepheard-Walwyn.
Hopkins, Rob. 2019. *From What Is to What If: Unleashing the Power of Imagination to Create the Future We Want*. London: Chelsea Green Publishing.
Hunt, Nick. 2018. *Where the Wild Winds Are*. Boston, MA: Nicholas Brealey Publishing.
Intergovernmental Panel on Climate Change. 2022. Synthesis Report of the Sixth Assessment Report. United Nations. https://www.ipcc.ch/ar6-syr/ (Accessed 13 January 2023).
James, Lauren. 2021. *Green Rising*. London: Walker.
Jamie, Kathleen. 2005. *Findings*. London: Sort of Books.
Jamie, Kathleen. 2011. Tim Dee. In *Archipelago*, Issue 5, p. 19. London: Clutag.
Jamie, Kathleen. 2016. Author Statement. *British Council Literature*. https://literature.britishcouncil.org/writer/kathleen-jamie (Accessed 20 January 2023).
Jamie, Kathleen. 2020. *Surfacing*. London: Sort of Books.

Kagge, Erling. 2017. *Silence: In the Age of Noise*. London: Viking.
Kimmerer, Robin Wall. 2015. *Indigenous Wisdom, Scientific Knowledge and the Teachings of Plants*. Minneapolis: Milkweed Editions.
Krznaric, Roman. 2020. *The Good Ancestor: How to Think Long Term in a Short-term World*. London: Penguin.
Levin, Jonathan, Clare Virginia Eby, and Benjamin Reiss. 2011. Contemporary Ecofiction. In *The Cambridge History of the American Novel*, ed. Leonard Cassuto, 1122–36. Cambridge: Cambridge University Press. https://doi.org/10.1017/CHOL9780521899079.074.
Lewis-Stempel, John. 2018. *The Wood: The Life and Times of Cockshutt Wood*. London: Doubleday.
Lilley, Deborah. 2017. New British Nature Writing. *Oxford Handbooks Online*. https://doi.org/10.1093/OXFORDHB/9780199935338.013.155.
Liptrott, Amy. 2016. *The Outrun*. Edinburgh: Canongate.
Lodge, David. 2003. *Consciousness and the Novel*. London: Penguin.
Lopez, Barry. 2001 [1986]. *Arctic Dreams: Imagination and Desire in a Northern Landscape*. London: Vintage.
Macdonald, Helen. 2014. *H is for Hawk*. London: Vintage.
Macfarlane, Robert. 2005, March 26. *Only Connect. Guardian*. https://www.theguardian.com/books/2005/mar/26/featuresreviews.guardianreview33 (Accessed 20 January 2023).
Macfarlane, Robert. 2007. *The Wild Places*. Cambridge: Granta.
Macfarlane, Robert. 2017. *The Wild Places*. London: Granta.
Macfarlane, Robert. 2019. *Underland: A Deep Time Journey*. London: Hamish Hamilton.
Marsden, Philip. 2020. *The Summer Isles: A Voyage of the Imagination*. London: Granta.
Massey, D, and Pat Jess. 1995. *A Place in the World? Places, Cultures, and Globalization*. The Shape of the World: Vol. 4. Milton Keynes: The Open University.
Maxwell, Gavin. 2014 [1960]. *Ring of Bright Water*. London: Unicorn.
McIntosh, Alastair. 2004. *Soil and Soul: People versus Corporate Power*. London: Aurum.
McNulty, Daru. 2020. *Diary of a Young Naturalist*. Beaminster: Little Toller Books.
Monbiot, George. 2019, September 5. The new political story that could change everything. TED Talk. https://youtu.be/xDKth-qS8Jk (Accessed 20 January 2023).
Moreno-Garcia, Silvia. 2020. *Mexican Gothic*. London: Jo Fletcher Books.
Morton, Timothy. 2013. *Hyperobjects: Philosophy and Ecology After the End of the World*. Minneapolis, MN: University of Minnesota Press.
Munteanu, Nina. 2021. Ten Eco-Fiction Novels Worth Celebrating. Tor.com. https://www.tor.com/2021/04/22/ten-eco-fiction-novels-worth-celebrating/ (Accessed 27 May 2023).
Murray, John A. 2003. *Writing About Nature*. Albuquerque, NM: New Mexico Press.

Nanson, Anthony. 2021. *Storytelling and Ecology: empathy, enchantment and emergence in the use of oral narratives*. London: Bloomsbury Academic.

Nichols, Jeff, director. 2011. *Take Shelter*. Sony. https://www.imdb.com/title/tt1675192/?ref_=nv_sr_srsg_0_tt_6_nm_2_q_Take%2520Shel.

Okri, Ben. 2021, November 12. Artists Must Confront the Climate Crisis—We Must Write as if These are the Last Days. *Guardian*. https://www.theguardian.com/commentisfree/2021/nov/12/artists-climate-crisis-write-creativity-imagination (Accessed 17th February 2022).

Oziewicz, Marek, Brian Attebery, and Tereza Dedinová, eds. 2022. *Fantasy and myth in the Anthropocene: Imagining futures and dreaming hope in literature and media*. Bloomsbury Publishing.

Parham, John, ed. 2021. *The Cambridge Companion to Literature and the Anthropocene of Cambridge Companions to Literature*. Cambridge: Cambridge University Press.

Parnell, Edward. 2020. *Ghost Land: In Search of a Haunted Country*. London: William Collins.

Porrit, Jonathan. 2013. *The World We Made: Alex McKay's Story from 2050*. London: Phaidon.

Prentiss, Sean, and Joe Wilkins. 2016. *Environmental and Nature Writing: A Writer's Guide and Anthology*. London: Bloomsbury.

Read, Rupert, and Marc Lopatin. 2022. Will the Passing of 1.5 Degrees See the End of Cruel Optimism? *Resilience*. https://www.resilience.org/stories/2022-04-08/paging-climate-justice-tragically-1-5s-time-is-up/ (Accessed 27 May 2023).

Reddy, Jini. 2021. *Wanderland: A Search for Magic in the Landscape*. London: Bloomsbury Wildlife.

Roanhorse, Rebecca. 2021. *Black Sun*. New York: Saga.

Roy, Anita, and Marland, Pippa. 2021. *Gifts of Gravity and Light: a nature almanac for the 21st century*. London: Hachette.

Schrader, Paul, director. 2018. *First Reformed*. A24. https://www.imdb.com/title/tt6053438/?ref_=nv_sr_srsg_0_tt_8_nm_0_q_First%2520Ref.

Sethi, Anita. 2021. *I Belong Here: A Journey Along the Backbone of Britain*. London: Bloomsbury Wildlife.

Shahwar, Durre, and Sarwar-Skuse, Nasia. 2024. *Gathering: women of colour on nature*. Edinburgh: 404 Ink.

Smith, Jos. 2018. *The New Nature Writing: Rethinking the Literature of Place (Environmental Cultures)*. London: Bloomsbury.

Solnit, Rebecca. 2023, January 12. If You Win the Popular Imagination, You Change the Game: Why We Need New Stories on Climate. The Long Read. *Guardian*. https://www.theguardian.com/news/2023/jan/12/rebecca-solnit-climate-crisis-popular-imagination-why-we-need-new-stories (Accessed 16 January 2023).

Somerville, Christopher. 2017. *The January Man: A Year of Walking Britain*. London: Transworld.

Spivak, Gayatri. 2017. Cited in Majumder, Auritro, 'Gayatri Spivak, Planetarity and the Labor of Imagining Internationalism'. *Mediations: Journal of the Marxist Literary Group, 30*(2). Post-Humanisms Reconsidered. https://www.mediationsjournal.org/articles/planetarity (Accessed 12 August 2021).

Steinberg, Saul. 1976. *'View of the World from 9th Avenue'*. The New Yorker. March 29 1976.

Stibbe, Arran. 2021. *Ecolinguistics: Language, Ecology and the Stories We Live By*, 2nd ed. London: Routledge.

Strayed, Cheryl. 2015. *Wild: A Journey from Lost to Found*. London: Atlantic Books.

United Nations. 2019. *Climate Change*. United Nations. Available from: https://www.un.org/en/globalissues/climatechange#:~:text=Climate%20Change%20is%20the%20defining,scope%20and%20unprecedented%20in%20scale. [Accessed 1 July 2024]

Waidner, Isabel, ed. 2018. *Liberating the Canon: An Anthology of Innovative Literature*. Manchester: Dostoyevsky Wannabe.

Warner, Marina. 1995. *From the Beast to the Blonde: On Fairy Tales and Their Tellers*. London: Virago.

Wynn, Raynor. 2019. *The Salt Path*. London: Penguin.

Zipes, Jack. 1983. *Fairy Tales and the Art of Subversion: The Classical Genre for Children and the Process of Civilisation*. London: Heinemann.

Part II

Branching Out

2

The Ground Beneath Your Feet

Starting From Where You Are

The fledgling writer of ecofiction need not leave their nest to begin. Material is all around them to stimulate the senses and generate ideas—sights, sounds, smells, tastes, and tactile sensations. Indeed, the primary source is *right there*, not just at their fingertips, but *in* the fingers: the skin, blood, bone, muscle, and nerves. For the first and perhaps most important realisation is that *we are nature* too, and the first environment we inhabit is our own body. Our relationship with it could be said to be a microcosm of our relationship to the planet. Whatever our history with it thus far—be it nurture, neglect, or abuse—we can improve that relationship right now by bringing awareness to it. It is the first ecosystem we get to study intimately and the only one literally over a lifetime. Before we go any further, consider this remarkable fact—the sine qua non of your existence. Your body, and your beingness: the messy miracle of it all, and the sheer luck of being alive. Why not write reflectively on this for a while: the 'natural history of your body'? (see 'Writing the Body' in **Spores**).

A hard, 'objective' description of one's physicality, however detailed, would not do one justice; neither would a self-portrait focused purely on one's thoughts and feelings alone. We are not just corporeal bodies; nor are we abstract consciousness. We are indubitably both. Therefore, would a hybrid approach—blending the hard data of the material world with the soft data of 'affect'—create a fuller picture? Daniel Torday argues that our five senses are augmented by a sixth and seventh: proprioception, the 'sense of where we are in space'; and enteroception, 'our sense of what's happening *inside* us, physically, in our guts' (Torday 2022). Proprioception becomes a gateway to the other senses, and 'makes the immediacy of any moment in a story grow vibrant' (ibid.). And enteroception helps establish a protagonist's line of desire (from basic physical needs—food, water, shelter, warmth; to more existential ones—love, status, revenge, enlightenment) and thereby create narrative traction ('the hungrier my character, the hungrier we are to read through a scene', ibid.). *Both* are useful for situating your protagonist as a narrator in a body in a particular time and place, with a strong sense of interiority, which anchors the narrative and enhances reader engagement—the 'relatability'.

Thus, interiority is just as vital as exteriority in any piece of writing—we don't just live in the world of the senses; and we don't just live in our heads. We co-exist in multiple 'worlds' simultaneously—and to capture that polysemous complexity is a technical challenge for any wordsmith, but for now, writing about your own flesh and blood—your own situatedness—is a good place to start.

To some, this may feel uncomfortable; not what you signed up for. Perhaps you had an idea of ecofiction being something outward-looking, and a chance to wax lyrical about beautiful places? A chance to travel, to explore anywhere *but* home, anything *except* yourself? That can certainly be an option, but if we are unable to connect with our own physicality and authentic self (which is a complex and debatable concept), then however far we go, however much natural history we learn, our writing will always lack a critical groundedness: a situatedness and bedrock of truth. Readers of nature writing (and its cousin, ecofiction) like to know how it felt in *this* time, *that* place—rendered in the hyper-specificity that elevates generic writing into the exceptional—but how can that be captured accurately if you are closed off from the sensorium of the self?

The next stage is to focus one's attention on what is in your immediate vicinity. Psychogeographer and novelist Iain Sinclair wrote in his account of walking in the footsteps of so-called peasant poet, John Clare (who, as a farm labourer, knew the natural world in a far more intimate, hands on way than any Romantic poet): 'We are never more than extensions of the ground on which we live' (1997). Clare lived and worked in the Fens of East Anglia, an unremittingly flat area of largely reclaimed land. The vast skies of this area were mirrored during his childhood by large swathes of unenclosed commons, but during in his lifetime Clare witnessed their parcelling up as a consequence of the early Eighteenth Century Inclosure Acts. This Clare took personally, as he beheld his precious childhood mythscape being changed beyond recognition (and shut off from the commoners). His keen-eyed poetry—a naturalist's field day—recorded the rich biodiversity of his locality in the kind of detail that only comes from a long association with a place, season after season, year after year. His rustic 'rhymes'—erratically punctuated and spelled, but highly sophisticated poetically—were eventually published and became popular among the literati of London. For a season Clare was the talk of the town, and found himself fêted by society (albeit in a patronising way). When he was dropped, the effect seemed to exacerbate his fragile mental health. He became convinced he was married to another woman, and at times identified as Lord Byron, a boxer, Napoleon, and other figures. He was placed in an asylum in Epping Forest—a relatively benign hospital for its day, but being exiled from his beloved Fens worsened his condition, for to be away from the land he knew so intimately literally made him 'out of his mind'. He absconded from the asylum and walked back to Helpston in Northamptonshire, sleeping in ditches and eating grass to stave off starvation. His family soon realised his condition was even worse, and eventually Clare was taken to the Northampton General Hospital and Lunatic Asylum, where he remained for the rest of his life, devastatingly cut off from the nourishing terra firma of his homeland.

Clare's tragic story is perhaps an extreme example of how important our formative landscape is to our sense of identity. Its nutrients forge who we are—literally. Certainly this would have been true historically, when our diet would have been largely based upon local produce: the minerals extracted from the soil in which this was grown would end up—via the food imbibed—in the enamel of our teeth. This fact enables archaeologists to identify the origins of prehistoric remains to within a certain site-specific geology. With greater mobility, the drinking of bottle or filtered water, and a diet drawing upon many air miles of imported foodstuffs, this is less the case, but there is still a deep truth here. Where we live influences us in many ways—the terroir of childhood in particular, where a landscape, urban, rural, or both, can be charged with a mythopoeiac numinosity, one that can linger inside us for the rest of our life, either as the arcadia we long to return to, or as the place that we are continually running away from.

For now, begin to observe your immediate surroundings, starting with exactly where you are while reading this. If you are at home, this is your 'natural' habitat—your nest, your lair, or your den. What surrounds you? Cushions, photos of loved ones, souvenirs, family heirlooms, a favourite mug, piles of books, a laptop or plasma screen, housemates, partner, pet? Try to see it all with the eyes of an extra-terrestrial visitor, like Craig Raine's 'Martian poetry'. Describe it in a defamiliarized way.

If you have a view, now describe that. What can you see? What's in the immediate vicinity; the middle distance; further afield? Open the window, and listen. What can you hear? Notice the complex interlacement of different sounds—the natural *and* the man-made. Write them as you notice them, filtering nothing out.

Once again, it is important to remember that 'nature' is not elsewhere, and the 'environment' is everywhere. We may be able to control the climate within our living spaces, but this is only a little bubble—and if the external climate is extreme, e.g. a long-term drought causing wildfires, then there is ultimately no escaping it. And many (especially in the 'Global South') are not privileged enough to even have the respite that such a bubble affords and are exposed to all that our changing climate can throw at us: heavy rain, floods, high winds, blizzards, heat waves, and so forth.

Ultimately, if we are to develop as writers—a path entwined with one's own personal maturation—we all need to step outside our front door; look beyond our particular garden fence (although many riches can be discovered in a garden, if you are lucky enough to own or have access to one where you live—spending time there with your notebook can be very rewarding). Beyond the picket fence; and ultimately beyond the pale of 'acceptable' behaviour' (in terms of the hegemonic culture of Anglocentrism). The Pale, or 'English Pale', was an area in the environs of Dublin controlled by England in the Late Middle Ages. Anything external to this colonial jurisdiction was deemed unruly. To the majority of Irish true freedom existed outside of this control zone—beyond the pale their own culture flourished freely. There is always a need for craft, but writing colonised by rules remains stiff and unoriginal. Good writers must be willing to stray from the path, to go the edges, and further—to push themselves, their chosen form, and their craft as far as possible. To seek out frontiers of practice. To go, as the poet Gary Snyder puts it, 'off the trail': '"Off the trail" is another name for the Way, and sauntering off the trail is the practice of the wild. That is also where—paradoxically—we do our best work' (1990: 165). Yet Snyder adds the caveat: 'we need paths and trails and will always be maintaining them. You must be on the path, before you can turn and walk into the wild' (ibid.). And so the apprentice writer must learn their craft and familiarise themselves deeply with the field they are venturing into. This is a form of mindfulness mirroring the various guidance for accessing wild places, from indigenous wisdom to modern mnemonics like the Countryside Code of the UK. One does not simply traipse into a natural habitat, heedless of what dwells there—rare orchids, nesting birds, reptiles, insects, and so forth. You are joining a (human and more-than-human) conversation, one that has been going on for a long time, and the conscionable visitor needs to sensitize themselves to the discourse; to be respectful of what is already extant.

To carefully find one's niche within the ecosystem.

For now, let us go for a mindful walk around our 'neck of the woods' (personification can be one device for rendering nature, as long as we avoid a default framing nature in an anthropocentric way). Try to experience your neighbourhood from the more-than-human (Abram 2017 [1997]): the perspective of a cat, dog, fox, or whatever habitually frequents it. You will start to notice all kinds of nooks and crannies you perhaps didn't before—sly little access points in hedgerows called 'smeuses'; desire paths cutting across lawns. These can be made by humans too. Notice how we customise our environment, e.g. graffiti is a key feature of the urban landscape, and can, at its best, be dazzlingly inventive and brilliantly executed. Of course, there can be unpleasant graffiti to, and other negative signs of urban life—the litter, vandalism, homelessness, drug addiction, ugly buildings and behaviour. For better or worse, it is all part of the urban ecosystem. While being always mindful of your own safety, don't filter anything out. Record it all, via your notebook, voice recorder on your phone, camera, or (even better) combination thereof. Practise adjusting your gaze to lower than usual (e.g. gutter level) or higher (while still watching where you are going). You may be surprised by what you discover: the 'weeds' in the pavement cracks; the orchid in the scrubland; the stag beetle making its slow, steady way on the path before you; the songbird singing defiantly from the satellite dish; the giddy bee, drunk on stolen nectar; or moth immolating itself against a streetlamp.

Explore your neighbourhood via different routes, at different times of the day (and, if you feel safe, at night). Sonia Overall has devised a 'Drift Deck' (2017) with prompts to encourage psychogeographical 'dérives'—Guy Debord's term for exploring an urban environment by 'drifting' between and recording its different ambiences—through your immediate environment. Note what you consider to be natural, and what you define as human-made—and how the two intertwine more than we realise. Much of what we think of as the natural landscape is the result of human activity and long-term agricultural and industrial practices, and much of what is artificial is colonised by nature. Nature doesn't behave or play by our rules. It continually transgresses, cross-fertilises, and hybridises. As the best writers should. Take a leaf from its book, find a smeuse, and wriggle through.

Acts of Perception

Writing is first and foremost an act of perception. Whether it is with the mind's eye, or with acute observation of the world around us, unless we notice things, we won't have much to write about—certainly such writing will risk weak specification: it will be generic and out of focus. There is a place for the contemplation of the abstract—and philosophy does that with a high degree of sophistication and nuance; but it generally is not in ecofiction (which will be used as a catch-all term for all stripes of *creative* writing about the environment/climate crisis; and the natural world—which includes the urban just as much as the wilderness). As with nature writing, ecofiction is at its best in keen-eyed observation of a *particular* habitat, species, or ecosystem. Not that it cannot shift magnitude several times within a chapter or even short story. The Linnaean System of classification, developed by Carl Linnaeus in the Eighteenth Century, and which frames all naturalist enquiry, encourages this: kingdom; phylum; class; order; family; genus; species. Metaphorically, this could extended to any place, person, situation, or concept. Things never exist just on one level. The closer one looks the more one discovers: infinitesimal granularity. This is best summed up by the visionary poet and artist, William Blake (1757–1827), who, in 'Auguries of Innocence' wrote:

> To see a World in a Grain of Sand
> And a Heaven in a Wild Flower
> Hold Infinity in the palm of your hand
> And Eternity in an hour

For Blake (and his wife, Catherine), vision was fundamental to their livelihoods (although they barely scraped a living as an engraver and colourist). References to 'visions' and forms of seeing recur frequently in Blake's poetry and art. The seminal quote, from 'The Marriage of Heaven and Hell' (which has inspired Aldous Huxley, The Doors, and many others) seems to encapsulate a kind of artist's statement: 'If the doors of perception were cleansed every thing would appear to man as it is, Infinite'. Blake perhaps implies that his own doors of perception had been cleansed, for certainly a sense of the infinite pervades his oeuvre, which seeks to chart a vast cosmology. And yet for most of us, our vision is limited, as the second part of his poetic aphorism, declares: 'For man has closed himself up, till he sees all things thro' narrow chinks of his cavern'. This image evokes Plato's cave—we only perceive the shadows on the wall, and mistake those for reality. And so our first challenge as writers is to open our senses fully—this can simply a case of stepping outside the door, and *experiencing* the world around you. This best works outside, as it allows for both daylight and our remarkable stereoscopic vision to work its wonders. There is no replicating this on a flat screen, however sophisticated the computer graphics or high the resolution. Our vision is three-dimensional, and can best be experienced in an immersive way—by being physically present in the world, not just viewing it second-hand in two dimensions. That may seem normative for many who spend a great deal of their lives online, but it is not the actual world: only the shadows on the cave wall.

So, step outside. Open the senses. Of course, the visual sense is only one of five—it is worth spending time focusing on each, but for now, let us dwell on sight. Depending on the strength and quality of your eyesight, by gazing at the world outside your door you will experience gradations of light, colour, depth, and an incredible amount of detail—more than a legion of computer animators and the most powerful servers could render. Just take some time to savour this incredible visual experience. Fully experience the sensation of *seeing*. We are so accustomed to it: it is so easy to take it for granted (until it is damaged or taken away entirely). For a while it was thought that we emitted beams of light from our eyes, which lit up whatever we beheld—beauty in the eye of the beholder, literally (an idea first posited by Plotinus in AD 270). Although this has been long disproved, it is a startling image—and could be appropriated as a metaphor for one kind of 'seeing'. Wherever we place our awareness comes into focus—not just visually, but mentally. As Abram has pointed out, perception is an act of translation, an approximation of what is actually there (1997); an idea echoed by Haskell in his exploration of the evolution of the sense of hearing: 'What passes into conscious perception is an interpretation, not a transcript' (2022: 28). Our awareness is, at best, a telephoto lens, although often we are viewing it down the wrong end: life—at the distance of our presumptions or distractedness. Spend some time *observing*—let your gaze linger on a leaf, a flower, an odd-shaped bush or tree, a particular landmark in this distance, a cloud passing overhead, or an insect right by your foot. How much detail can you observe? Try recording this in your notebook. Spend five minutes on a single observed 'thing' and describe it as accurately as you can; then move onto another; and another. Try half a dozen of these mini word sketches. Practise this 'conscious-seeing' thirty minutes every day and you will build up not only a rich resource of natural description, and hone your writing, you will also train your eye like a good wildlife photographer. Whether you like photography or not, you don't need a fancy state-of-the-art camera to 'take photos' like this (with your own eyes) every time you are out and about. This attention to the natural world—to observable phenomena—is a foundational skill for any writer, but especially a budding writer of ecofiction, and is perhaps the single most important one. Train your eye (and your pen) to describe what is *there*, rather than just a lazy shorthand of what we casually glance—a generic 'tree', say, rather than a specific species that has been wind-pruned in a particular way, with moss and lichen growing on one side of the trunk, a broken branch—perhaps shattered by a lightning strike, and regular visitors such as a certain slightly overweight squirrel (fat on stealing food from the birdfeeder), or a mating pair of corvids, one with a slight limp. Usually, when we glance at a scene, or 'take in' a view, we form a composite picture in our minds from countless, brief snapshots our eyes take. And yet a lot of this is visual shorthand, rapidly filled in, and often based upon what we are used to seeing: trees, grass, sky, buildings, et cetera, rather than *what is actually there*, as Robert MacFarlane noted: '…when we look at a landscape, we do not see what is there, but largely what we think is there' (2003: 18). It takes an effort (at first) to start to really see what is in front of us, and to begin to differentiate the details (of *this* shade of green from *that* shade of green, and so forth). To train your eye is an essential skill for writers of ecofiction, in the same way having a good ear for dialogue is for a short story writer and novelist. Learn to see what is really there, and practise recording it as accurately as possible.

The art critic John Berger famously explored 'ways of seeing' influential in the television series and book of that name (1972). He interrogated the voyeuristic act, and how this is often sanctified by art (notably the painters of nudes and landscapes in which the proprietorial gaze is culturally sanctioned). He deconstructed the implicit power discourses encoded into the compositions and subjects of such 'status art', and encouraged a more conscious, critical form of seeing—one that fully sees what is there, but also looks beyond the surface. He said: 'If we can see the present clearly enough, we shall ask the right questions of the past' (ibid.). This is an essential next stage, in terms of analysing what a certain sensory experience means. True perception is about going beyond the surface of things (while not forgetting to render their actuality in exactitude). William Stafford captured this bifocalism perfectly in his poem 'Bi-Focal'. The last two verses read:

> As fire burns the leaf
> and out of the green appears
> the vein in the center line
> and the legend veins under there,
>
> So, the world happens twice—
> once what we see it as;
> second it legends itself
> deep, the way it is. (1998)

The focus on the minutiae of the leaf—its 'vein'—leads to a deeper intravenous realisation: beneath the surface of things a core of 'legend' exists. And in Stafford's mind, legend here means something fundamental, not fabricated—a bedrock of authentic being that is 'deep, the way it is'. To train one's eye and mind to perceive *both*—the leaf and its vein of legend—is a more advanced skill, but one to work towards. Many spiritual traditions offer insight and training in this area, but anyone can read a cross-section of world myths, legends, folk tales, and fairy tales to get a sense of this. In such narratives there is a quality of immanence—of things meaning more than they appear: the numinous atmosphere of a dream where everything is charged with metaphoric significance. This heightened awareness is often foreshadowed by a transition into a realm of preternatural wonders—succulent fruit hang heavy on the bough, birds break forth into paradisal singing, flowers ooze forth their heady perfume, crystalline streams scintillate with hypnotic light. It is tempting to see such visions (often literary end-products of long oral traditions) as a glimpse of a shamanistic, animistic way of being in the world. Although that may be the case with some (e.g. in the Finnish epic, the Kalevala, which draws on an indigenous shamanic tradition) we have to be careful not to read too much into them. However, as writers of ecofiction we can perhaps allow a certain magic to creep into our prose—for do we not want to weave a spell, one that will re-enchant the natural world (however it manifests) for the reader: to make them see the world anew? Not all 'nature writers' would agree—it's a broad church after all—but certainly Robert Macfarlane and Jackie Morris, in their very successful children's book, *The Lost Words* (2017) and its sequel, *The Lost Spells* (2020), deliberately set out to create such an effect with their 'spell-charms'—acrostic poems that helped to recover words describing the natural world in risk of being lost from the vocabulary of the young after being jettisoned from the *Children's Oxford English Dictionary*: acorn, otter, wren, and others. For any writers of ecofiction to achieve such instauration may seem too ambitious for some, and yet Macfarlane and Morris' project has inspired a remarkable proliferation of collaborative and intergenerational creative responses—music, artwork, concerts, grassroots projects, and more. The acts of perception that inform the writing can lead to influence the perception and behaviour of the reader—not by telling them what to think, but by helping them to see anew what is before their eyes. And from this (re)newed awareness, practical action may result—a community environmental project such as planting an orchard. Such initiatives begin as an 'apple of the eye'. Perception leads to appreciation, by the simple but powerful act of awareness.

The Nature Table of the Notebook

The most valuable resource for any writer is a notebook. It does not matter what brand it is or what pen you use—a cheap jotter and a biro will do—as long as you use it. It may seem low-tech, but it is the perfect qualia-capture device, *qualia* (from 'quale', coined by philosopher C.S. Peirce in 1866 [1982, para. 223]) being the phenomenal character of an experience. So, not just observing sunlight streaming through an avenue of trees early one morning, but what that *feels* like—what is also known as the 'affect'. This can only be gleaned, in the above example, by *actually walking* along that avenue, not just Google Mapping it. A digital version, however detailed, is only ever a representation of reality—never the real thing, akin to the difference between a cheap reproduction of a famous oil painting and standing before it. If you have time to really look (which sometimes is difficult with iconic masterpieces) then you will start to notice the impasto texture of the oil paint, the lustre of the pigment, cracks of age, a barely legible signature, an exquisite highlight, or particular weave of the canvas … in short, the telling details. This is the benefit of actually getting out there with your notebook, going for a walk—even if it is to your modest local park—and starting to record what you see/hear/feel/touch/and perhaps even taste.

You will be in good company. Great writers and artists throughout the centuries have kept the equivalent of the notebook—whether in diary, journal, sketchbook, commonplace book, or some other form. Many are digitised these days and available through the respective library, although if you get a chance to see one in person it can be thrillingly visceral and occasionally revelatory. Some, like Leonardo da Vinci's, William Blake's, Derek Jarman's, or Guillermo del Toro's, are works of art. One of the most astonishing (and apposite for our purposes here) is Dorothy Wordsworth's. Unpublished in her lifetime and never intended for eyes other than her and her brother's (the famous Lake Poet, William Wordsworth), her journals are full of clear-eyed and beautifully captured descriptions of her walks around the Quantocks or the Lake District. In their pages, from an entry dated 'Thursday 15th April, 1802', we see the account of the 'host of golden daffodils' that provided the aide-memoire for her brother's iconic poem.

> …When we were in the woods beyond Gowbarrow park we saw a few daffodils close to the water side. We fancied that the lake had floated the seeds ashore and that the little colony had so sprung up. But as we went along there were more and yet more and at last under the boughs of the trees, we saw that there was a long belt of them along the shore, about the breadth of a country turnpike road. I never so daffodils so beautiful they grew among the mossy

stones about and about them, some rested their heads upon these stones as on a pillow for weariness and the rest tossed and reeled and danced and seemed as if they verily laughed with the wind that blew upon them over the lake, they looked so gay ever glancing ever changing. There was here and there a little knot and a few stragglers a few yards higher up but they were so few as not to disturb the simplicity and unity and life of that one busy highway. (*Journals of Dorothy Wordsworth* 1971: 109)

Even if her brother had not composed his poem a couple of years later—able to retrieve the precise *qualia* of that memory thanks to Dorothy's journal—there is genuine literary merit in such writing by itself: specificity, rhythm, energy, life. And this is the benefit of using a notebook in situ: to capture such moments while they are fresh. Perhaps flower-pressing is not the best analogy, but hopefully it conveys something of the transference of life onto the page—albeit without its illegal destruction: that is what writers of ecofiction *ideally* should aspire to (while, that is, acknowledging a plurality of approaches and agendas). A notebook should be a bit messy—a fecund record of life with pages perhaps a little grubby from mud, coffee, wine, thumbprints, and rain smudges. It can even have a tactile, almost semi-sculptural quality to it if crammed with feathers, flowers, buttons, tickets, wrappers, postcards … anything that catches the eye of the writer with a 'magpie mind', or as a follower of what Margaret Atwood calls the 'ways of the jackdaw' (2003: xviii). Line this literary nest with shiny words and phrases—place-names, street names, quotes, eavesdropped conversation, titles for stories, for characters, plot and character sketches, vivid vignettes… Anything and everything. A healthy notebook should aspire to be a catholic, heterotopian space (Foucault, 1967)—a place of playful otherness, mirroring the world back to itself in creative, subjective, even transgressive ways. The borders of the notebook are semi-permeable—looking both inward and outward, but there should be something sacrosanct about its pages: this is *your* private dreaming space, to experiment, to 'fail', and to 'fail better'. It should (ideally) be a place of rigorous creative enquiry, but if it is just used to capture, to reflect, and to put down for the first-time tentative ideas, plans, and visions, then you will be using it fine. There is no right or wrong with a notebook, other than not using it.

Over time a well-used notebook will acquire a rich texture—an incremental accretion of different qualities of text (and possibly image). Emulating the mulch of the forest, this inky sediment is a fertile compost of inspiration. Concealed within it may be a rhizomatic network of connections—like the subterranean fungal network of a forest—which lead to eruptions of new ideas in all manner of shapes and sizes: the strange fruit of the subconscious, perhaps, but one facilitated by this steady absorbing and recording of qualia.

This texture of text—a nutrient-rich soil of telling details, anecdote, proper nouns, dialect words, ecolectical terms, quotes, dialogue, and self-reflexive observation—is often a good combination for a piece of creative non-fiction, and, in some instances, ecofiction. Good prose should flow, yes, but also feel toothsome—should have 'bite' to it—so that sentences snag with memorability. In terms of style the sentences should ideally emulate the affect of a place, an experience. So, a description of a journey across a glacier could be full of hard, jagged words: icy prose that glints with both beauty and the threat of violence. The account of a desert journey might feel full of immense spaciousness, oppressive heat, sublime dawns and starfields, exhaustion, mirages, and oases of unexpected reward. And the same for other biomes—mountain, forest, ocean, coastal zones, savannah, tundra, and so forth—with the caveat that the writing is always individuated by the specificities of *that* place, at *that* time. It is the exceptions to the expected that make for good writing. Subverting the clichés of place can only be achieved through careful research—chiefly the field visit, the notebook, and the camera. Only through the experiential approach can the telling detail be unearthed—the micro-texture you only notice by being there, by having that experience, by being fully present in the moment, hyper-alert to the sensory twitch of the web of embodied being.

Scottish writer Nan Shepherd, who lived her entire life within the Cairngorms range, recorded with loving exactitude the situated sensuality of her locale. An English teacher and writer of novels, it is in her non-fiction classic, *The Living Mountain,* that she captures in a series of vivid vignettes the subtle observation of the best nature writing. For example, in a chapter on 'Water', she describes the discernment possible from hyper-attentiveness:

> The sound of all this moving water is as integral to the mountain as pollen to the flower. One hears it without listening as one breathes without thinking. But to a listening ear the sound disintegrates into many different notes – the slow slap of a loch, the high clear trill of a rivulet, the roar of spate. On one short stretch of burn the ear may distinguish a dozen notes at once. (2011 [1977]: 26)

When Shepherd drinks from the source of a mountain burn she notes 'the sting of life is in its touch' (ibid.). It is to this 'sting of life' that the budding writer of ecofiction should aspire—and such a quality of prose comes from first experiencing, and then recording it as accurately as possible.

Deep Mapping

A concept useful for the apprentice nature writer is what has been called 'deep mapping', a term that has several antecedents—e.g. in John Muir's Yosemite (1911); Henry David Thoreau's Walden (1854); Gilbert White's Selborne (1789); and Annie Dillard's Tinker Creek (1974) to name a few famous examples; and variants, such as 'psychogeography' (Debord, 1954); 'counter-mapping (Vaughan-Lee 2019); 'deep topography' and 'place-hacking' (Coverley 2018)—and yet is hard to pin down. Les Roberts has attempted a scholarly pathology of it for those who wish to delve into its complex roots (2016). A standard definition is lacking, although it generally implies an alternative, creative cartography of a particular locale—one that is highly subjective and phenomenological, and informed by exhaustive research or long-term engagement. Key aspects include a kind of gumshoe level of close, incremental observation; a sense of verticality, of depth rather than distance; of a hyper-awareness of the palimpsest of history—the accretion of narratives in a place, of the cross-hatch of sometimes conflictual versions of a place jostling for attention in a simultaneity of perception. Iain Biggs's suggestion that it is a kind of 'essaying of place' (drawing upon the full sense of an 'essay'—to attempt a composition on a subject; try out an idea, from *essais*: to venture forth)—provides a useful shorthand definition (Biggs 2010), which is helpful, as with anything psychogeographical it can so easily become enmired in its own solipsistic intellectual obfuscation (Manwaring 2019). As Kathleen Jamie suggests, in talking about what in her mind is the better kind of environmental literature, it should ideally be 'towards', not 'about' nature—this important caveat suggests a certain humility, an awareness of the flawed nature of the endeavour, the myriad compromises and fallibilities of the text and its author, rather than a hubristic totalising.

Any writer can attempt their own version of 'deep mapping' from their doorstep. You don't have to live somewhere 'picturesque', you just need a curiosity about where you live. Just set off with your notebook, but slowly, lingeringly, noticing everything as you go. As the artist Paul Klee said, it's akin to 'taking a line for a walk' (Macmillan 2000). The key is not to filter anything out—to be promiscuous in one's attention. Nothing is too trivial or unbeautiful to be recorded. Try to describe a particular route impressionistically via a stream-of-consciousness outpouring; or create discreet creative responses to personal nodes of interest—these do not have to be landmarks or scenic spots, but places that snag your attention in some way: an old doorway, ghost sign, footpath, derelict property, tree, empty lot, crossing, or aperture. These literary snapshots could be combined with actual photographs, audio recordings, video footage, or other forms of documentation—but see these as secondary responses, perhaps to help you 'retrieve' the experience later. For our purposes, words are our primary form of qualia-capture.

In this way, you could start to build up an impressionistic, highly individualised 'map' of your chosen area. Revisiting it at different times of the day, night, or year can help to defamiliarize it further and reveal new qualities or details. Exploring one's local universe can be endlessly fascinating—it can reward a lifetime of close, patient observation. Fewer of us are remaining so close to home compared to even a hundred years ago—although some still do. Yet for many migration—caused by financial, political, environmental, or personal factors—is a significant part of Twenty-first Century life. Placelessness or 'deterratorialization' (Deleuze and Guattari 1988) is something we shall explore in later chapters (**Voices of the Global Majority**; and **The Rhizomatic Writer**). If one has been separated from one's homeland/city/town/village then that can actually create an even stronger sense of place: the mythscapes of our childhood, of our mother country, can be intensely vivid and affective. Homesickness, longing, or 'hiraeth' (Welsh) can create the most poignant 'maps' of all. And now, in the age of the Anthropocene, environmental destruction can create a new, disturbing variant of this: solastalgia, Glenn Albrecht's term for: 'the distress that is produced by environmental change impacting on people while they are directly connected to their home environment' (Albrecht et al. 2007). With the escalating impact of the Climate Crisis globally, solastalgia will become increasingly common (e.g. the devastation caused by wildfires in Australia and California are only two examples), which, beyond all the essential actions required to ameliorate such incidences on an international level, makes deep mapping more poignant, and perhaps more urgent.

The Weather in You

Crime writer Elmore Leonard offered this piece of harsh writing advice in his 'Rules for Writing':

> Never open a book with weather. If it's only to create atmosphere, and not a character's reaction to the weather, you don't want to go on too long. The reader is apt to leaf ahead looking for people. (Leonard 2010)

This may seem bad news for nature writers of all stripes, including writers of ecofiction, but fortunately, Leonard offers a caveat:

There are exceptions. If you happen to be Barry Lopez, who has more ways than an Eskimo to describe ice and snow in his book *Arctic Dreams*, you can do all the weather reporting you want. (ibid.)

Unfortunately, no one is Barry Lopez, except Lopez himself (sadly departed in late 2020, the master nature writer left acknowledged classics of his field, and is an almost impossible act to follow). Nevertheless, weather is intrinsic to most writers of ecofiction, especially so in an age of Climate Crisis—when in fundamentals ways it is the only game in town. Indeed, to *ignore* the weather (or, in a wider sense, climate) is perhaps unconscionable in the light of scientific consensus and stark warnings from the IPCC (2021): a noxious brand of Climate Denial-Lit. This sobering consideration casts an eerie new light on meteorological writing, especially on the literary technique known as 'pathetic fallacy', a Ruskinian term with an (initially) pejorative implication to describe 'the attribution of human characteristics to inanimate objects' (1961: 159), most commonly the natural world. While no doubt scenes that unthinkingly go to the default description of inclement weather as a way of mirroring the internal emotional state of the protagonist/s (e.g. raining at a funeral) are as clichéd as 'It was a dark and stormy night…' for an opening gambit, a heightened awareness of climactic conditions in contemporary ecofiction seems essential. The weather no longer mirrors our anxiety, it can be the *cause* of it. It is no mere convenient backdrop for adding emotional depth to a scene. It is a protagonist too, even possibly an *antagonist* (although in truth, unless we subscribe to Lovelock's Gaia hypothesis (1987 [1979]), any personification risks romanticising or eliding the problem). Yet to avoid any critical engagement with prevailing meteorological conditions in a piece of modern ecofiction is worryingly myopic. Great nature writing can be generated in this way without it becoming an environmental diatribe, as can be seen in *Rain* (Harrison 2017), *Where the Wild Winds Are* (Hunt 2017), *The January Man* (Somerville 2017), *The Salt Path* (Winn 2018), *The Summer Isles* (Marsden 2019), and others. It is even possible to make a virtue out of such so-called 'pathetic fallacy', as the scholar Justine Pizzo has argued in her repurposing of the spurious misogynistic claims of 'atmospheric exceptionalism', levelled against women in the Nineteenth Century (2016: 84–100).

Whoever or wherever we are, the weather—be it seasonal or unseasonal, normal, anomalous, or extreme—is a key element of our day. As always, the body is the place to start—our own personal weathervane or barometer of senses, skin, muscle, and bone—and a notebook is a good place to record it. Try to discern the different qualities of rain, wind, heat, cold, and so forth. Learn to distinguish between cloud types. Study lore and local expressions for different kinds of climate, e.g. the Derbyshire saying: 'It's gone dark over Bill's

Mother's' (2019). Learn to read the weather, and to write it. Study classic examples of weather-writing (e.g. Susan Fenimore Cooper; Mary Austin; Thomas Hardy; Charles Dickens; Richard Jefferies; Herman Meville; Joseph Conrad; Ann Haymond Zwinger; Rachel Carson; Annie Dillard; Annie E. Proulx, et al.), but if you need somewhere to start, start from where you are.

However, one should not be bound by the accidents of birth and geography—a form of literary essentialism. As human beings we are far more plural and porous than that, and certainly as writers we contain multitudes. So, in the next chapter we look at going *beyond* what you know.

Mycelia: Connections to Other Writers, Texts, and Resources
- Baden, Denise. 2021. *Habitat Man.* Southampton: Habitat Press.
- Doyle, April. 2022. *Hive.* Kibworth: The Book Guild.
- Christie, Michael. 2020. *Greenwood.* Brunswick, Victoria: Scribe.
- Shepherd, Nan. 2011 [1977]. *The Living Mountain.* Edinburgh: Canongate.
- Thorpe, Adam. 2014. *On Silbury Hill.* Beaminster: Little Toller.
- Jansson, Tove. 2022 [1972]. *The Summer Book.* London: Sort of Books.

Spores: Writing Activities
Writing the Body
- Start by describing how you are feeling in this moment—sleepy, hungry, restless, anxious, distracted, etc. Let your pen be your diagnostic tool.
- Dig deeper into the story of your body—one only you can tell. How did you get that scar, that ache or odd bump? How do you 'get on' with your feet, legs, back, neck, bowels, lungs, or other organs?
- Imagining looking in a mirror. Describe objectively what you 'see', being as precise as possible, but critically *non-judgemental*—just provide an accurate description like a neutral police report.
- Now write a self-portrait based upon how your body *feels from the inside*—highly subjective, emotive, and real.
- Which one is more accurate? Which one captures your 'nature' better?

Using the Senses
- Begin to observe your immediate surroundings, starting with *exactly where you are while listening to this.* If you are at home, this is your 'natural' habitat—your nest, your lair, or den. What surrounds you? Cushions, photos of loved ones, souvenirs, family heirlooms, a favourite mug, piles of books, a laptop or plasma screen, housemates, partner, pet? Try to see it

all with the eyes of an extra-terrestrial visitor, like Craig Raine's 'Martian poetry'. Describe it in a defamiliarized way.
- If you have a view, now describe that. What can you see? What's in the immediate vicinity, the middle distance, further afield? Open the window, and listen. What can you hear? Notice the complex interlacement of different sounds. Write them as you notice them, filtering nothing out.

References

Abram, David. 2017 [1997]. *The Spell of the Sensuous: Perception and Language in a More-Than-Human World*. Vintage Books: New York, NY.
Albrecht, Glenn, Gina-Maree Sartore, Linda Connor, Nick Higginbotham, Sonia Freeman, Brian Kelly, Helen Stain, Anne Tonna, and Georgia Pollard. 2007, February. Solastalgia: The Distress Caused by Environmental Change. *Australasian Psychiatry* 15 (1_suppl): S95–98. https://doi.org/10.1080/10398560701701288.
Atwood, Margaret. 2003. *Negotiating with the Dead: A Writer on Writing*. London: Virago Press.
Beckson, Karl, and Ganz, Arthur. 1961. *A Reader's Guide to Literary Terms*, p. 159. London: Thames & Hudson.
Berger, John. 1972. *Ways of Seeing*. London: Penguin.
Biggs, Ian. 2010, July 9. Deep Mapping as an 'Essaying' of Place. Illustrated talk Given at the Writing Seminar at the Bartlett School of Architecture. http://www.iainbiggs.co.uk/text-deep-mapping-as-an-essaying-of-place/ (Accessed 12 May 2021).
Blower, Lisa. 2019. *It's Gone Dark Over Bill's Mother's*. Brighton: Myriad.
Coverley, Merlin. 2018. *Psychogeography*. Harpenden: Old Castle Books.
Debord, Guy-Ernest. 1954. *Exercise in Psychogeography*. Potlatch No. 2, June 1954. Paris: L'internationale Lettriste.
Deleuze, Gilles, and Félix. Guattari. 1988. *A Thousand Plateaus: Capitalism and schizophrenia*. London: Bloomsbury.
Dillard, Annie. 2011 [1974]. *Pilgrim at Tinker Creek*. Norwich: Canterbury Press.
Elmore Leonard's Rules for Writing. 2010, February 24. *The Guardian*. https://www.theguardian.com/books/2010/feb/24/elmore-leonard-rules-for-writers#:~:text=1%20Never%20open%20a%20book,leaf%20ahead%20looking%20for%20people (Accessed 12 May 2021).
Foucault, Michel. 1984 [1967]. Of Other Spaces (1967) Heterotopias. In "Des Espace Autres," *Architecture /Mouvement/ Continuité*, October, 1984. Trans. Jay Miskowiec. https://foucault.info/documents/heterotopia/foucault.heteroTopia.en/ (Accessed 13 May 2021).

Harrison, Melissa. 2017. *Rain: Four Walks in English Weather*. London: Faber and Faber.
Haskell, David George. 2022. *Sounds Wild and Broken: Sonic Marvels, Evolution's Creativity, and the Crisis of Sensory Extinction*. London: Faber and Faber.
Hunt, Nick. 2017. *Where the Wild Winds Are: Walking Europe's Winds from the Pennines to Provence*. London: Nicholas Brealey Publishing.
Intergovernmental Panel on Climate Change. 2021. https://www.ipcc.ch/ (Accessed 13 May 2021).
Lovelock, James. 1987 [1979]. *Gaia: A New Look at Life on Earth*. Oxford: Oxford University Press.
MacFarlane, Robert. 2003. *Mountains of the Mind* 18. London: Granta.
MacMillan, Duncan. 2000, October 14. "Taking a Line for a Walk": The Art of Paul Klee. *The Lancet* 356 (9238): 1361. https://doi.org/10.1016/S0140-6736(00)02831-2. https://www.thelancet.com/pdfs/journals/lancet/PIIS0140673600028312.pdf (Accessed 2 June 2023).
Manwaring, Kevan. 2019. Unpacking Psychogeography, Kevan Manwaring. https://thebardicacademic.wordpress.com/2019/06/07/unpacking-psychogeography/ (Accessed 12 May 2021).
Marsden, Philip. 2019. *The Summer Isles: A Voyage of the Imagination*. London: Granta.
Moorman, Mary, ed. 1971. *Journals of Dorothy Wordsworth*. Oxford: Oxford University Press.
Muir, John. 2014 [1911]. *My First Summer in the Sierra*. Edinburgh: Canongate.
Overall, Sonia. 2017. *Drift Deck*. http://www.soniaoverall.net/walking-psychogeography/ (Accessed 2 June 2023).
Peirce, C.S. 1982 [1866]. *The Writings of Charles S. Peirce: A Chronological Edition, Volume 1: 1857–1866*. Bloomington, Indiana: University of Indiana Press.
Pizzo, Justine. 2016. Atmospheric Exceptionalism in Jane Eyre: Charlotte Brontë's Weather Wisdom. PMLA/Publications of the Modern Language Association of America 131 (1): 84–100. https://www.cambridge.org/core/journals/pmla/article/abs/atmospheric-exceptionalism-in-jane-eyre-charlotte-brontes-weather-wisdom/8BD54C7047FAF109E1870682B9AB373E (Accessed 12 May 2021).
Plotinus. 1820 [AD 270]. *The Enneads*. Trans. Stephen MacKenna and B. S. Page. http://people.bu.edu/dklepper/RN413/plotinus.html (Accessed 13 May 2021).
Roberts, Les. 2016. Deep Mapping and Spatial Anthropology. *Humanities* 5 (1): 5. https://doi.org/10.3390/h5010005.
Sinclair, Iain. 1997. *Edge of the Orison*. London: Penguin.
Snyder, Gary. 1990. *The Practice of the Wild*. Berkeley: Counterpoint.
Somerville, Christopher. 2017. *The January Man: A Year of Walking Britain*. London: Transworld.
Stafford, William. 1998. Bi-Focal. *The Way It Is: New and Selected Poems*. St Paul, Minnesota, Graywolf Press, St. Paul, Minnesota. https://www.poetryfoundation.org/poems/42779/bi-focal (Accessed 13 May 2021).
Thoreau, Henry David. 2008 [1854]. *Walden*. Yale University Press.

Torday, Daniel. 2022, September 30. On Proprioception, the Sixth Sense of Storytelling. The Millions. https://themillions.com/2022/09/on-proprioception-the-sixth-sense-of-storytelling.html (Accessed 2 June 2023).

Vaughan-Lee, E., and A. Loften. 2019. 'Counter-Mapping' by Adam Loften & Emmanuel Vaughan-Lee. *Emergence.* https://emergencemagazine.org/story/counter-mapping/ (Aaccessed 24 January 2021).

White, Gilbert. 1789. *The Natural History of Selborne*. London: Benjamin White.

Winn, Raynor. 2018. *The Salt Path: A Memoir*. London: Penguin.

3

Going Beyond What You Know

Refuting the adage peddled out in numerous creative writing workshops, 'write what you know'—which only has some value as a writing *prompt*, but not as a writing *ethos*—in this chapter we consider the benefits of writing what you *want* to know. Acknowledging the complex considerations around cultural appropriation, which we shall reflect upon in detail in the next chapter, imagine how restrictive and essentialising it would be to *only* be allowed to write about one's family, ethnicity, gender, upbringing, or neighbourhood. For some writers, this is their DNA, their modus operandi, and can produce exceptional work—but such restrictions would stifle the human imagination; the writer's capacity to imagine other lives and other worlds vastly different from their own is limitless: and is for some, *their* modus operandi. To escape from the accidents of one's birth, inherited characteristics, heritage, schooling, life circumstances, and so forth, is for some writers a strong motivator. In a similar way to the appeal and benefits of reading fiction, poetry, and non-fiction from paradigmatically different perspectives—something that many consider to be enriching—so to can writing beyond what we know be enormously beneficial–deepening our compassion, cross-cultural empathy, and understanding of the world. A book can be a portal to absolutely anywhere; so should a blank page. The opportunities that the *tabula rasa* of a fresh sheet of foolscap, a new journal, or a blank document affords are one of the few true freedoms left in this world—and even then, some regimes curtail this, alongside the barbarism of imprisoning writers and censoring books. So, it is a freedom we should never take for granted, but should make the most of while we have it, and defend it at all costs. The thrill of the blank page is akin to being confronted within a new continent—one that you as writer will be the first one to explore. At this moment, this threshold moment charged with powerful potential, one should feel utterly unlimited by anything except your imagination and your ability to communicate it. Be unbound in your boldness.

However, there are risks and challenges in writing beyond what you know. One risks being out of one's depth due to a lack of expertise, resulting in work that is unconvincing, inaccurate, or worse: deliberately misleading. Such writing can come across as inauthentic, a poor ventriloquist act, that may result in the reader losing faith in your ability and stopping reading. As well as getting it wrong, one also risks running dry—while as if you are writing about a subject or experience you know well, this should not be an issue. In that case, one may have the parallel challenge of keeping it concise, relevant, and engaging.

And yet—creative innovation and excellence comes from taking risks. The photographer Diane Arbus said, 'My favo[u]rite thing is to go where I have never been' (2004). Picasso made a career out of taking creative risks, continually pushing his art as far as it would go. In an interview, David Bowie suggested that when you are out of your depth, 'when your feet no longer touch the bottom' (Morgen 2022), *that* is when creatively, you are most alive. The science fiction author Ray Bradbury would concur, saying 'Living at risk is jumping off the cliff and building your wings on the way down'. Helen Keller, author of *The Open Door* (1957), suggests, 'Life is either a daring adventure or nothing at all'. Ralph Waldo Emerson, perhaps with a tad more caution, advised, 'Don't be too timid and squeamish about your actions. All life is an experiment. The more experiments you make the better'. And over a century later Neil Gaiman wrote, 'If you dare nothing, then when the day is over, nothing is all you will have gained'.

As a writer one must be prepared to take risks—to go out on a limb.

The Farthest Apple

Proximity and reach can be useful concepts when considering inspiration—that is, in terms of ideas generation rather than anything esoteric. Although inspiration can strike, it more often than not doesn't. It cannot be cajoled, forced, blackmailed, or demanded, and there is no point sitting around waiting for it, except in terms of showing up to the desk, as Philip Pullman emphasises: 'Habit is the writer's best friend. Habit has written far more books than talent has' (2019). Cultivating a regular, disciplined writing practice is a far more reliable methodology than wandering lonely as cloud (or gazing daydreamily out of the window) and hoping the muse will visit. Every writer needs to discover their own best way of working—as long as it produces results that is all that matters. There are various approaches to ideas generation, and one can read hundreds of creative writing books and not produce one original idea. But here is one method that works—proven in countless creative writing classes. I call it 'The Farthest Apple'.

Imagine a tree, an apple tree. It is late summer and the branches are laden with fruit, ripe for the picking. Yet this is no ordinary apple tree, for upon it grow ideas. Unfortunately, the ones nearest the ground have already been scrumped, or have fallen and been nibbled by maggots, or lay rotting—creating a slightly woozy atmosphere. When starting a new piece of writing, it is effective to jumpstart it with a bit of brainstorm. For visual learners a good technique is to use a form of spider diagram. This allows for non-linear connections and avoids thinking in straight lines. Here is a variation on this classic diagrammatic approach. On a blank sheet of paper draw a basic apple tree—roots, trunk, and branches. On the trunk write a core word: it can be anything—love; trust; surrender; moon; elephant; milk-shake. Now go along the branch and draw another apple and add the first-word that comes to you. Don't overthink it. Write your first response. Now respond to *that* word with the first one it suggests—draw this as a third apple, further along the branch. Keep repeating this—for a chain of association—further and further along the branch until you run dry. Now, look at the end-word and compare it with the first-word. It *is* possible that no one has ever considered those two concepts or words side-by-side before. The end-word reinvigorates the first-word. It tilts it and shows it in a fresh way. This is your farthest apple. Try this a few times. Create a personal harvest of original takes on existing concepts. As a writer aspiring to write in a fresh way aspire to scrump these farthest apples. Don't go for the ones easiest to reach: these are clichés. Over-used, tired, a bit mouldy, and maggoty. You can set a core subject on the trunk, then create a cluster of 'first bite' words around it. Then expand outwards in each direction. Once you've created your outer harvest of original slants see if you can identify any echoes or affinities. Link with lines, arrows, snaking squiggles, etc. You've created a semantic ecosystem. Use this in your writing project to reinvigorate your conceptual and linguistic range. Repeat this exercise a few times at the start of a new writing project. With practice you will start to make synaptic leaps naturally across the arborescent folds of your cranial hemispheres. You will train your mind to think originally—and like Isaac Newton you may even have the odd 'Eureka!' moment.

Ecology Without Theory

In *Ecology Without Nature* (2007) Timothy Morton argues that we need to reconceptualise ecology, decoupling it from 'nature', which has become in his mind romanticised and fetishized. Adopting his contrarian, post-structuralist, 'postmodern nihilist' approach, one could advocate an ecology *without* theory (while acknowledging the paradox that ecology involves the *study* of living systems, and thus theoretical contextualising; in the same way that it situates the natural world at its heart: one really cannot have an ecology without nature or theory, whatever semantic games philosophers play). Sometimes it seems you cannot see the wood for the (eco-critical) trees—that we risk being buried beneath the obfuscations and posturings of cultural theorists who seem to only operate within their own sphere, endlessly echoing and critiquing each other's outpourings far removed from the actuality of the subject: nature itself (or however we like to define the organic world). While as an 'ecology of theory' advocates a return to the body, to the senses, to direct experience, not other people's interpretation of it. Anything that helps us appreciate, protect, and preserve the fragile, precious biodiversity of the planet (including studying it) is part of the general good work that needs to be done (alongside environmental education, conservation, lobbying of governments, and sometimes non-violent direct action), but at some point you simply need to step outside and open one's senses. As Bob Dylan sang, 'You don't need a weatherman. To know which way the wind blows' (1965).

Beyond Your Geography

In *Maps of the Imagination* (2004) Turchi draws comparison between the creative process in writing and cartography—playfully mapping one onto the other. Finding mapping to be a 'potent metaphor' (2004: 24), he argues that writing is a form of mapmaking, but one that creates its own rules as it goes along—a rebellious mode of creative-critical enquiry. He insists that '…while some writers may appreciate lists and categories, catalogs of options and examples, others resist the prescriptive, inclined toward analogy rather than explication, exceptions rather than rules' (2004: 24–25).

The writer delineates uncharted territory through their creation of characters, setting, and plot in prose; the poet, playwright, and screenwriter do the same in their own forms.

In ancient maps, such as the Thirteenth Century Mappa Mundi, the largest surviving medieval map carefully preserved at Hereford Cathedral, the edges of the known world were often populated with monsters, most famously dragons, flagged up by the warning: *hic sunt dracones*—a metaphoric firing range not to stray too close to. The notion that dragons, wyrms, or serpents patrolled the outermost limits of the (known) world echoes the motif found in world myths of the primordial embodiment of chaos such as Tiamat, and best known in Norse mythology as Jörmungandr, the Midgard Serpent—who engirdled the world, biting its own tail like Ouroborous. Seemingly awaiting the unwary, these cthonic 'critters', as Haraway might call them (2016), could be restored not as the ultimate threshold guardians warning us not to stray from the fold (as centred around the Holy Land in medieval maps) but as an invitation to the bold to plunge into the terra incognita of the unconscious or subconscious of our minds, where untold riches await—Hy Brasils and Northwest Passages of inspiration. In the spirit of Marco Polo and other early explorers, the writer needs to metaphorically venture over the horizon of the known, of the familiar if they are to discover virgin territory (as long as colonialist notions of superiority, precedence, and claim are jettisoned). Of course, like the so-called New World and other colonised lands, one could argue that these 'undiscovered countries' have long existed—for indigenous people, the ancestors of humankind, and before the first bipeds walked upon them. Jung framed this as the Collective Unconscious—a sense of an autonomous archive of all that humankind has ever dreamed, feared, desired, and worshipped, that exists beyond the individual and even possibly before humanity even walked onto the world's stage. Whatever its nature, the essential truth is one must be prepared to stray beyond the 'known world' of oneself, one's chosen genre or form, school or tradition, to truly innovate. The neurologist McGilchrist would perhaps say we need cultivate greater synaptic connections of the hemispheres of our brain—to be 'bihemispheric writers' (2012), and go beyond the false dichotomy of 'left' and 'right' brain. Fellow neurologist, Alice W. Flaherty (2005) would argue for the efficacy of fugue states—insomnia, intoxication, extreme mental states—to bypass any kind of writer's block and to access inspiration. Liminal states such as the hypnogogic or hypnopompic are especially conducive to this, as are the pink noise of running water, the twilight of dawn or dusk, certain music and sensations. This is evidenced by countless examples in literature—to use just one example, the Nobel Prize-winning poet, W.B. Yeats was inspired to write 'The Lake Isle of Innisfree' while in the middle of busy London street, when the trickling of a fountain on Fleet Street reminded him of the 'lake water lapping' of his native Sligo:

> I hear lake water lapping with low sounds by the shore;
> While I stand on the roadway, or on the pavements grey. (Yeats 1989)

In many world myths and legends, the hero or heroine protagonist must venture beyond their familiar territory to defeat the monster; save the damsel, village, or nation in distress; find the Grail or the elixir that will heal the people and the land. This has been taxonomized by Joseph Campbell as *The Hero's Journey* (1993 [1949]). His approach—an erudite, but sweeping 'First World' comparative mythology that risks being neo-colonialist and culturally appropriating in its exhaustive use of other cultures to serve as examples in one (white man's) Monomyth—has been critiqued since; although the push-back against The Hero's Journey is perhaps more to do with its ubiquity and success as a useful guide for creative writing students, novelists and screen-writers largely thanks to Christopher Vogler's repurposing of it for Hollywood (1999). For there are some fundamental truths in the basic pattern—of the protagonist leaving their Ordinary World (often through circumstance—bereavement, war, flood, famine, poverty, illness, etc.) and venturing into the Special World to win the 'elixir' or treasure that will help heal the wound in their own world. This is evidence in some of the earliest written narratives such as *The Epic of Gilgamesh*, or the Anglo-Saxon poem, *Beowulf*. In the Thirteenth Century medieval poem, *Sir Gawain and the Green Knight*, King Arthur's nephew is obliged to venture into the wild north to retain his honour, after participating in a deadly 'beheading game', when the Green Knight arrived at King Arthur's court one Christmastide with axe in hand and invitation to cut off his head. Going beyond the relative safety of court, which was at risk of becoming bourgeois and complacent in its success as a 'stable state' (prospering on the hardwork of others, via a punitive feudal system), the young knight needs to venture beyond the etiquette and peacockery to reconnect with something wilder and more authentic, as did Gilgamesh long before him, and many have done since. The Aarne-Thompson-Uther (ATU) Index and Stith-Thompson's Motif-Index of Folk-Literature identify many examples of this in fairy tales and folk tales from across Europe and beyond. In a bold act of narratological syncretism, Christopher Booker has attempted to boil down this to 'seven basic plots' (2004)—a structuralist approach that is totalising and reductive (such neat ideas sell books and 'masterclasses', but do not truly chart the limitless capacity of the human imagination)—but without claiming an ur-story or universality there *is* something archetypal about this tension. Jonathan Bate, in *The Song of the Earth* (2000), suggests this is to do with the semantic and ontological tension between the concepts of 'nature' and 'culture', a tension which humanity has been caught in ever since the dawn of civilisation.

Thresholds geographical—fords, bridges, ports, tunnels, caves, doorways, coasts, and cliff edges; physical—hunger, insomnia, illness, intense heat or cold, drowning, violence, childbirth; and psychological—racism, sexism, classism, ableism, injustice, bullying, bereavement, torture, blackmail, punishment, abuse, examination, interrogation, imprisonment—offer not merely obstacles for protagonists, but opportunities for growth. For mettle to be tested and to shine forth. One grows when one is forced to the edge and beyond—ontological exploration and expansion. Travel expands the mind, and for a writer can be a powerful motivating factor—to take roads less travelled, to 'boldly go', to traverse frontiers as Gary Snyder describes them: 'A frontier is a burning edge, a frazzle, a strange market zone between two utterly different worlds' (1990: 15). These liminal zones, where we are often at our most vulnerable, are where cathartic regeneration can occur—not in the comfort zones of stasis. There is great risk involved in venturing beyond the known, as Sean Penn's film, *Into the Wild* (2007), based upon the biography by Jon Krakauer (1996) relating the misadventure of the young malcontent, Chris McCandless dramatizes vividly. And yet in that risk, one feels more fully alive—even as one puts oneself in life-threatening situations—a paradoxical state that Macfarlane captures in his examination of what draws mountaineers to perilous summits (*Mountains of the Mind* 2008); M. John Harrison's novel of obsession (*Climbers* 1989), and in Barry Lopez's seminal examination of what has drawn people to the far north, *Arctic Dreams* (2014 [1986]).

On a metaphorical level, this awareness of what can be discovered by venturing into terra incognita has paid dividends in countless works that imagine what lays beyond—from classic adventure stories like *Journey to the Centre of the Earth* (Verne 1864), *The Call of the Wild* (1903), *The Lost World* (Doyle 1912) and *Lost Horizons* (Hilton 1933); to almost every science fiction novel. A particularly fine example of the latter can be found in Jeff VanderMeer's Southern Reach Trilogy (*Annihilation; Acceptance; Authority*— republished as *Area X: The Southern Reach Trilogy* 2014). In *Annihilation*, a group of unnamed scientists go on a mission (the latest in a series of failed attempts with fatal or life-changing consequences) into a restricted area in Florida where biomorphic mutations and other anomalies have transformed the flora, fauna and landscape, and anyone who ventures there, into something entirely other and alien. VanderMeer defamiliarises 'nature' gives it sentience and agency, and destabilises discreetist notions of humans being apart from that. The novel foreshadows the posthuman, or perhaps acknowledges the pre-human. Area X acts as a hothouse for a primal deliquescence (often precipitated by fungal cross-fertilisation) that seems to be encoded within us, merely awaiting the sporal trigger. The scientists stumble upon barely recognisable figures that have been reclaimed by the wild, and in the inverted tower of the Lighthouse, at the epicentre of the extra-solar incursion, a slug-like Crawler writes an endless gnomic gospel upon the walls—apparently all that remains of the transmogrified lighthouse keeper. As Haraway exhorts, we are 'symbionts' by nature, and 'ecological assemblages' (2016)—hosting and being hosted by biocommunities in a complex, glorious entanglement. As though pre-empting Morton, VanderMeer's eco-weird posits an ecology without *us*.

In terms of more mimetic ecofiction, narratives that explore the outer reaches of the known world include Stef Penney's *The Tenderness of Wolves* (2006) and Iain Sinclair's *The Gold Machine: Tracking the Ancestors from Highlands to Coffee Colony* (2021). Each adopts a very different approach in terms of research.

Penney's Costa Prize-winning debut novel is set in Canada in the 1860s, and involves a murder mystery around the death of a trapper. Penney suffers from agoraphobia, and so conducted her research remotely via London libraries. Having never stepped foot on Canadian soil (at the time) Penney was still able to convincingly evoke a sense of place—for her many fans at least. How convincing for Canadians remains unclear, and the depiction of First Nations peoples by white writers remains problematic, however sensitively handled. A novel that tackles the challenges of that head on is Harry Whitehead's *The Cannibal Spirit* (2011)—the result of painstaking anthropological research and a hyper-awareness of the pitfalls of representation. This muscular novel dramatizes the real-life story of George Hunt in turn-of-the-century Victorian Canada. Of mixed-race (European/indigenous) heritage, straddling the worlds of the anthropological collector and that of the medicine man, Hunt is a problematic figure. Is he the exploiter of First Nations people, misappropriating their heritage for his patron, Professor Boaz in New York; or is he their advocate, helping to perpetuate their wisdom? Janus-like he straddles these two paradigms, one ostensibly representing the future (rapacious 'Progress') and the other the past. The tectonic plates of their conflict collide in him with devastating effect—on himself and those around him. Rendered in a visceral, embodied style, he is a massive figure in many ways—a grotesque 'dark father' archetype, who prowls the pages of the book, lurking in the shadows of the forest, like some tormented and monstrous boar from legend. Yet is he the bringer of doom, or the deliverer? The death of his son, David, provides the inciting incident, triggering a perilous chain of events. The manner of his son's burial proves a bone of contention—emblematic of the schism between the pagan and the Christian fault-lines of frontier Canada. Hunt manages to offend both the proselytising missionary and his own tribe. His son-in-law, Harry Cadwallader, a sailor-of-fortune with a dark past, is forced to play the stooge, and track his erstwhile 'father-in-law-from-hell' down. This triggers a Conradian adventure as Harry and his sidekick, the deceptively happy-go-lucky Charley Seaweed—hunchback and vulgar ways masking real wisdom and power—journey into the heart of the Canadian darkness. Whitehead knows his onions—the depth of the research shines through in the texture of the world he evokes and the authentic tang of his prose, providing a bedrock of reality over which he casts the fallibility of his characters' knowledge and beliefs. His depiction of the exotic 'other' is deliberately provocative and iconoclastic. There are no noble savages here. Everyone is culpable; each paradigm, subjective. No one stands fully in the light. In many ways each of the characters is struggling to emerge out of the forest of their own 'ignorance'. But what is discovered in the gleaming cities penetrating the skies of the virgin century is the true manifestation of the cannibal spirit—the ravenous machine of progress and profit that devours people, cultures, histories, and our humanity.

In contrast to Penney's stay-at-home approach, another Londoner, Iain Sinclair, who has forged his distinctive brand of psychogeography through an exhaustive charting of the capitols deep history and edgelands—*Lud Heat* (2012 [1975]); *White Chapell, Scarlet Tracings* (1987); *Downriver* (2004 [1991]); *Lights Out for the Territory* (1997); *London Orbital* (2003); *Ghost Milk* (2012); and *The Last London: True Fictions from an Unreal City* (2017)—decided to consciously travel far beyond his literary purview in *The Gold Machine* (2021), in which, prompted by his daughter, he retraces his great-grandfather's journey to Peru and his involvement with the coffee plantations there. In doing so, Sinclair steers fully into the skid of colonial culpability.

Sinclair's process is an intrinsically situated one—an embedded approach akin to a detective going 'undercover', or a war journalist spending time with troops in the theatre of conflict. He puts himself at risk, not physically but ontologically. There is a slippage of self, of history; the factual elides into the fictional—the truth is continually contaminated, and not allowed to get in the way of a good story. The words take on a life of their own, and each foray is a free dive—each paragraph a long breath, which the author returns to the surface of the page with, clutching strange findings from the deep.

Whatever one's methodology it is demonstrable that going beyond your geography as a writer can bear fruit. Another 'creative transgression' for writers who wish to repudiate the 'write what you know' edict, is to go beyond not only your place, but your time.

Beyond Your Temporality

Benjamin Myers, author of *The Gallows Pole* (2017)—a gripping, bleak historical novel with a strong sense of place, about the notorious David Hartley and the Cragg Vale Coiners, a real-life Eighteenth Century gang of working class forgers who became local folk heroes in their resistance to the authorities—lives 'smack bang' in the middle of the area the gang once operated in, but nevertheless, he still had to take a leap of faith to go beyond the historical material available to bring alive their story:

> Research was everything early on – not just the basic facts of the story, but in the smaller details, for example the nuances of regional dialect, the dietary details of characters or in site-specific scenes and the role that landscape played in the story. At some point though an author has to take a leap into the unknown and impress their own ideas onto the story. The main character David Hartley exists in public records, local history, legal documents and so forth, but very little was actually known about his personality, his politics and his philosophy, and that is when artistic license is applied. At that point historical writing, memoir, fiction and – in this case – a twisted sort of poetry all merged into one, and splashes of colour were hopefully added to the grey areas of the shadowed past. (Myers 2018)

Examples of this empathic temporal 'leap into the unknown' include William Morris' classic utopian fantasy, *News from Nowhere* (1890); George Stewart's *Earth Abides* (1949); and Anthony Doerr's *Cloud Cuckoo Land* (2021) (among many others). Historical Fiction is a hugely popular form with countless examples of this—and some, like Hilary Mantel's *Wolf Hall* trilogy, are of exceptional quality. But the focus here is ecofiction and so I have chosen examples that have the qualities highlighted in the introduction.

George Stewart's 1949 novel, *Earth Abides,* is singular in both senses—it is the only science fiction the University of California Professor of English ever wrote, and also a remarkably prescient and deeply moving epic. Set in the aftermath of a virus that decimates the global population—the Great Disaster that derails the human project catastrophically (at least in terms of what we think of as 'civilisation')—the opening chapters depict an eerily quiet and depopulated land that could easily be one in lockdown. Yet as the protagonist, Isherwood Williams, (or 'Ish' as he becomes known) makes his solitary way back from the wilderness where he had been undertaking field research, it soon becomes apparent that a devastating plague has swept the land, leaving fly-ridden corpses in lonely gas stations, mummified ones in the desert, and rendering the former population clusters of cities as no-go zones. And the near mass extinction event of humankind allows for a rewilding of America, in a similar way to how Victorian nature writer Richard Jefferies imagined a 'wild England' in his post-apocalyptic novel of 1885, *After London*. Yet, unlike in Jefferies, where the first half of the novel is a detailed natural history survey sans character or plot, in Stewart's narrative, Ish is our viewpoint character who has agency. We experience this biological apocalypse through his thoughts and senses—an academic, he reflects upon what he beholds stoically. Used to his own company and absorbed by his own preoccupations, he is able to cope with a depopulated California, until finally jarred out of his solipsism by first a dog, and then by chance encounters with the diseased, deranged, or decadent few who have also survived. He embarks upon a bleak road trip to the East Coast, only to be unimpressed by the remnants he encounters. Returning to the West Coast and his former childhood home, he settles down to a quiet life, until … well, I'll leave that for you to discover. What is refreshing about Stewart's post-apocalypse is the anthropological approach he takes in charting the vicissitudes of the remaining survivors. He takes the long view of history, and prophesies a circularity to it … the survivors subsist upon what they can scavenge, but eventually the shelves empty or are overrun by the swarms of ants, rats, and feral canines, and the scattered tribes regress into a future primitive state. The novel shows its age in some places—most notably in its problematic descriptions of people of colour, the handicapped, and of women. And yet Stewart nearly redeems himself by lauding the main female (and mixed race) character—who is shown to have greater strength and stamina than the men. She is rather put on a pedestal and is frequently referred to as the 'mother of nations'—and so this idealised feminine is just as problematic in its own way. Stewart also is far off the mark in his disavowal of climate studies as being of any relevance to future life on Earth: 'Climatic change was not a practical problem'. Yet for a novel written in the late 1940s, we can hardly blame the author for *that* blindspot, and in many ways Stewart's sole foray into the speculative is a seminal work of Climate Fiction, and in that sense it is far ahead of the curve. It rightly won the first International Fantasy Award in 1951. So, despite its weaknesses of representation, the novel has many strengths—not just the breadth of its vision, but in its non-anthropocentric shifts, and its proto-ecological tone. It foregrounds the importance of environment, and exhorts (of the earth): 'There is nothing else by which men live'. Stewart emphasises the Earth will survive us, and is indifferent to our plight. He destabilises our imagined position as the pinnacle of creation; he also challenges the vanity of ambition, the empty intellectualism of academe (whenever it ceases to have practical purpose), and the myth of progress. All that matters, he seems to infer, is our immediate community of connections, the family (or 'Tribe' in its extended form), our inner resilience, adaptability, and capability. Simple skills of survival become more important than the vainglorious dreams of betterment and posterity. And yet although this heartbreakingly charts the end of the Enlightenment Project and western civilisation's brief moment in the sun, this is ultimately a humanist and humanitarian novel, and there is deep poetry and compassion here—in the poetic, pseudo-Biblical epigraphs; and in the loving record of marriage and friendship. A haunting vision of a plague-stricken America, there is nevertheless a quiet beauty here that lingers long after the book has been put down.

Cloud Cuckoo Land (2021) by Pulitzer Prize-winning American author Anthony Doerr is a storytelling tour-de-force that should appeal to anyone in love with fabulation and the fantastic. It is a novel about stories and a praise-song to libraries, archives, and the endless possibilities of language and the imagination.

The multi-linear narrative is set over three time periods—medieval Constantinople, modern-day Idaho, and aboard an intergenerational starship in the not-too-distant future. Each era is focalized through the travails of a small cast of characters: a Christian seamstress and Muslim cattle herder caught on either side of the siege of Constantinople; an ecofanatic malcontent and octogenarian autodidact stuck in a hostage situation in a public library in Lakeport, Idaho; and teenage interstellar native who finds herself aboard a plague-bound starship. Confinement, restriction, and obligation are explored through these three alternating threads—and linking them all together is an apparently lost Greek epic by Diogenes, about a foolhardy traveller who stumbles into a quest for the titular utopia.

Cloud Cuckoo Lands of different calibres motivate all the characters—from a warm bed and hot meal amid war-torn hardship and displacement; the consolatory refuge of a book; an eco-Valhalla for the hard-line martyr; to an Earth-like planet on the far side of the galaxy. Sehnsucht of varying intensities haunts all of the characters, and its presence rather than its fulfilment seems to be fundamental to the human condition, Doerr seems to suggest. We are motivated by what is absent, what is over the horizon, by the unattainable—so many fool-knights on Grail quests that will never be accomplished. And yet, in the striving, in that perpetual, ever-expanding liminal zone between where we are and where we want to be, life is lived. One half riding Baron Munchausen-like to the moon, the other half grounded in the harsh actuality of home-grown terrorism, religious warfare, environmental destruction, the struggles of a single parent raising a child on zero-hour contracts, resource scarcity and pandemics, Doerr's mercurial novel dances an elegantly fine line between the visionary and the mundane, the didactic and the aesthetic.

Yet, unlike so many 'literary' novels, this is eminently readable, has narrative traction. The six hundred plus pages fly by. For a novel that covers so much, that has such scope and depth and daring, it never becomes turgid or preachy. The prose is infused with a delight in storytelling, in the infinite (and redemptive) power of the imagination.

And for something that may seem so frivolous—like so many mainstream 'fantasy-lite' novels that exploit tropes of the genre without ever really fully committing, *Cloud Cuckoo Land* feels like the real deal: a novel of *true* Fantasy, in the manner of, say, John Crowley's *Little, Big* (2000 [1981]). Multi-layered but not dense, its architectural structure is never intrusive: it is cathedral-like in its complexity—that is, it never loses sight of the spire. Everything is perfectly balanced, with this single goal always in mind.

Beyond its technical brilliance, the core of the novel seems to be ecological—in the true sense of the word: it explores and celebrates 'the relation of living organisms to one another and to their physical surroundings'. With its long view of the human story, it is a Fantasy novel of the Anthropocene—relating to humans and their impact upon the environment. It hints at the ultimate Cloud Cuckoo Land—a preindustrial, prelapsarian Earth: 'an older and undiluted world, when every barn swallow, every sunset, every storm, pulsed with meaning'. In a way, Doerr's novel attempts to restore that meaning through an extended act of re-enchantment: by making us appreciate the everyday wonder beneath our feet.

These three novels, *News from Nowhere*, *Earth Abides*, and *Cloud Cuckoo Land*, each share an ecological sensibility, and each demonstrate the advantages of going beyond one's temporality. But what about other transgressions across societal borders?

Beyond the White Picket Fence

Writing beyond one's ethnicity can produce powerful results, as seen in Bruce Chatwin's *The Songlines* (1987); David Mitchell's *Cloud Atlas* (2008); and Octavia Butler's *Parable of the Sower* (2019 [1993]). In the latter, Butler writes not just from an African-American perspective, but brings alive the intersectional challenges of other non-white Americans. As a writer of colour herself, Butler is in a stronger position to do this (and she does it with great aplomb)—what I call translateral representation. The opposite of this is when a white writer chooses to write *on behalf of* a marginalised community, capitalising upon their experience. A recent, notorious example of this is *American Dirt* (2020), by Jeanine Cummins, about a Mexican bookseller who is forced to flee to North America as an illegal immigrant. Even though it became an 'Oprah Book of the Week', it accounted a lot of criticism for apparently exploiting the experiences of Mexican immigrants: what has been called 'trauma porn'—an aspect of cultural appropriation I will look at in more detail in the next chapter.

In sharp contrast, and as a good example of how to write beyond the pale, let us consider Butler's novel in more detail.

Butler's near future climate dystopia, written in 1993, chillingly starts in 2024, and convincingly depicts the breakdown of society from the perspective of an African-American family, who live in a satellite town of Los Angeles—part of a small neighbourhood who strive to defend themselves against the encroaching violence and chaos. Water is more expensive than food; jobs are scarce. Outside the gated communities there are lawless no man's lands ruled by gangs and 'pyros'—shaven-headed painted arsonists. The story focuses on Lauren Olamina, the daughter of a preacher, who has the gift of 'sharing'—the ability to feel other's pain. As the wave of anarchy breaks over the walls of her neighbourhood, Lauren is forced to accelerate her plans to leave and seek a better life in the north, where there are rumours of paid work and better conditions. Although only a teenager, Lauren shows remarkable leadership skills, resilience, and vision—attracting to her a ragged band of survivors, who join her in her journey and dream of starting a community founded on a form of Christo-Stoicism she calls 'Earthseed', which has the ultimate agenda of taking humanity to the stars—a kind of anthropocentric panspermia. This newly-forged religion is related in epigraphic poems and aphorisms featured in 'The Books of the Living', written by Lauren in her notebook, mirroring Butler's own remarkable self-affirming juvenilia in which she imagined herself as the successful writer she became. The use of this religiose paratext and subtext elevates Butler's novel from the schlew of dreary dystopias that have since been published—it is a spiritual, redemptive vision that provides the escape hatch from the grimdark nihilism pervasive in the early Twenty First Century. Thirteen years before Cormac McCarthy's unrelentingly bleak vision of a burnt America in *The Road* (2006), Butler vividly imagined a First World apex economy descending into dysfunctional savagery—the shock of the derelict mall and abandoned freeway providing a jolt of fear more effective to those enmired in the Capitalist fever-dream than holes in the O-zone layer or collapsing ice-shelves. A burnt-out Amazon warehouse would have more impact to some than the actual destruction of vast swathes of the Amazon rainforest. As Frederic Jameson has been often misquoted as saying: 'It is easier to imagine the end of the world than the end of capitalism' (Fisher 2012). Yet Butler manages *both*. Her novel depicts not the well-trodden tropes of 'post-apocalypse' but a 'thrutopia' (Rupert Read's term for narratives that dramatize the transition into a different, powered-down future 2017). In her scenario, there is no complete societal collapse—yet. Economy and technology still function. Elections still take place. A populist candidate promises sweeping changes. The police still exist but are more likely to take a bribe, beat you, or ignore your cries for help, than 'protect and serve'. Butler's thrutopia is predicated on the African-American experience—one that experiences prejudice and police brutality on a regular basis. Two years before the publication of her book, Rodney King was beaten to death by members of the LAPD in 1991, triggering riots across the country, and Butler's novel seems informed by not only the resulting aesthetic of that in news footage, but by the angry fire fuelled by centuries of exploitation and persecution. There is no Seventh Cavalry coming to save you—indeed, they may be coming to lynch you. And so you have to take it upon yourself to save your own skin. *Parable of the Sower* teaches the reader how to survive in a brutal world. It is empowering and defiant, unflinching in its depiction of the casual violence meted out by life, and yet celebratory of the simple acts of kindness that forge community and (re)build civilisation. It also celebrates the everyday miracles of nature—as when it rains for the first time in six years. In the title and throughout, Butler uses natural imagery and analogies as a tonal counterpoint to the brutalised sub/urban landscape. Practical acts of conservation (such as saving seeds) combined with biomimetic acts of 'sowing seeds' of hope, love, and faith, are the stepping stones to a better world. Consequently, *Parable of the Sower,* not only joins the ranks of first-class dystopias, alongside George Orwell's *Nineteen Eighty-Four* (2019 [1949]), and Margaret Atwood's *The Handmaid's Tale* (2010 [1985]), but outshines them in terms of its ecological sensibilities.

* * *

Writing beyond social norms has produced some other electrifying classics of ecofiction: Edward Abbey's *The Monkey Wrench Gang* (2000 [1975]) and Diane Cook's *The New Wilderness* (2020) in particular, which we shall look at in **Art versus Activism.**

Gender is becoming increasingly perceived as a construct, with pushback from so-called TERFs, etc and other gender-critical discourse. However, a fluid a concept or 'construct', writing beyond one's (original) gender can produce powerful work—whether one writes a central protagonist with a different gender or makes gender politics central to the plot: *The Ministry for the Future* as can be seen in (2020); *The Lamplighters* (2021); and Le Guin's classic *The Left Hand of Darkness* (1981 [1969]).

Other impressive results can be generated by writing beyond one's discipline or 'subject specialism', e.g. April Doyle's apiarist novel, *Hive* (2022); and beyond one's species e.g. Richard Adams' *Watership Down* (1972), or Richard Powers' *The Overstory* (2018).

It needs to be acknowledged that writing *within* one's identity—be it intersectional (Crenshaw 1989) or otherwise—can produce some of the most powerful work to see print: *I Belong Here* (Sethi 2022); *Planetwalker* (Francis 2009); *Undercurrents* (Carthew 2023); and *Braiding Sweetgrass* (2013), to give a few examples.

It is also critical to acknowledge that writing beyond one's ethnicity, gender, class, societal norms, discipline, or even species all bring with them a range of challenges and possible benefits. In the next chapter, we will look at these.

Ultimately, if we are to develop as writers—a path entwined with one's own personal maturation—we all need to step outside our front door, and look beyond our particular garden fence (although many riches can be discovered in a garden, if you are lucky enough to own or have access to one where you live—spending time there with your notebook can be very rewarding). Beyond the picket fence—that is, beyond the pale of 'acceptable behaviour' (as delineated by the hegemonies of Anglocentrism) wild riches await the boldest of writers. The Pale, or 'English Pale', was an area in the environs of Dublin controlled by England in the Late Middle Ages. Anything external to this colonial jurisdiction was deemed unruly. To the majority of Irish true freedom existed *outside* of this control zone—beyond the pale their own culture flourished freely. There is always a need for craft, but writing colonised by rules remains stiff and unoriginal. Good writers must be willing to stray from the path, to go the edges, and further—to push themselves, their chosen form, and their craft as far as possible. This requires taking creative and ontological risks and writing beyond one's knowledge and identity. But such an endeavour comes with responsibility, as we shall consider next.

Mycelia: Connections to Other Writers, Texts, and Resources

Excellent examples of writing 'beyond the pale', include:

- Davidson, Robyn. 2013 [1980]. *Tracks*. London: Bloomsbury.
- Griffiths, Jay. 2008. *Wild: An Element Journey*. London: Penguin.
- Liptrott, Amy. 2016. *The Outrun*. Edinburgh: Canongate.

- Macdonald, Helen. 2014. *H is for Hawk*. London: Vintage.
- Strayed, Cheryl. 2015. *Wild: A Journey from Lost to Found*. London: Atlantic Books.
- Wynn, Raynor. 2019. *The Salt Path*. London: Penguin.

For other kinds of 'going beyond', it would also be worth looking at:

- Bowles, Paul. 2000 [1949]. *The Sheltering Sky*. London: Penguin.
- Clare, Horatio. 2022. *Heavy Light: A Journey Through Madness, Mania, and Healing*. London: Vintage.
- Clarke, Lindsay. 2010. *The Water Theatre*. London: Alma Books.
- Fermour, Patrick Leigh. 2013 [1977]. *A Time of Gifts*. London: John Murray.
- Fermour, Patrick Leigh. 1986. *Between Wood and Water*. London: Penguin.
- Fermour, Patrick Leigh. 2014. *The Broken Road*. London: John Murray.
- Frazier, Charles. 1997. *Cold Mountain*. London: Sceptre.
- Garner, Alan. 1996. *Strandloper*. London: Harvill Press.
- Hayes, Nick. 2021. *The Book of Trespass: Crossing the Lines that Divide Us*. London: Bloomsbury.
- Lee, Laurie. 1970 [1969]. *As I Walked Out One Midsummer Morning*. London: World Books.
- Ondaatje, Michael. 1992. *The English Patient*. London: Picador.

Spores: Writing Activities
- The Non-Anthropocentric—in this exercise you are challenged to give voice to the non-human, or more-than-human: animals, trees, landmarks, bodies of water, natural phenomena. Ideally be in view of or in close proximity to (if safe) the more-than-human you wish to give voice to: sit by a stream, under a tree, or in view of a wildlife compound or nature reserve; failing that, use an image or object to inspire you: a feather, shell, antler tine, bone, seed, etc. Use all your senses to closely commune with your subject. Now begin to write, letting it speak through you. Avoid the anthropomorphic if you can and let it sound as 'other' as you are able to articulate—using onomatopoeia, neologisms, and feral sounds if it feels right. Rewild your language.
- Researching the Unknown—pick a subject you would like to know more about (something that could provide fertile ground for a narrative, e.g. the petrochemical industry; fast fashion; factory farming; GMO). Conduct

some initial research. Identify key sources and resources. Is there a particular museum, or study centre where you could access special collections? Are there any major exhibitions coming up or conferences? Once you have made some notes, consider if there is scope here for a creative response—a flash fiction, short story, or novel. How will you dramatise the issue or area and make it engaging for your readers?
- Going Beyond the Pale—it is essential to take risks in pursuit of true artistry. Sometimes we have to let the dangerous voices speak, going beyond the pale of etiquette, of societal norms. This is not to give a platform to hate-speech, but to allow the anger, frustration, despair, etc., of the disenfranchised to be heard: to give voice to the voiceless. Not to speak over them, or for them, but with them—in solidarity. This requires courage: to be the heretic, to say the thing that no one has said; to be the child in the Emperor's New Clothes—the one who sees truly, and not just what they have been socially conditioned to see. Speak up now. Give voice to what needs to be said. Don't hold back, but *do* consider carefully how you could use such a venting of spleen (if that's what you end up writing) in your fiction. Could you create a character who embodies this particular viewpoint? If so, include a cross-section of others too—and let the reader triangulate between them. Avoid unexpurgated diatribe.

References

Abbey, Edward. 2000 [1975]. *The Monkey Wrench Gang*. New York: Perennial.
Adams, Richard. 1972. *Watership Down*. London: Rex Collings.
Arbus, Diane. 2004. *Magazine Work*. New York: Aperture.
Atwood, Margaret. 2010 [1985]. *The Handmaid's Tale*. London: Vintage.
Bate, Jonathan. 2000. *The Song of the Earth*. London: Picador.
Booker, Christopher. 2004. *The Seven Basic Plots: Why We Tell Stories*. London: Continuum.
Butler, Octavia E. 2019 [1993]. *Parable of the Sower*. London: Headline.
Campbell, Joseph. 1993 [1949]. *The Hero with a Thousand Faces*. London: Fontana Press.
Carthew, Natasha. 2023. *Undercurrents: A Cornish Memoir of Poverty, Nature and Resilience*. London: Hodder and Stoughton.
Chatwin, Bruce. 1987. *The Songlines*. London: Picador.
Crenshaw, Kimberlé. 1989. Demarginalizing the Intersection of Race and Sex: A Black Feminist Critique of Antidiscrimination Doctrine, Feminist Theory and Antiracist Politics. *University of Chicago Legal Forum*: Vol. 1989, Article 8. https://chicagounbound.uchicago.edu/uclf/vol1989/iss1/8 (Accessed 7 February 2023).

Crowley, John. 2000 [1981]. *Little, Big*. London: Gollancz.
Cook, Diane. 2020. *The New Wilderness*. London: Oneworld.
Cummins, Jeanine. 2020. *American Dirt*. New York: Flatiron Books.
Doerr, Anthony. 2021. *Cloud Cuckoo Land*. London: Fourth Estate.
Doyle, April. 2022. *Hive*. Kibworth: The Book Guild.
Dylan, Bob. 1965. *Subterranean Homesick Blues*. New York, NY: Columbia Records.
Fisher, Mark. 2012. *Capitalist Realism: Is There No Alternative?* Portland, OR: Zero Books.
Flaherty, Alice W. 2005. *The Midnight Disease: The Drive to Write, Writer's Block, and the Creative Brain*. Boston, MA: Houghton Mifflin/Mariner Books.
Francis, John. 2009. *Planetwalker: 22 Years of Walking. 17 Years of Silence*. Washington, DC: National Geographic.
Haraway, Donna J. 2016. *Staying with the Trouble: Making Kin with the Chthulucene*. Durham and London: Duke University Press.
Harrison, M. John. 1989. *Climbers*. London: Orion.
Jefferies, Richard. 1980 [1885]. *After London, or Wild England*. Oxford: Oxford University Press.
Keller, Helen. 1957. *The Open Door*. New York: Doubleday.
Kimmerer, Robin Wall. 2013. *Braiding Sweetgrass: Indigenous Wisdom, Scientific Knowledge and the Teachings of Plants*. London: Penguin.
Krakauer, Jon. 1996. *Into the Wild*. New York: Random House.
Le Guin, Ursula K. 1981 [1969]. *The Left Hand of Darkness*. London: Orbit.
Lopez, Barry. 2014 [1986]. *Arctic Dreams*. London: Vintage.
Macfarlane, Robert. 2008. *Mountains of the Mind: A History of a Fascination*. London: Granta.
McCarthy, Cormac. 2006. *The Road*. London: Picador.
McGilchrist, Iain. 2012. *The Master and His Emissary: The Divided Brain and the Making of the Western World*. New Haven and London: Yale University Press.
Mitchell, David. 2008. *Cloud Atlas*. London: Random House.
Morgen, Brett, director. 2022. *Moonage Daydream*. Featuring David Bowie. Universal Pictures. https://www.imdb.com/title/tt9883832/?ref_=nv_sr_srsg_0_tt_5_nm_0_q_Moonage%2520Daydream.
Morris, William. 1890. *News from Nowhere, or An Epoch of Rest, Being Some Chapters from a Utopian Romance*. Oxford: Kelmscott Press.
Morton, Timothy. 2007. *Ecology Without Nature: Rethinking Environmental Aesthetics*. Cambridge, Mass: Harvard University Press.
Myers, Benjamin. 2017. *The Gallows Pole*. Hebden Bridge: Blue Moose.
Myers, Benjamin. 2018. Shortlist Spotlight: Benjamin Myers, Sir Walter Scott Prize for Historical Fiction. https://www.walterscottprize.co.uk/shortlist-spotlight-benjamin-myers/ (Accessed 2 February 2023).
Orwell, George. 2019 [1949]. *Nineteen-Eighty-Four*. London: Penguin Classics.
Penn, Sean. 2007. *Into the Wild*. USA: Paramount Vantage.
Penney, Stef. 2006. *The Tenderness of Wolves*. London: Quercus.
Powers, Richard. 2018. *The Overstory*. London: William Heinemann.

Pullman, Philip. 2019. "Habit is the writer's best friend. Habit has written far more books than talent has." Twitter, Jan 21.
Read, Rupert. 2017. 'THRUTOPIA: Why Neither Dystopias Nor Utopias Are Enough To Get Us Through The Climate Crisis, And How A 'Thrutopia' Could Be'. *Huffington Post*. 6 November 2017. Available from: https://www.huffingtonpost.co.uk/rupertread/thrutopia-why-neither-dys_b_18372090.html. [Accessed: 3 June 2024]
Robinson, Kim Stanley. 2020. *The Ministry for the Future*. London: Orbit.
Sethi, Anita. 2022. *I Belong Here*. London: Bloomsbury Wildlife.
Sinclair, Iain. 1987. *White Chapell, Scarlet Tracings*. London: Goldmark.
Sinclair, Iain. 2004. *Downriver*. London: Penguin.
Sinclair, Iain. 1997. *Lights Out for the Territory*. Cambridge: Granta.
Sinclair, Iain. 2003. *London Orbital*. London: Penguin.
Sinclair, Iain. 2012. *Ghost Milk*. London: Penguin.
Sinclair, Iain. 2017. *The Last London: True Fictions from an Unreal City*. London: Oneworld Publications.
Sinclair, Iain. 2012 [1975]. *Lud Heat: A Book of the Dead Hamlets*. n.p.: Skylight Press.
Sinclair, Iain. 2021. *The Gold Machine: Tracking the Ancestors from Highlands to Coffee Colony*. London: Oneworld.
Stewart, George. 1999 [1949]. *Earth Abides*. London: Millennium/Gollancz SF Masterworks.
Stonex, Emma. 2021. *The Lamplighters*. London: Viking.
Snyder, Gary. 1990. *The Practice of the Wild*. Berkeley: Counterpoint.
Turchi, Peter. 2004. *Maps of the Imagination: The Writer as Cartographer*. San Antonio, Texas: Trinity University Press.
VanderMeer, Jeff. 2014. *Area X: The Southern Reach Trilogy*. New York, NY: Farrar, Straus and Giroux.
Whitehead, Harry. 2011. *The Cannibal Spirit*. London: Penguin.
Yeats, W.B. 1989. *The Collected Poems of W.B. Yeats*. London: Collier Books.

4

Voices of the Global Majority

How can voices that eschew the western, Anglophone, and the economic elite help to defamiliarise and revitalise fiction about environmental issues? In this chapter we will look at diverse voices that articulate and epitomise the so-called 'Global South'—a problematic term, in the way it is totalising; elides vast diversity; and is suggestive of a 'First World' bias and superiority complex, but one that has provided a useful counterbalance for shifting perspectives from the 'Global North'—voices which destabilise existing power structures, and offer a spectrum of diverse paradigms and positions from across the globe.

However, to acknowledge and redress the inequalities that a term such as the 'Global South' perpetuate, I propose an alternative: the Global Majority. This reframing is substantiated by the plethora of information available that shows the vast disparities of wealth, population, and geography (United Nations, 2015). As energy and climate change expert, Professor Kevin Anderson, has advocated (#AltCop 2020), we need 'new narratives', ones that reframe our current thinking, behaviour, and policies.

Also, this chapter considers an essential area that all writers of conscience must engage with: the ethics of representation. Every writer must consider their position regarding 'cultural appropriation'. What could be called 'The Lionel Shriver position' will be considered alongside more sensitive ones. Mindful of Gayatri Chakravorty Spivak's Subaltern Position, and Edward Said's Orientalism, we will consider the importance of empowering marginalised voices, representing indigenous rights, and other post-colonial considerations—perspectives that have problematised the Anthropocene:

another term that has been critiqued for its apparent eliding of the disproportionate actions, needs, and impacts of the Global North (Haraway 2016; Macfarlane 2019; Bould 2021). Acknowledging the reality of intersectionality for many of these voices, and the key role that has to play in helping us to overcome the systemic biases that perpetuate colonialism and capitalism, we will look at the challenges and rewards of 'writing the other' (Shawl and Ward 2005).

* * *

The Climate Crisis is another sweeping umbrella term for a global phenomenon with multiple manifestations (extreme weather events; melting of glaciers and ice-shelves; thawing of permafrost; acidification of the oceans; deforestation; habitat loss; loss of biodiversity; mass extinctions; exhausted and eroded soil; pandemics; floods; heat waves; wildfires; and so forth) that impacts upon peoples disproportionately across the globe. Those with the lowest incomes and least impact upon the environment (in terms of carbon footprint) are being affected *more*, unprotected by the buffer zones wealth affords, and the majority of these are BIPOC (Black Indigenous People of Colour) populations in the Global Majority. The acknowledgement of this and the many efforts to redress it is known as Climate Justice, which Dr Farhana Sultana describes as, 'fundamentally about paying attention to how climate change impacts people differently, unevenly, and disproportionately, as well as redressing the resultant injustices in fair and equitable ways' (2020).

Ecofiction in the Twenty-first Century needs to acknowledge the Global Majority if it is to offer an accurate representation of the issues we face, and the way they affect people differently. To do otherwise is to perpetuate a neo-colonialist perspective of the world—one that can only conceptualise such problems if they impact a white, middle-class family, say, in the 'Global North' (the dramatic focus of many Hollywood re-imaginings of the Climate Crisis, such as Ric Roman Waugh's 2020 *Greenland*, which uses the trope of the 'planet-killing comet' to create an accelerated climate apocalypse scenario where only certain privileged families get to survive—chiefly, it seems, North Americans of the techno-industrialist class). Their experience of the Climate Crisis will be significantly different to that of, say, a subsisting indigenous family on the low-lying Marshall Islands in the Pacific (whose lives are not deemed worth dramatising either in big budget ways, or in fiction, thus far).

An impactful, if imperfect, example of a novel that foregrounds the experience of the Global Majority is Kim Stanley Robinson's *The Ministry for the Future* (2020). The opening chapter is set in an 'ordinary town in Uttar Pradesh', a state in India, which experiences a lethal wet-bulb temperature (a deadly combination of heat and humidity) of 38/35 Centigrade. An American aid worker, Frank May, is caught in it while staying at a hotel. At first his air conditioning still works, and he allows people to take shelter in his room, but eventually, they are all forced into the swimming pool, where all but he die in a harrowing scene. Robinson seems to be using this gruelling opening to shock the reader into the reality of Climate Change and its deadly effect, dramatizing the familiar analogy of frogs being boiled alive in increments (by the time they realise, it is too late for them to hop out). Robinson is saying, unequivocally, that humanity is at risk of suffering the same fate—a dramatisation of one of David Wallace-Wells' chilling worst-case scenarios (2019). The plot focuses mainly on the efforts of former Irish minister, Mary Murphy and her fictional UN agency, The Ministry for the Future, to ameliorate the catastrophic effects of the Climate Crisis, forcing through emergency measures to radically change the damaging policies of governments across the globe. India, having been devastated by the deadly heatwaves, leads the way in embracing sustainable energy solutions.

Although written by a non-BIPOC author, Robinson—a successful, white, American writer—the novel demonstrates an acute awareness to the impact of the Climate Crisis on the Global Majority, and a concerted effort to foreground it. This may not be as 'ideal' as BIPOC voices of the Global Majority speaking for themselves—and, critically, it doesn't replace or silence those—but it makes more overtures to acknowledge lives beyond the Global North than many other novels. And it's impact was considerable—the novel was cited by former US President Barack Obama as one of his 'books of the year', and was widely discussed at COP26, with Robinson himself giving talks at parallel events taking place in Glasgow (COP26 TED Countdown).

Yet Robinson, however well-intentioned can never be more than a white 'ally' to BIPOC writers, and it is their voices, most of all, that urgently need to be heard, to be published, read, discussed, celebrated, and promoted. Fortunately, the more conscionable publishers have widely-acknowledged the need to diversify. Much work needs to be done still, but lists are becoming slowly more representative and diverse. And more novels in translation are appearing on the shelves too—some with clear acknowledgement of the co-creative act of translation. World literature is growing popularity, although it is has precedents in the pioneering work of authors like Isabelle Allende, Jorge Luis Borges, Patricia Grace, Keri Hulme, Witi Ihimaera, Halldór Laxness, Gabriel García Marquez, VS Naipaul, Helen van Neerven, Salman Rushdie, Alexis Wright, and many more (some of whom I discuss in more detail below). In the last two decades writers of colour from the Global Majority have grown in prominence, with an impressive 'new wave' from Africa: such as

Chimamanda Ngozi Adichie, Abi Dare, Aminatta Forna, Laila Lalami, Leila Aboulela, Sarah Lapido Manyika, and Sefi Atta, to name but a few.

As many of these so-called Developing Countries are already experiencing the sharp end of the Climate Crisis it is more vital than ever that such voices—representing a healthy cross-section of backgrounds, ethnicities, genders, and politics, and not being bound to a single issue or subject—are given a platform.

Indigenous perspectives are also much needed in this conversation. In *Braiding Sweetgrass* (2016), bryologist and enrolled member of the Citizen Potawatomi Nation, Professor Robin Wall Kimmerer interweaves her scientific training with her First Nations cultural heritage to resonant effect. She gently but firmly insists: 'We need acts of restoration, not only for polluted waters and degraded lands, but also for our relationship to the world. We need to restore honour to the way we live, so that when we walk through the world we don't have to avert our eyes with shame, so that we can hold our heads up high and receive the respectful acknowledgment of the rest of the earth's beings' (ibid.). This 'relationship to the world', what Donna J. Haraway calls 'making kin' (2016) is fundamental to many indigenous cultures. It is a way of being in the world, being with the world, that David Abram explores, advocating a phenomenological (after Merleau-Ponty) approach:

> It may be that the new "environmental ethic" toward which so many environmental philosophers aspire—an ethic that would lead us to respect and heed not only the lives of our fellow humans but also the life and well-being of the rest of nature – will come into existence not primarily through the logical elucidation of new philosophical principles and legislative strictures, but through a renewed attentiveness to this perceptual dimension that underlies all our logics, through a rejuvenation of our carnal, sensorial empathy with the living land that sustains us. (2017 [1996]: 69)

In the West we need to relearn to speak that language, but first and foremost, we need to listen—to the Earth, and to those who live close to it. Often these voices are overlooked, but like the small Himalayan nation of Bhutan, which is not only carbon neutral but carbon negative, they can lead the way, as its former prime minister, Tshering Tobgay, eloquently demonstrated in his 2016 TED talk:

> I thank you for listening to our story, a story of how we are keeping our promise to remain carbon neutral, a story of how we are keeping our country

pristine, for ourselves, our children, for your children and for the world. But we are not here to tell stories, are we? We are here to dream together. ...

Tobgay, and his country, are guided by their Buddhist beliefs—which illustrate how important a core ethos is to any endeavour. In Latin America, such a tenet that is gaining traction, despite the extreme hostility from some of the governments, is 'buen vivir'—an umbrella term for a whole host of social and climate justice initiatives, but one that focuses on the quality of the 'end', rather than just the 'means', as Eduardo Gudynas, one of its key exponents, explains: 'These are not equivalents at all. With buen vivir, the subject of wellbeing is not [about the] individual, but the individual in the social context of their community and in a unique environmental situation' (interviewed by Oliver Balch, 2013). This reframing from the individualistic to the communitarian, which in the Global North may seem radical, is key to the movement's success. No one person can stand alone against the capitalist industrial machine. We are entangled beings, 'creative assemblages' as Haraway calls us, and to think in discreetist terms is to be part of the problem. And in a similar way, we are not one-dimensional either—defined by a single essentialist characteristic, but multi-faceted. This dimensionality has been called 'intersectionality'.

Intersectionality

In her seminal article for the *University of Chicago Legal Forum*, Kimberlé Crenshaw critiqued the 'single-axis framework' (1989: 139) dominant in antidiscrimination law, but also, she argues, in feminist theory and antiracist politics that does not reflect the 'multidimensionality of Black women's experience' (ibid.). In doing so, Crenshaw provided a focalising concept that has been influential in discourse around gender, sexuality, ethnicity, politics, class, and beliefs ever since. Since Crenshaw such 'protected characteristics' (to use the terminology of Equality, Diversity, and Inclusivity which has been adopted by many publically-funded organisations, especially within Higher Education) could not be seen in isolation, especially among 'marginalised' groups whose lived reality is often a near perpetual, debilitating convergence of multiple prejudices and pressures, which those who do not share their intersectionality rarely have to consider. Racism, sexism, ableism, classism, homophobia, religious hatred, and so forth are egregious by themselves, but in combination can create massive obstacles for those who endure them— a crossfire of persecution and restricted options: the opposite of privilege. Of course, such intersectional experiences have been around for a long time, but Crenshaw's articulation of the concept helped to provide an essential framework for discussion.

Since Crenshaw's seminal article, intersectionality has been seized by many as the critical frame needed to defend rights and to campaign for systemic change.

Naisha Khan, a young Canadian racial and climate justice campaigner, exhorted the importance of intersectionality in the Climate Movement in her talk, 'The Sustainabiliteens: Creating an Intersectional Climate Movement' (CBC Radio, Vancouver 2021). Khan argues that the Climate Movement is largely predicated upon a white, First World, cis-gendered, heteronormative perspective that marginalises BIPOC voices and experience and unknowingly perpetuates the very problems it campaigns against—'systems of oppression' that perpetuate colonialism and capitalism—and until these are addressed the systemic change desired will not be truly effective or representative. Khan, seeing Crenshaw's intersectionality as the key critical reframing required, proposes the following solutions: centre and uplift BIPOC voices; unlearn white supremacy ('but not at the cost of my emotional labour'); incorporating hope; and celebrate BIPOC joy.

Although focused on the Climate Movement, Khan's criteria could be applied to ecofiction that aspires to give voice to the Global Majority. No one is ever going to get it all right, but awareness of such issues and a willingness to address them—through better representation and opportunities—is definitely a step in the right direction.

However, there are sections of society—including writers—who resist this.

Cultural Appropriation—The Lionel Shriver Position

Cultural appropriation is a phenomenon that has been happening for centuries, as the ongoing debates around the repatriation of national treasures such as ghost shirts belonging to First Nations tribes, the Benin Bronzes, or the Elgin Marbles have shown. As a specific concept, it has only been in existence since the 1970s, emerging from discourse around western colonialism. Although no one has been credited as the sole author, the British academic Kenneth Coutts-Smith discussed a near identical concept, 'cultural colonialism', and this filtered down from academic circles into popular consciousness via the tabloid favourite, 'political correctness', which the Right-Wing press quickly leapt upon as a symbol of all that was wrong in modern society—any sensitive awareness of 'other' peoples' perspectives (that is, not white, middle class, Conservative and Anglophone) being seen as killjoy and kowtowing to 'bleeding heart liberals'. With the advent of Tim Berners-Lee's World Wide Web and the Internet, in particular social media, this divisive debate has been exacerbated, with algorithms promoting controversial posts, as they generate more 'engagement' (views; likes; reposts; comments)—which advertisers value greatly. In the early Twenty-first Century, traditional print media, having to compete with digital platforms of endlessly streaming, and updating content, manufactured the so-called Culture Wars (which the tabloid-friendly 'Mods versus Rockers' and 'Beatles versus Stones' rivalry of the 1950s and 1960s foreshadowed in a more transparently anodine way), in which the 'Woke' Left are castigated for being unpatriotic, weakling 'snowflakes'. The Anti-Fascist movement, shortened to 'Antifa' in North America, created a pushback among Trump supporters during his Presidency: summarised as 'Anti-Anti-Fa', which essentially means 'Pro-Fascism'. The bitter irony is the original 'Antifa' were not marginalised and demonised members of the liberal left, but the entire Allied Forces of the Second World War. Yet the 'Anti-Antifa' discourse continues, perpetuated by many descendants of Second World War liberators in complete cognitive dissonance, disingenuity, or devilment. This is supported by the co-opting by the Alt-Right of Nazi iconography and signalling, including White Supremacy hand signals used by Republican sympathisers in Congress, and the 45th President himself 'dog-whistling' his so-called Proud Boys into mass shootings and ram-raiding of citizens, and the assault upon Capitol Hill on January 6th, 2021. Angry critiques of cultural appropriation by Right-Wing commentators such as Katy Hopkins and Nigel Farage are the thin end of the wedge. Intelligent, informed debate is always needed, and nothing should be beyond criticism, but the silencing of any complaint about libertarian 'freedom' to say and do whatever one chooses, whatever the consequences, is perpetuated by those protesting against 'Cancel Culture'. It is also a bitter irony that true Cancel Culture is the kind that bans books, criminalises protest, erodes human rights, and leads to concentration camps—something Alt-Right commentators choose to forget, or outright deny the existence of.

One of the most outspoken critics of any kind of *mindfulness* (which is perhaps a better way of putting sensitivity of representation and ethical responsibility for what one creates) in publishing has been the novelist Lionel Shriver, whose speech lambasting the very idea of cultural appropriation clearly positioned her against the Left. Defiantly wearing a sombrero, Shriver said, 'I hope the concept of cultural appropriation is a passing fad' (2016).

The late British journalist and author Christopher Hitchens adopted a similar antagonistic stance in a talk: 'My opinion is enough for me, and

I claim the right to have it defended against any consensus, any majority, anywhere, any place, and any time. And anyone who disagrees with this can pick a number, get in line, and kiss my ass' (2006).

The fact is that many Left-wing writers would *defend* the right of the Hitchens and Shrivers of this world to have the freedom to express their opinion, such as Shami Chakrabarti, the former Director of the human rights organisation, Liberty:

> I defend your right to foam at the mouth from the pulpit or soapbox and to irritate, offend and insult me, even to the point that I am a lesser creature than you. You should be able to bar me from your home, church or clergy, if that is your taste, view or faith. That is your freedom of speech, conscience, association and your private life. That is your loss not mine. (2014: 120)

In discussing his novel, *The Good Man Jesus and the Scoundrel Christ* (2010), Philip Pullman, former Chair of The Society of Authors, expressed a connected sentiment—the right to shock, and even to offend:

> It was a shocking thing to say and I knew it was a shocking thing to say. But no one has the right to live without being shocked. No one has the right to spend their life without being offended. Nobody has to read this book. Nobody has to pick it up. Nobody has to open it. And if you open it and read it, you don't have to like it. And if you read it and you dislike it, you don't have to remain silent about it. You can write to me, you can complain about it, you can write to the publisher, you can write to the papers, you can write your own book. You can do all those things, but there your rights stop. No one has the right to stop me writing this book. No one has the right to stop it being published, or sold, or bought, or read. (2010)

There are complexities and nuances to this debate, as when authors or artists deliberately intend to cause offense (which tragically played out in the 2015 massacre of *Charlie Hebdo* staff in Paris), but in a time when libraries are being eviscerated of classic and contemporary literature, which has been banned by fundamentalist civic authorities in North America, the restriction of creative freedom or its 'policing' needs to be carefully watched.

And yet it is still possible to be mindful of alterity, be skilled at representation, and be a good ally wherever possible to BIPOC communities without feeling curtailed; and without shamelessly appropriating whatever one fancies.

This antithesis to the Shriver (or Hitchens) Position is articulated by Nisi Shawl and Cynthia Ward in their book, *Writing the Other* (2005).

Approaching Writing the Other

When a student at the 1992 Clarion West Writers Workshop expressed the opinion that 'it is a mistake to write about people of ethnic backgrounds different from your own because you might get it wrong, horribly, offensively wrong, and so it is better not even to try', Nisi Shawl, who was in attendance with Cynthia Ward, decided to write an essay addressing the problem—for the opinion was one many writers, both published and aspiring, seemed to share. Just don't go there. This results in a paucity of representation and thin-blooded fiction that does not represent the diversity of the world. Even if such stories are set on Secondary Worlds, in a pocket universe, or in a distant part of the galaxy, readers need to see themselves on the page. It is a generosity to the world to look beyond your own particular picket fence—conceptually, culturally, ethnically, economically, and in terms of one's beliefs and politics. You could just call it good writing.

Initially focusing on the 'challenges' of writing characters marked by racial and ethnic differences, Nisi Shawl realised that writers encounter similar issues when trying to create characters who differ significantly in age, gender, and sexual preferences from their own. Working with Cynthia Ward, Shawl developed a workshop to tackle the rewards and challenges of 'writing the other'. Out of this coalesced their book, *Writing the Other* (2005), in which they bring together core teachings and techniques from their classes. Some of the key principles include giving yourself permission to get it wrong—in the first draft at least, and being prepared to 'revise, rewrite, and redraft!'. Another is to avoid the 'unmarked state' when characters have no definable character-istics—this creates a void in which a lot of assumptions are made, and biases and privilege can be perpetuated, such as 'liberal perception fallacy', when well-intentioned predominantly white, middle-class writers assume people in the real world always act nice towards one another just because that may be their reality: in doing so failing to acknowledge the intersectional issues that many people face everyday. A key way of avoiding the unmarked state is to identify in some way what Shawl and Ward call ROAARS (Race; Orientation; Ability; Age; Religion; Sex). They say it is vital to *acknowledge* differences, not elide them, while at the same time avoiding essentialism and tokenism. Ensure diverse characters are *rounded* characters most of all, not defined by a single characteristic. If writing beyond one's experience, do you research and ask sensitivity readers to check your work-in-progress—for although it is forgivable to 'get it wrong' in that first draft, you need to be willing to get it right if it is to be published, for once it is in the public domain ill-considered writing can cause damage, not least to the writer's own reputation.

This happened with former teacher, Kate Clanchy, who was accused of racial and ableist stereotyping in her memoir, *Some Kids I Taught and What They Taught Me* (2019). A tweet criticising her book exploded into a damaging public spat on social media between former President of The Society of Authors, Philip Pullman, and Chimene Suleyman, Monisha Rajesh and Sunny Singh. The fallout of this included Clanchy and her publisher 'parting ways', and Pullman stepping down from his presidency after apologising for jumping in to defend Clanchy initially. Not wanting to defend Pullman, it seems clear that the blame sits primarily on both Clanchy's shoulders and those of her editor. There was a stage of the creative process where Clanchy would have been forgiven for getting it wrong, but by the time it sees print, it's too late. As Shawl and Ward emphasise: 'Writing is *considered* speech. It gives you the opportunity to rewrite and revise. It gives you the opportunity to override the reptile brain and the lazy forebrain' (2005). Yet, despite such cautionary tales, Shawl and Ward encourage us to not turn away from the challenges of writing the other: just to put the work in, be prepared to fail, fail better, and, with each rewrite, reach closer towards more accurate representation. No one wants to be another's tokenistic or monolithic 'type'. Avoid lazy, shorthand character traits. Just try writing about real people in all of their flawed complexity—however imaginary the context.

Let All Voices Be Heard

One cannot help the accidents and serendipities of genetics, geography, parents, upbringing, early education, and cultural influences; and one should not apologise for them either. We are all 'intersectional' in the broadest sense—the sum of our inherited characteristics and influences, initially, at least, until one is free to forge one's own path in life, if that is indeed possible (it is a privilege not available to all, unfortunately). So, not all of us are voices of the Global Majority, but we can choose to align ourselves with them in a number of ways. We can actively support them by championing writing authored and published by them; write reviews; ask libraries and bookshops to stock them; literary festivals to book them, and then support their readings and talks; read, listen to, and watch interviews with them; campaign for our educational institutions to decolonise their curricula. Open doors. Drop down ladders. Be good allies.

But what if we want to write about the 'other'?

Well, first of all, question your motives for wishing to do so: are you the best person to tell their story? What is your connection to the 'material' (which, unless purely fictional, is drawing upon the lived reality of others and can therefore risk being exploitative)? What is your motivation? Are other writers, BIPOC writers of the Global Majority, already telling the story or stories you wish to tell? If so, what do you feel you can add, if anything? Consider your position—where does the power lie (or as Shawl and Ward put it, where does the privilege lie)? If you are eliding authentic voices, drowning them out in favour of your own perspective, then reconsider: why not draw upon your own heritage instead? If it is recent, it is likely to be raw—and you run the risk of offending someone; if it is in the past, then you'll need to undertake serious research. Are you willing to go to archives? conduct interviews? undertake field research? acknowledge the input of others? Consider co-authoring something, or creating an anthology or other kind of creative platform for the voices you wish to celebrate. Why should your name go on somebody else's story? Whatever your decision, make sure your project—if you proceed—is done with respect, with integrity, and with skill. Enlist the help of sensitivity readers, or as I heard them called at a festival ('Writing Marginalised Villains', Fantasycon, London, September 2022), 'accountability readers'. Make sure you are accountable for what you write, aware as possible of the possible impact. We cannot control precisely how people react to our writing, but consider your intentions—if it is done to insensitively shock, to hurt, to 'punch down', then reconsider the wisdom and ethics of your actions. If it is done to honour, to celebrate, to raise awareness, to explore, and champion, then most people would value that—especially the stakeholders (as long as they have been consulted, if possible).

The human imagination is limitless, and with skill, integrity, and serious research *anything* is possible. As Chimamanda Ngozi Adichie has eloquently argued ('Freedom of Speech', BBC Reith Lectures 2022), our imaginations should not be 'policed'. It is an act of great compassion to imagine the lives of others. To look over your own particular garden fence; to walk in another's shoes. To learn someone's story and pass it on (well). Imagine if Shakespeare only wrote about the family of a whittawer (glove-maker) in Stratford-upon-Avon instead of the myriad, complex lives of kings, queens, princes, knaves, rogues, fools, merchants, drunkards, lovers, and villains? The world would be a poorer place. Do whatever your 'muse' calls you to do—with all the above caveats—just do it well. The further from yourself the purview of your material, the more work you will have to do. Be prepared to spend years, if necessary, to get it right. Consider how much research Hilary Mantel had to undertake to bring to life vividly, convincingly, the world of Thomas Cromwell (in her twice-Booker Prize-winning *Wolf Hall* trilogy: *Wolf Hall* 2009; *Bring Up the Bodies* 2012; *The Mirror and the Light* 2020). In terms of the theme of this chapter, could you convincingly write *The Famished Road* (1991), *Midnight's Children* (1981), *Whale Rider* (1987), and so forth, as well as those authors who were writing from within their culture? If not, one can risk accusations of 'trauma porn that wears a social justice fig leaf' (as activist Myriam Gurba put it), as happened to the author of *American Dirt* (2020), Jeanine Cummins, who received a critical backlash as a white American woman of Irish and Puerto Rican heritage writing about the Mexican immigrant experience. The scale of this (thousands of articles, tweets, and blog posts) seems not unrelated to the hype surrounding the book's release. Lauded as 'a *Grapes of Wrath* for our times', by novelist Don Winslow, featured on Oprah Winfrey's Book Club, and promoted by a marketing campaign that many saw as 'tasteless and misleading', (Shapiro 2021) *American Dirt* was a high-profile publication that seemed to make bold claims about authenticity, realism, and social conscience. It provides a salutary warning about undertaking such endeavours with care.

Examples of the Global Majority in Ecofiction

Ecofiction has been aligned with voices of the Global Majority since its earliest days, although as a literary label it is sometimes applied retrospectively. With hindsight it is possible to identify nascent themes that may not have been so apparent at the time. Magic Realism is a genre of literature that emerged out of Latin American countries in the 1980s—a heady blend of dirty realism and supernaturalism, it intoxicated Western publishers and reviewers for a while, at a time when Globalisation was very much the dominant ideology of the marketplace, and multiculturalism, world music, and the popularity of globetrotting welcomed in a warm, spice-laden breeze, brightening up fashion, festivals, and publishers' lists. Not all Magic Realism could be classed as ecofiction, although the animistic atmosphere that often pervades such titles as *Eva Luna* (Allende 1988) and *The Storyteller* (Marquez 1991) is a step in the right direction.

In New Zealand, Keri Hulme, an author of Maori-Scottish/English descent, won the 1985 Booker Prize with *The Bone People* (1984), her unflinching portrayal of Māori and Pākehā (New Zealand European) culture and mythology. Although drawing upon the distinctive terrain of South Island, Hulme's novel could not be described as primarily ecological, focusing as it does on the lives of three characters who in microcosm represent the ethnic influences of Aotearoa, who between them forge a multiculturalist identity which seeks to heal the wounds of colonialism. However, another novel from Aotearoa/New Zealand, *The Whale Rider* (1987), by Witi Ihimaera, a well-respected Māori author, draws upon the strong cultural connection between Māori tribes and cetaceans. As campaigns by environmental NGO, Greenpeace, 'Save the Whale', was very much in public consciousness in the late 80s, the book struck a chord. It was adapted into a successful film by Niki Caro in 2002. Another contemporary Kiwi author, Elizabeth Knox, weaves ecological sensibilities into *The Absolute Book* (2021 [2019]), although the blending of mythologies and folklore (Norse; Celtic; British) is tonally jarring and unconvincing, even within a Fantasy frame—a Narnia-esque pick-and-mix.

A postmodern bricolage may be reflective of our late perspective of history, but could also be indicative of late Capitalism—where everything seems available (for now) at the tap of a 'buy now' icon. Yet, just because something is available that doesn't mean consuming it is wise; that hoovering up the world's riches—like so many bottom trawlers scraping the seabed raw—is a good thing.

Writers who shamelessly plunder in such ways may be part of the problem contributing to the Climate Crisis—a certain rapacious mindset. Late Capitalism writers are faced with the virtual accessibility and fathomlessness of world history and culture through the internet and, as such, are sometimes spoilt by choice (while paradoxically living within a paradigm that is self-consuming and destructive): the existential crisis of the Anthropocene. And yet this too can provide material.

The Wandering (2020 [2017]) is an interactive novel by Intan Paramaditha, written in her native Indonesian before being published in translation in 2020. Drawing upon the basic ergodic elements of 'choose-your-own-adventure' type stories commonly used in young adult genre fiction, Paramaditha evokes the ontological emptiness of a protagonist caught within a transnational existence. With its materialist trappings—a kind of phenomenological windowshopping, in which the protagonist is willingly trapped within the global mall culture of the upwardly mobile—*The Wandering* could only be called 'ecological' in terms of its depiction of 'connections between living systems'—everything in Paramaditha's novel is interconnected and entangled. Choices create consequences, and actions have impact. One's carbon footprint is entwined with one's karmic footprint, and there is no escaping this legacy.

A speculative approach allows the writer to dial-up the impact of current trends—often with disturbing effect. Paolo Bacigalupi lives in Colorado, but in his debut, *The Wind-up Girl* (2010), which won both the Hugo and Nebula awards, he imagines a refreshingly non-Western Post-Peak Oil future where elephants drive giant turbines. The story is set in Thailand and foregrounds the experiences of BIPOC characters, with white characters as the neo-colonialist interlopers. Its key themes are entanglement and evolution. Through bio-engineering such as genetically-modified organisms (GMOs) humankind has unleashed autonomous, anarchic forces that cannot be controlled:

> That is the nature of our beasts and plagues. They are not dumb machines to be driven about. They have their own needs and hungers. Their own evolutionary demands. They must mutate and adapt, and so you will never be done with me, and when I am gone, what will you do then? We have released demons upon the world, and your walls are only as good as my intellect. Nature has become something new. It is ours now, truly. And if our creation devours us, how poetic will that be? (2009)

Baciagalupi's wound-down near future world seems to exist in the ontological tension between William Paley and Benoit Mandelbrot, between a mechanistic and chaos mathematics view of the universe.

Paley, an English 18th clergyman, Christian apologist and philosopher, in his teleological argument about what makes nature 'tick', used the analogy of God a watchmaker: 'Just as watches are set in motion by watchmakers, after which they operate according to their pre-established mechanisms, so also was the world begun by the God as the Creator, after which it—and all its parts have operated according to their pre-established natural laws' (Paley 1802).

In contrast, Mandelbrot's famous set provided a stunning visual model of Chaos Theory, which emerged in the 1980s as a radical 'new' way of seeing the universe—one that is embedded in the geometry of Nautilus shells, leaves, and coral on a microcosmic level, and weather patterns, global financial markets, pandemics, and nebula on a macrocosmic one. In this metonymic paradigm, the part does not only embody the whole, but can have spiralling consequences, which led to the famous analogy that if a butterfly flaps its wings on one side of the globe it can create a storm on the other. In such a universe, the smallest changes (say on a genetic level) can have a multilinear domino-chain of escalating impacts. And yet some, locked within the mechanistic paradigm, still wish to be watchmakers.

Another speculative fiction novel written in a similar hard-boiled, violent, cyberpunk-ish style is *Zoo City* (2018 [2010]) by Lauren Beukes, a white

South African. In her near future thriller set in a corrupt, decaying Johannesburg, a new underclass is created of 'animalled' citizens. Anyone prosecuted for criminal activity has an animal magically attached to them, which provides a visible sign of their guilt. This creates an entanglement of the human and the more-than-human, in which nature is literally hanging around the necks of the characters—which in the central protagonist's, Zinzi December's, case is a sloth. Echoing Baciagalupi's teleological chaos, at one point Zinzi acknowledges:

> I really wanted to believe that there were these magic celestial bodies that would direct my life, tell me what to do, and it turns out it's not stars, it's some bits of screwy DNA. I'm just meat with faulty programming. (2018 [2010])

In Beukes' novel, nature is definitely red in tooth-and-claw, human nature most of all. As an ecofiction, it is anti-pastoral to the extreme—claustrophobically so. The city is monolithic, all-consuming. There is no escape from its corruption. Everyone and everything is compromised. Even though magic exists, it feels like a closed entropic system. There is no exit from the urban and from the materialist.

A more explicitly ecologically-minded novel, which does not just use the more-than-human as a trope, but as intrinsic to its 'animist realist' sensibilities, is *The Famished Road* by Ben Okri, a writer of Nigerian descent who, at 32, was the youngest recipient of The Booker Prize at the time (1991). Okri later made explicit his concerns for the environment, and advocated for a concerted effort on the part of writers to address it: 'We need a new philosophy for these times, for this near-terminal moment in the history of the human' (2021). He defined this approach as 'existential creativity':

> How do I define it? It is the creativity wherein nothing should be wasted. As a writer, it means everything I write should be directed to the immediate end of drawing attention to the dire position we are in as a species. It means that the writing must have no frills. It should speak only truth. In it, the truth must be also beauty. It calls for the highest economy. It means that everything I do must have a singular purpose (ibid).

One emerging writer of Solarpunk from Nigeria of Igbo-heritage, Somto Ihezue, is authoring short fiction in the speculative spectrum, informed by environmental sensibilities. Ihezue finds in the speculative a 'literature of hope' (to use Solnit's term). It offers him, 'An escape into futures that are kinder, spaces where we are allowed to be brave… be afraid. Escape into places that are home. My writing is resistance' (**Interviews**).

In terms of the more speculative end of ecofiction, the most exciting work at the moment is coming from non-Anglophone countries, such as *Revenge of Gaia: Contemporary Vietnamese Ecofiction* (2021), edited by Chi P. Pham, and Chitra Sankaran.

In their anthology Pham and Sankaran selected fiction published since 1986, 'The Reform Year', 'when Vietnamese artists and writers were politically and culturally 'liberated' and engaged with great commitment in criticizing, among other things, the government's environmental policies and ways in which these were enmeshed in economic strategies and schemes for so-called national progress. Thus, modernization and industrialization that were the chosen paths of the postcolonial Vietnamese government, become the major targets of contemporary Vietnamese ecofiction' (2021). Unsurprisingly, such post-reform narratives adopt a critical stance against anything perceived as being a legacy of the Communist regime. Offering a counter-narrative that 'challenges socialist goals of development and modernisation', the selected stories 'articulate and affirm a more holistic vision, where man is no longer a predator but a participant of nature. These stories therefore are politically charged and pave the path for a more visionary future' (ibid.).

Such narratives offer modes of resistance to the hegemonic that are endlessly inventive and vibrantly polyphonic—and therein lies their strength and resilience. As a result, Solarpunk has become something of a Rebel Alliance within writers of the Global Majority, providing a creative hack to the dominant discourse, changing the narrative from an extractive economy to a regenerative one (Just Transition framework, Synergia 2023).

Authors in Latin American countries in particular seem to have embraced the concept of Solarpunk, as demonstrated by the participants of SolariseCon 2022, a live-streamed YouTube symposium, which asked 'Is Solarpunk Just Another Style?'; and showcased by anthologies such as *Ecological and Fantastical Stories in a Sustainable World* (2018) edited by Gerson Lodi-Ribeiro, and Roberta Spindler.

Within China, it is gaining traction too (Climate Fiction in SFFH, Fantasycon panel 2022). The most successful film in China at the time of its release, *The Wandering Earth* (2021), based upon the 2000 short story by bestselling author of *The Three-Body Problem* (2015) and subsequently re-released as a full novelisation (2021), Ciu Lixin, imagines catastrophic climate events across the globe triggering an extinction-level crisis. The solution—to move the Earth to better climes—is pure, outlandish technofix, but the huge platform the film gave to such imagery straight from the Apocalyptic Sublime of John Martin at least brings the reality of ecological disaster into popular consciousness, which in a nation the size of China cannot be dismissed. In the thought experiments of speculative fiction, Chinese SF authors can perhaps express freedoms denied to them elsewhere in a country notorious for its poor human rights record. Chinese science fiction (kēxué huànxiǎng, commonly abbreviated to 科幻 kēhuàn, literally 'scientific fantasy') is 'genre of literature that concerns itself with hypothetical future social and technological developments in the Sinosphere' (Wikipedia). As such, it is predicated upon current converging crises around dwindling resources and the sustainability of the biosphere. It provides an important, influential platform, with some of the most exciting work in the field emerging both from Chinese authors and those of Chinese descent.

Solarpunk is not without its problems—as any form that foregrounds agenda over aesthetics encounters (something we will explore in the next chapter)—and yet it does serve a vital purpose for current creative practitioners from the Global Majority: it offers a creative space for antihegemonic narratives, especially indigenous speculative perspectives such as MesoFuturism, as depicted by Brazilian artist @Q1R0Z (SolariseCon 2022).

Sometimes, voices of the Global Majority can be articulated brilliantly within novels written in and set in the Global North. One example of this is *Tyger* (2022a) by SF Said, a British Muslim author based in London, who draws upon the poetry, art, and mythopoeia of William Blake, alongside an explicit acknowledgement of the colonial legacy of Great Britain, foregrounding the lives of intersectionally marginalised protagonists. Set in a counterfactual version of London, *Tyger* begins by stating: 'It happened in the Twenty-first Century, when London was still the capital of an Empire, and the Empire still ruled the world…' (ibid). This defamiliarisation technique enables Said to look at *modern* fault-lines in society between white and BIPOC, male and female, rich and poor, Western and non-Western—and in its depiction of inequality, slums, privilege, and lack of social mobility suggests the 'post' of post-Colonial may not be such a definite thing. By creating his own version of London, with its own mythology Said was able to ask some fundamental questions about existence without any predetermined fault-lines and shibboleths: '*Who are we? Where do we come from? Where do we go? What does it mean? How should we live?* (2022b: 32).

Although ostensibly Fantasy, Said's novel has distinctive ecological sensibilities, thus qualifying it as ecofiction: 'tygers' being thought extinct in the storyworld (and *this* world's most endangered big cat), along with many other animals: a few token species are kept in the chief villain's zoo—a symbol of all those trapped by the 'mind-forg'd manacles of man'. At one point, the Tyger seems to address the reader: 'What kind of world could kill them all? And what kind of future can such a world have?'.

(Not) Another Brick in the Wall

As we have seen, problems around representation of voices from the Global Majority are indicative of wider societal issues around equality, diversity, and inclusivity—issues which require systemic change. Acknowledgement of intersectionality is one step forward. Greater opportunities for BIPOC voices, especially from the Global Majority, would be even better—through anthologies, festivals, showcases, interviews, features, book contracts, translations, and adaptations. As Naisha Khan has emphasised Climate Justice will not truly occur until intersectionality is addressed. Much of this work begins in the classrooms, and not just in the decolonising of the curriculum. A key deconstruction of systems of oppression in education—as advocated in Paulo Freire's *Pedagogy of the Oppressed* (1968), and its update, *Pedagogy of Hope* (1992)—is highly recommended as a way of rethinking the implicit and explicit hierarchies and colonialist discourses that still exist in educational institutions around the world (with a few shining exceptions). We need to rigorously critique all 'lore' of the classroom, the workshop, and the creative writing programme, as Vanderslice (2011), Webb (2015), and Whitehead (2016) have argued. *The Anti-Racist Workshop* (Chavez 2021) and *Craft in the Real World* (Salesses 2021) are much-needed re-imaginings of the creative writing workshop: the forge of ecofiction, and so a key place to address any problems before they see print—a safe, supportive space where it is permissible to get it wrong, before you get it right.

MYCELIA: Connections to Other Writers, Texts, and Resources

Authors:
Brannavan Gnanalingam (NZ) author and lawyer; Hone Tūwhare (NZ) poet; Hinemoana Baker; Patricia Grace (Maori), author of Potiki; Witi Ihimaera (Maori), author of *The Whale Rider* (who co-edited *Pūrākau* with Whiti Hereaka); Rajorshi Chakraborti (Indian-New Zealand cli-fi writer); Janu (India), a tribal activist; Mahasweta Devi (India), a mainstream writer and social activist; Anita Agnihotri (India), an officer of the Indian Administrative Services and a creative writer; Zakiya Mecca (Jamaican-British); Mya-Rose Craig (Bangladeshi-British); Jessica L. Lee (Canadian-Chinese-British), author of *Turning: a swimming memoir* (2017); Professor Wangari Maathai (Kenyan), environmental activist, Nobel Prize-winner; Satish Kumar (Indian), founder of *Resurgence* magazine, and author of *Earth Pilgrim* (2009); Helen van Neerven (Aboriginal), author of *Heat and Light* (2014); Alexis Wright (Aboriginal), author of *The Swan Book* (2015).

Other Resources:

- *Emergence* is a magazine and podcast that is particularly good at providing a platform for voices from the Global Majority and from BIPOC writers and activists. It has a great selection of essays in print, audio, and video format. https://emergencemagazine.org/.
- *Waterbear* is free digital-streaming platform for environmental and social justice documentaries. https://www.waterbear.com/watch.
- *Panorama: the journal of travel, place, and nature* is another great platform celebrating voices and perspectives from the Global Majority. https://panoramajournal.org/.
- Synergia Institute. 2023. Just Transition Framework Infographic. Toward Co-operative Commonwealth: Transition in a Perilous Century. Synergia Institute 2023 MOOC.
- United Nations. 1948. Universal Declaration of Human Rights. https://www.un.org/en/about-us/universal-declaration-of-human-rights (Accessed 7 February 2023).
- United Nations. 2015. Sustainable Development Goals. https://sdgs.un.org/goals (Accessed 6 February 2023).

SPORES: Writing Activities

- Behind the News—select a recent climate-related news item that has affected the Global Majority, e.g. a devastating flood, famine, heat wave, drought, wildfire, tornado, etc. Research it. Zoom in on the impact on individual lives. Listen to interviews if possible; watch eye-witness footage. Imagine what it would be like to be in their shoes. Changing details out of respect, take the key facts of what happened and create a fictional character, family, or group of friends who live through it. Give them a voice: write in first person and describe what you witness. Make it as vivid as possible. Bring in specific sensory description drawn from the news reports and testimonials. Focus on the close-up, the small scale. Avoid back-extrapolation. Remember, people on the ground at the time will have only a limited perception of what is going on. Even afterwards there will be probably conflicting reports, unless captured on film or recorded by monitoring stations.

References

Abram, David. 2017 [1997]. *The Spell of the Sensuous: Perception and Language in a More-Than-Human World*. New York, NY: Vintage Books.

Adichie, Chimamanda Ngozi. 2022. Freedom of Speech. BBC Reith Lectures. https://www.bbc.co.uk/iplayer/episode/p0dhrlhm/the-reith-lectures-2022-the-four-freedoms-1-chimamanda-ngozi-adichie-freedom-of-speech (Accessed 9 February 2023).

Allende, Isabel. 1988. *Eva Luna*. New York, NY: Knopf.

Anderson, Kevin. 2020, November 16. AltCop. https://altcop.earth/ (Accessed 8 June 2023).

Bacigalupi, Paolo. 2010. *The Wind-up Girl*. London: Orbit.

Balch, Oliver. 2013, February 4. Buen vivir: The Social Philosophy Inspiring Movements in South America. *Guardian*. https://www.theguardian.com/sustainable-business/blog/buen-vivir-philosophy-south-america-eduardo-gudynas (Accessed 8 June 2023).

Balch, Oliver. 2013, February 4. Buen vivir: The Social Philosophy Inspiring Movements in South America. *Guardian*. Available from: https://www.theguardian.com/sustainable-business/blog/buen-vivir-philosophy-south-america-eduardogudynas [Accessed 4 July 2024]

Beukes, Lauren. 2018 [2010]. *Zoo City*. Nottingham: Angry Robot.

Bould, Mark. 2021. *The Anthropocene Unconscious: Climate Catastrophe Culture*. London: Verso.

Chakrabarti, Shami. 2014. *On Liberty*. London: Allen Lane.

Chavez, Felicia Rose. 2021. *The Anti-Racist Workshop: How to Decolonize the Creative Classroom*. Chicago, IL: Haymarket Books.

Clanchy, Kate. 2019. *Some Kids I Taught and What They Taught Me*. London: Picador.

Crenshaw, Kimberlé. 1989. Demarginalizing the Intersection of Race and Sex: A Black Feminist Critique of Antidiscrimination Doctrine, Feminist Theory and Antiracist Politics. *University of Chicago Legal Forum*: Vol. 1989, Article 8. https://chicagounbound.uchicago.edu/uclf/vol1989/iss1/8 (Accessed 7 February 2023).

Cummins, Jeanine. 2020. *American Dirt*. London: Headline.

Fantasycon. 2022, September. Writing Marginalised Villains. London: Fantasycon.

Paulo, Freire. 1992. *Pedagogy of Hope*. London: Bloomsbury.

Paulo, Freire. 1996 [1968]. *Pedagogy of the Oppressed*. London: Penguin.

Gurba, Myriam. 2019, December 12. Pendeja, You Ain't Steinbeck: My Bronca with Fake-Ass Social Justice Literature. Tropics of Meta. https://tropicsofmeta.com/2019/12/12/pendeja-you-aint-steinbeck-my-bronca-with-fake-ass-social-justice-literature/ (Accessed 8 February 2023).

Haraway, Donna J. 2016. *Staying with the Trouble: Making Kin with the Chthulucene*. Durham and London: Duke University Press.

Hitchens, Christopher. 2006. *Free Speech*. Available from: https://www.youtube.com/watch?v=zDap-K6GmL0 [accessed 8 June 2023].
Hulme, Keri. 1984. *The Bone People*. London: Hodder and Stoughton.
Ihimaera, Witi. 1987. *The Whale Rider*. London: Heinemann.
Khan, Naisha. 2021. 'The Sustainabiliteens: Creating an Intersectional Climate Movement'. Vancouver: CBC/Radio-Canada. Available from: https://youtu.be/YJhAdI1jne4 [accessed: 7th February 2023]
Kimmerer, Robin Wall. 2016. *Braiding Sweetgrass: Indigenous Wisdom, Scientific Knowledge and the Teachings of Plants*. London: Penguin.
Knox, Elizabeth. 2021 [2019]. *The Absolute Book*. London: Michael Joseph.
Lixin, Ciu. 2015. *The Three-Body Problem*. London: Head of Zeus.
Lixin, Ciu. 2021. *The Wandering Earth*. London: Head of Zeus.
Lodi-Ribeiro, Gerson, and Spindler, Roberta. 2018. *Solarpunk: Ecological and Fantastical Stories in a Sustainable World*. World Weaver.
Macfarlane, Robert. 2019. *Underland: A Deep Time journey*. London: Hamish Hamilton.
Mantel, Hilary. 2009. *Wolf Hall*. London: Fourth Estate.
Mantel, Hilary. 2012. *Bring Up the Bodies*. London: Fourth Estate.
Mantel, Hilary. 2020. *The Mirror and the Light*. London: Fourth Estate.
Marquez, Gabriel Garcia. 1991. *The Storyteller*. London: Faber and Faber.
Okri, Ben. 1991. *The Famished Road*. London: Anchor Books.
Okri, Ben. 2021, November 12. Artists Must Confront the Climate Crisis—We Must Write as if These are the Last Days. *Guardian*. https://www.theguardian.com/commentisfree/2021/nov/12/artists-climate-crisis-write-creativity-imagination (Accessed 8 February 2023).
Paley, William. 1802. *Natural Theology: Or Evidence of the Existence and Attributes of the Deity, Collected from the Appearances of Nature*. Philadelphia: J. Faulder.
Paramaditha, Intan. 2020 [2017]. *The Wandering*. London: Harvill Secker.
Pham, Chi P., and Chitra Sankaran. 2021. *Revenge of Gaia: Contemporary Vietnamese Ecofiction*. London: Penguin.
Pullman, Philip. 2010, April 1. On Freedom of Speech. Sheldonian Theatre. https://www.youtube.com/watch?v=QnMW9sLTQfI (Accessed 8 June 2023).
Robinson, Kim Stanley. 2020. *The Ministry for the Future*. London: Orbit.
Rushie, Salman. 1981. *Midnight's Children*. London: Jonathan Cape.
Said, S.F. 2022a. *Tyger*. London: David Fickling Books.
Said, S.F. 2022b. Tyger. *Vala*, vol. 3. The Blake Society. https://blakesociety.org/wp-content/uploads/2022/12/VALA-issue-3.pdf (Accessed 8 June 2023).
Salesses, Matthew. 2021. *Craft in the Real World: Rethinking Fiction Writing and Workshopping*. New York, NY: Catapult.
Shapiro, Lila. 2021, January 5. Blurbed to Death: How One of Publishing's Most Hyped Books Became its Biggest Horror Story—And Still Ended Up a Best Seller. *Vulture*. https://www.vulture.com/article/american-dirt-jeanine-cummins-book-controversy.html (Accessed 8 February 2023).

Shawl, Nisi, and Cynthia Ward. 2005. *Writing the Other: A Practical Approach*. n.p.: Aqueduct Press.

Shriver, Lionel. 2016, September 13. Lionel Shriver's Full Speech: 'I Hope the Concept of Cultural Appropriation is a Passing Fad'. *Guardian*. https://www.theguardian.com/commentisfree/2016/sep/13/lionel-shrivers-full-speech-i-hope-the-concept-of-cultural-appropriation-is-a-passing-fad (Accessed 7 February 2023).

Shukla, Nikesh. 2016. *The Good Immigrant*. London: Unbound.

Singh, Vandana. 2018. *Ambiguity Machines and Other Stories*. Easthampton, MA: Small Beer Press.

SolariseCon. 2022. Is Solarpunk Just Another Style? https://www.youtube.com/watch?v=U20OFV-M8V0 (Accessed 9 February).

Sultana, Farhana. 2020. Political Ecology 1: From Margins to Center. *Progress in Human Geography*, 1–10. https://cssn.org/wp-content/uploads/2020/11/Political-ecology-1-From-margins-to-center-Farhana-Sultana.pdf (Accessed 8 June 2023).

Synergia Institute. 2023. Just Transition Framework Infographic. Toward Co-operative Commonwealth: Transition in a Perilous Century. Synergia Institute 2023 MOOC.

Tobgay, Tshering. 2016. This Country Isn't Just Carbon Neutral—It's Carbon Negative. TED talk. https://www.youtube.com/watch?v=7Lc_dlVrg5M (Accessed 9 February 2023).

United Nations. 2015. THE 17 GOALS: Sustainable Development Goals. Available from: https://sdgs.un.org/goals [accessed: 3 June 2024].

Vanderslice, Stephanie. 2011. *Rethinking Creative Writing*. Wicken, Ely: Creative Writing Studies/NAWE.

Wallace-Wells, David. 2019. *The Uninhabitable Earth*. London: Allen Lane.

Waugh, Ric Roman, director. 2020. *Greenland*. STX Films. https://www.imdb.com/title/tt7737786/

Webb, Jenn. 2015. *Researching Creative Writing*. Newmarket: Frontinus Press.

Whitehead, Harry. 2016. The Programmatic Era: Creative Writing as Cultural Imperialism. *Ariel: A Review of International English Literature* 47 (1): 359–390.

5

Activism versus Art

At the very core of ecofiction there is a fundamental problem—how to reconcile agenda with art. An agenda in fiction could be anything, but in this context if we consider it to be a desire to raise awareness about environmental issues (in early ecofiction) and the urgency of the climate and biodiversity crisis (in more recent work) then we have what risks becoming didacticism, which may be instructional and educational, but may backfire in its very wish to communicate, persuade, and even motivate, by its school-teacherly manner. Worse, it could smack of finger-wagging, or even 'Bible-thumping', risking the spectre of the preacher. An intention to proselytise rarely goes well with great art. Such an endeavour will preach to the converted, but seldom succeeds in reaching beyond its particular faith community—because no one likes to be preached to (unless they go to their place of worship for that reason). Now, it could be argued that those who buy ecofiction books perhaps 'want to be preached to', but are more than likely already converted to the environmental agenda. Their interest draws them to work that aligns with their world view, their values. This is 'natural'. Only the boldest of readers reads beyond their comfort zone, beyond their value system—except if it is their job. Critics, scholars, and competition judges do this a lot, but they are a narrow section of society, a fraction of the eight billion potential readers on the planet (even if literacy was universal, and translations widely available). With ultra-Conservative, Right-Wing lobby groups putting pressure on educational institutions, libraries, and bookshops in the USA and other countries experiencing a rise of the 'Alt-Right', as well as in traditional hard-line theocracies and regimes, the chances of reading literature from outside one's belief systems dwindles with every book ban and burning. Dogma actively attacks that which offers alternatives: the heterodoxies and heresies that celebrate diversity, tolerance, resistance, and other modalities. Therefore, dogma, at its worst, is the enemy of art. As the novelist John Fowles said, 'When literature serves dogma, it ceases to be literature' (1998).

Yet this in itself is a hard-line stance.

If we can consider art in the broadest sense, dogma has been a great patron of the arts for centuries, as the cathedrals of Europe stand testimony too. Going back even further, the earliest temples show how the didactic and the aesthetic can often work together: Angkor Wat, the Pyramids of Giza, Luxor, Carnac, Petra, Stonehenge, Machu Piccu, Nazca lines, Taj Mahal, Uluru. One could argue (as Peter Fuller has done: 1990a, 1990b) that when art is aligned with a higher purpose, it becomes sublimated and ennobled: The Book of Kells, the Lindisfarne Gospels, the Dresden Codex, The Last Supper, the Cistine Chapel, Hildegard von Bingen's Canticles of Ecstasy, Michelangelo's David, Picasso's Guernica, and so forth. Sometimes it brings out the best in us, even if it does not forgive reprehensible behaviour—the House of Borgia was great patrons of art in the Renaissance even while they committed many crimes. Art does not provide a get out of jail card; but it can encourage the 'better angels of our nature' (Lincoln 1861).

And yet ecofiction, with its ecological sensibilities, can risk becoming an exercise in virtue signalling and Manichean characterisation—with the 'good' protagonists acting in environmentally-friendly ways, and the 'bad' antagonists leading deliberately destructive, carbon-burning lifestyles. Such is the case on Eleanor Catton's *Birnam Wood* (2023), which sets a group of eco-warriors against an unconscionable tech-billionaire. However well-written such a narrative on a microcosmic level, it risks perpetuating stereotypes and tropes—a modern Mystery Play with its saints and devils. As Kevin Powers points out in his review: '…our culture is already rife with calls for moral simplicity. Isn't it the duty of the literary novel to go deeper?' (*Guardian* 2023).

And yet if a writer—*especially* one of ecofiction—fails to engage with the myriad challenges the world faces in the Anthropocene (not merely charting some of the impacts, but interrogating the systemic issues that have contributed to them) they risk a form of political quietism: using the shock and awe of ecocatastrophe to just sell books and thereby becoming complicit in the very problem, as Nanson posits:

> Artists can be wary of agendas of commitment because of the danger these will suck the life out of art and reduce it to propaganda. But the claim to have no such agenda may make you complicit with a default ideology, such as one endorsing an unsustainable or unjust status quo. (2021: 3)

Are activism and art mutually exclusive, or can they be allies? How can we, as writers, negotiate the challenges of writing with conviction? Is it possible to write ecofiction that is uncompromising in its agenda while being a great read? It is undoubtedly a tricky tight-rope to negotiate. This chapter explores these tensions.

The Environmental Agenda

Of course, there is no single agenda in the environmental movement, but a multiplicity of causes—all worthwhile, whether it is to reduce carbon emissions; promote sustainable farming practices; encourage recycling; save the whale; stop fracking; ban GMOs; stop deforestation, the acidification of the ocean, and holes in the ozone layer; improve air quality; protect the Antarctic; increase animal welfare; secure clean water for all; campaign for climate justice, and so forth. For some it is about personal lifestyle choices, awareness-raising, or creating resilient 'transition' communities and socio-economic structures and initiatives. For others it may be to do with having more empathy with the biosphere and the more-than-human. Some adopt non-violent direct action tactics, some utilise a blend of art and activism, and some lobby via NGOs and large-scale campaigns. For many, exhausted and frustrated by decades of environmental campaigning, a more direct, interventionist approach is required, as embodied by Extinction Rebellion and Just Stop Oil—which encourages disruptive actions which lead to arrest as part of its tactic for raising awareness about the urgency and primacy of the Climate Emergency. For an growing number climate justice is the fundamental concern, but increasingly many acknowledge that 'You can't have climate justice without gender equality' (Nakate 2022). That unless intersectionality is factored into the environmental movement it risks perpetuating the colonialist and capitalist ethos that has been instrumental in creating the climate emergency in the first place. Therefore, to try to reduce the movement to one monolithic agenda is problematic and inaccurate. Perhaps a useful analogy would be to liken it to a rainforest—in which multiple organisms compete for life, but in a way that creates a healthy biodiversity. All turn towards life in the way all plants yearn for light. It is the complexity and polyphony that creates resilience. The messy entangled assemblage(s) of it all. The 'trouble', as Haraway would put it (2016). And yet perhaps we can at least agree that a novel classed as 'ecofiction' is acknowledging there *is* a climate emergency, and that we do need to do *something* about it. That saving the biosphere and all of its biodiversity is a good thing. That the world is a beautiful, fragile place—one that needs defending. That not only would the world be a sadder place without particular species or habitats, but that we need to act *now* if we are to survive as well. Ultimately, the Climate Emergency is the issue that trumps all issues. One could argue it even challenges the validity of the whole project of publishing. Is that too subtle an endeavour to be relevant and fit-for-purpose when faced with the challenges that we are? Do we really need more books (even ones promoting good ideas and printed in accordance with the guidelines of the Forest Stewardship Council) when what really need, surely, is action? This was a dilemma the novelist Manda Scott articulates: 'Writing books takes a long time and the publishing process is too slow and why would I take years to get an idea into the world when I could put it out in an hour's podcast on a Monday afternoon?' (Scott, 2023).

Considering how many books on environmental issues have been published—along with all the attendant courses, writing programmes, festivals, and media—do we honestly need any more? Is the publishing industry, with its sizable carbon footprint—the 'book miles' of each of its products— even contributing to the problem? Let us consider literature to see if that's the case: whether art and the environmental are too counter-productive to co-exist, by now turning to consider the agenda of literature.

The Agenda of Literature

Literature, in particular the novel—our locus of interest here—is comprised, like the analogous 'rainforest' of the environmental movement, of myriad micro-agendas, as individualistic and idiosyncratic as those involved in its creation and consumption. Sometimes, the reasons why authors spend substantial parts of their life creating characters, settings, plots, and rich storyworlds are just as mysterious, opaque, or unconscious to the author. Creativity is rarely a purely rational process, as the neurologist Alice W. Flaherty, explores in her book (2005) on 'the midnight disease', (a phrase the novelist Michael Chabon coined in his 1995 campus novel, *Wonder Boys*) which explores what compels some to write, what 'blocks' this compulsion, and what is happening in the 'creative brain' when things are going well. And, accepting this—that each novel can be said to be its own sui generis manifesto for existence—we can perhaps at least agree on what literature does well.

Novels can purely entertain, providing escapism and contrast to our daily lives—and as Tolkien himself said, in his valedictory address as the retiring professor of Anglo-Saxon from Merton College, Oxford, the desire to escape is completely understandable if one feels as though one is living in a 'prison' (thought of as 'Real Life' to some): 'Why should a man be scorned, if, finding himself in prison, he tries to get out and go home? Or if, when he cannot do so, he thinks and talks about other topics than jailers and prison-walls?' (1997: 148).

Novels can provide consolation, companionship, and reassurance that somebody, somewhere understands what think, feel, or have gone through. There is a kind of community of intent created by the mutual love of a particular novel. Fiction excels at dramatising the lives of multi-faceted characters from across history. It encourages emotional and cultural literacy. It may not be the Grail that will heal the wasteland, but like Parsifal—the fool-knight whose cleansed perception 'pierces-the-veil' and helps him achieve the Grail Chapel—it is adept at asking the right questions. This is a quality Alex Clark emphasises: 'being a reader does not prevent you from also being a citizen; it might even help you to be a more empathetic, imaginative, compassionate one' (*Guardian* 2017).

As David Lodge suggests, the novel is perhaps the best medium for the representation and exploration of human consciousness (2003). It encourages empathy and helps us to explore the polysemous, intrinsically plural nature of truth and reality. As a vehicle for exploring ontological concerns it is beyond par. Because of the quiet, intimate act of reading, where the solitary individual makes meaning—rather than risk being drowned out by the hive-mind of social media with its echo chambers and algorithmic bias towards shock, scandal, and antagonism—it is a medium that encourages nuance and subtlety of thought. The novel enables us to travel the world in a few pages and imagine vastly different cultures—and so it is inherently *environmentally-friendly*, in a very practical sense, by being low-impact; and in a literal sense, by encouraging us to reflect upon relationships between living organisms, including humans and their natural environment. Unless read on an e-reader, or as an audio book, it requires no lithium battery, no device with built-in obsolescence—unless you count the shelf life on an average paperback (which is still significantly longer than a tablet or kindle). As a technology, the book has been serviceable for centuries, bringing literacy to the masses. The novel can influence a reader's thinking and even value system—inspiring a radical re-evaluation of morals and lifestyle. As Bertie Wooster was fond of declaiming: 'I am going to bed with an improving book!' (Wodehouse, 2008) The sense of 'improving literature' may have gone out of the window with the Victorians (except in some repressive regimes and states), and from its very earliest days the novel has been seen as somewhat disreputable, as Jane Austen satirizes in *Northanger Abbey* (1817), where Isabella Thorpe and Catherine Morland share the slightly scandalous thrill of the Gothic novel:

"Dear creature! How much I am obliged to you; and when you have finished Udolpho, we will read the Italian together; and I have made out a list of ten or twelve more of the same kind for you."

"Have you, indeed! How glad I am! What are they all?"

"I will read you their names directly; here they are, in my pocketbook. Castle of Wolfenbach, Clermont, Mysterious Warnings, Necromancer of the Black Forest, Midnight Bell, Orphan of the Rhine, and Horrid Mysteries. Those will last us some time."

"Yes, pretty well; but are they all horrid, are you sure they are all horrid?"

(Austen, Chapter 6)

Readers often seek the visceral hit of the vicarious thrill. The deep dive into other lives and ways of being in the world. The writer of ecofiction can use this.

Circulating libraries—the earliest form of public library where readers took out a subscription to access the rotating stock of novels, non-fiction, newspapers, and journals—were believed to be encouraging the lower classes into moral turpitude, due to the salacious nature of some of the material. This was satirise by the playwright Richard Brinsley Sheridan, in his Regency play, *The Rivals* (1775):

Madam, a circulating library in a town is as an evergreen tree of diabolical knowledge, —it blossoms through the year! And depend on it, Mrs. Malaprop, that they who are so fond of handling the leaves will long for the fruit at last. (Sheridan)

It is interesting that Sheridan's character draws upon a natural image, albeit one saturated in Judeo-Christian guilt. Abram (1997) argues that the 'flesh of language' contains vestiges of its ecological frame, and that the acts of writing and reading are inherently ecological. They reconnect us to our environment, conceptually and perceptually (via the subliminal biomorphism of the text). It makes us use senses that have evolved over millions of years to help us survive in the natural environment—to fight, flee, hunt, and gather; senses that help us perceive and interpret the vast complexity of our shared biosphere (Haskell 2022).

Yet beyond this, the novel can also contain images and messages that help attune our consciousness to the wider ecologies of the biosphere, as well as to our own biocommunities and 'creative assemblages', (Haraway 2016) as fellow holobionts upon this planet.

And so perhaps we can justify the project of literature as something of inherent value with intrinsically 'ecological' qualities in the broadest sense.

So, what specific examples are there—where the implicit environmental qualities of the novel become explicit?

Some Examples

There are numerous examples of novels and publishing projects that explore environmental issues. Throughout this book I draw upon a wide range, sometimes outside of what could be strictly defined as 'ecofiction' (which is after all a relatively modern label). This is reflective of nature—biodiversity builds resilience. We enrich our imagination and available reality by doing so. It widens the genre pool, otherwise you risk the law of diminishing returns, a kind of literary inbreeding. Furthermore, by pigeonholing both book and author—only reading 'ecofiction', and *only* setting out to write it too—one risks narrowing one's market and impact, as Irish writer Lynn Buckle explains in discussing her own work:

> …my primary aim is to target a much broader audience with my solution-based approach to climate change which is embedded into my literary fiction. I prefer not to restrict my appeal solely to readers who are already interested in ecofiction because the planet does not have time for us to preach to the converted. I am more interested in reaching those readers who are disinterested in climate change and hopefully disrupt their viewpoints. My publications are therefore defined by the publishing industry as literary fiction. They are solution-based, intersectional, fictional nature writing, within the genre of literary fiction. (from **Interviews**, 2023)

Not only should the modern writer wanting a wide audience to be genre-fluid, but also willing to look *beyond* the novel for inspiration: to find nutrients elsewhere to enrich the mulch of the imagination. If we were to widen our purview to include poetry then there is a whole swathe of writers we could draw up who foregrounded ecological sensibilities (so not just 'nature' as a pastoral backdrop, but awareness of the more-than-human, social justice, and the negative impact of human activity upon the environment): Basho, William Blake; Gerard Manley Hopkins, John Keats, William Wordsworth; Ted Hughes, Heathcote Williams, Gary Snyder, Mary Oliver, and Alice Oswald, to name a few.

The so-called 'Peasant Poet', John Clare of Northamptonshire (1793–1864) perhaps more than most, was a spokesperson and defendant of the more-than-human and the commons. Unlike his contemporaries, the Romantic Poets, he had a deep knowledge of the land as a farm labourer and amateur naturalist. He knew his beloved Fens like the proverbial 'back of his hand'. He walked them tirelessly and deep mapped his local vicinity around Helpston, noticing the incremental seasonal changes through such collections as *Poems Descriptive of Rural Life and Scenery* (1820), *The Shepherd's Calendar* (1827), and *The Rural Muse* (1835). Clare's most famous poem, 'I Am', written in Northampton's asylum, has been much anthologised, performed, and provided the title of Richard Flanagan's eco-novel, *The Living Sea of Waking Dreams* (2021) from the second stanza, yet it is the third stanza that provides a heart-rending cri-de-coeur from someone who had witnessed firsthand the enclosure of the Fens (as a result of the Enclosure Acts, which broke up much of the land classified as 'Commons' into private ownership):

> I long for scenes where man hath never trod
>   A place where woman never smiled or wept
>   There to abide with my Creator, God,
>   And sleep as I in childhood sweetly slept,
>   Untroubling and untroubled where I lie
>   The grass below—above the vaulted sky.

This poem could be seen as a personal manifesto, and his entire oeuvre is a form of activism. His life has inspired three novels to date, which could be classed as bona fide ecofiction: *Clare* by Kohn Mackenna (1993); *The Quickening Maze* (2009) by Adam Foulds; and *The Ballad of John Clare* (2010) by Hugh Lupton. Although each evokes Clare's milieu, none are as successful as John Crace's *Harvest* (2013), which portrays a vividly convincing, and moving version of the impact of the Inclosure Act upon a fictional English village.

Novels that foreground environmental issues go back at least far as Thomas Hardy, who dramatised the lives of rural, working-class people caught in the cat's cradle of poverty, morality, land reforms, and new technology. To take one example of his considerable oeuvre, *The Woodlanders* (1887), what Phillip Mallett calls a 'transitional work' (2004: vi) between his earlier work and his later, more fatalistic novels. As the title suggests, the story is set within a woodland, in this case a part of Hardy's fictionalised purview, 'Wessex', called Blackmoor Vale: 'some extensive woodlands, interspersed with apple orchards' (2004: 1). As so often in Hardy's novels, the landscape is introduced first and *then* his cast—the ancient and more-than-human is foregrounded and the anthropocentric dramas that follow are seen as passing shadows: a squall or flash flood of emotion at best.

Mallett points out how in *The Woodlanders,* as in many of Hardy's other novels, 'the human action takes place amidst the intensely realised processes of the natural world, a world which is clearly something more than 'setting' or 'background' (2004: vi). This could be a definition of ecofiction, although it would be necessary to add a qualification for Twenty-first Century fiction—that the novel shows awareness of the multiple ecological threats focalised and exacerbated by the Climate Emergency.

The story begins with Barber Percomb pausing to get his bearings amid the umbrageous solitude, which acts as a constant backdrop to the hopes and dreams, fears, and desires of the inhabitants and visitors to Blackmoor Vale. In myths, legends, folklore, and fairy tales, the forest is a place of archetypal power and narrative entanglement (Maitland 2012). The arborescence of its pathways—formed by human and other-than-human passage—suggests multiple, divergent plot-threads (Manwaring 2023), as well as a mycelial subtext of themes, allusions, and intertextuality. The trees and undergrowth conceal, confuse, disrupt, and aid—as Robin Hood and his Merry Men knew all too well. The wildwood belonged to all before, in Norman England at least, it became officially 'forest'—a fecund resource for the ruling classes and strictly controlled with severe punishments for any who transgressed the new law of the land. And yet, paradoxically, the forest became a place of social justice (in the many gests of Robin Hood), of narrative compression and karmic acceleration. And so for Hardy, the woods were never just a picturesque backdrop—like many of his rural settings, they were saturated with metaphoric resonance. In a note in his journal made a month before the completion of *The Woodlanders,* he articulated this: '….I don't want to see landscapes, i.e., scenic paintings of them … I want to see the deeper reality underlying the scenic' (Hardy 1887: 192). However apparently 'seductive' the pastoral is in Hardy—an aesthetic that most adaptations have leaned into, creating soothing comfort-viewing evoking a romantic nostalgism—the actual dialectic of the novel is *anti*-pastoral. As Mallett emphasises: 'Pastoral is an artificial form, which by playing with the idea of crossing the boundary between the sophisticated and the natural in fact asserts its permanence and inevitability' (2004: xiii). The organic and the inorganic, the 'natural' and the man-made, is in constant tension in Hardy's novel: the sole ambulant meets those on a carrier's van drawn by a single horse; Giles Winterbourne's 'five-tonne of oak' encounters the carriage of Mrs Charmond; noisy steam-powered machinery sets a demanding pace of human labour; a stultifying commercial imperative dominates and exploits natural resources, becoming the yoke the underclass must bear the burden of; the local beauty, Grace

Melbury, sent away by her ambitious father for education and social advancement, finds herself estranged from her community and ecosystem, no longer able to identify the varieties of apples, which are now 'just apples'. The ruthless zero sum of this schism is epitomised by the selling of Marty South's hair, which Barber Percomb set forth to undertake. He finds her, a local girl who has 'feelings' for Giles Winterbourne, working late on completing her father's workload, at 18 pence per thousand spars. Percomb tempts her with the money she would make by selling her tresses to him, on behalf of a lady who desired them. Marty refuses at first, but broken hearted by Giles' rebuttal, she eventually acquiesces. This brutal exploitation of natural resources sums up the theme of nature versus culture that permeates the novel, and much of Hardy's oeuvre (Lanone 2022).

In *The Return of the Native* (1878), Hardy spends the entire first chapter describing the dominant setting, Egdon Heath, inspired by the rise of land behind his 'former homes' (Max Gate and Hardy's Cottage) on the edge of Dorchester. This foregrounding of the more-than-human may seem stylistically bold, even ahead of its day (over a century later, Richard Powers was to win the Pulitzer Prize for Fiction for a similar foregrounding of the non-anthropocentric in his 2018 novel, *The Overstory*), but the Wiltshire nature writer and novelist, Richard Jefferies (1848–1887) was even more daring, giving over *half* of his pioneering post-apocalypse, *After London, or Wild England* (1885), to an extended expositional account of the rewilding of England (and according to the premise of the novel, the rest of the world), caused when a mysterious orb appears close to the Earth, affecting global tides and weather patterns. This is never expanded upon or explained, but it would be tempting to back-extrapolate it as a cypher for anthropogenic Climate Change, which was becoming discernible even in Jefferies' day: as a London-based reporter he had been dismayed by the impact of his fellow species upon the environment. With the Industrial Revolution at full speed ahead, Jefferies lamented its effect upon the quality of soil, water, and air. Jefferies imagined a post-industrial flooded England—a neofeudal future primitive scenario in which the advances of technology had been lost or forgotten. The protagonist, the malcontent Felix, explores the toxic ruins of London in his canoe—the capital buried beneath huge drifts of foetid silt: all that remains of the majority of the population, slowly coalescing into the fossil record—an early literary marker of the Anthropocene. It was as though Jefferies had foreseen The Great Smog of 1952, which killed 4000 Londoners within a week and catalysed the Clean Air Act of 1956; or even a nuclear apocalypse. His descriptions of an obliterated city could have been Hiroshima or Nagasaki. And yet Jefferies seems to see such devastation an inevitable consequence of the myth of Progress, which the concept of 'Doughnut Economics' (Raworth 2017) has shown to be an unsustainable one. There is a certain chilly schadenfreude to his coolly journalistic account of the rewilding of England—as though it was something he secretly longed for. This is perhaps at its most transparent in the story fragment, *The Great Snow* (1876), in which Jefferies describes an apocalyptic, mass-extinction-level event which wipes out most, if not all, of humanity. Forsaking the conceit of plot, or at least a protagonist-centred one, Jefferies merely relates the devastating unfolding of events—which begins benignly enough: a series of 'snow-days', snowball fights and sledding, until the severity of the constant snowfall leads to towns and cities being buried beneath Ice Age scale drifts, the end of food production and ensuing famine, the disabling of infrastructure, the freezing to death of livestock and countless individuals, and the reversion of any survivors to barbarism, cannibalism, and madness. Such scenes of post-apocalypse have become familiar to modern readers, viewers, and gamers in the plethora of dystopian novels, films, TV dramas, and games that have appeared since the late Sixties (when environmental issues began to filter into the public consciousness), increasing exponentially since the millennium, when many of the grim vistas imagined are not evoking the future, but current newsreels of climate disasters and resource wars. With eerie prescience, Jefferies knew the way the wind was blowing.

Other authors have also foreshadowed an ecological discourse in their work, more successfully (as novels) and with more impact (in terms of their popularity) arguably than Jefferies could have dreamed of, in particular, *Moby Dick* (1851) by Herman Melville; *Heart of Darkness* (1899) by Joseph Conrad, which has been called the first modern novel; and *The Call of the Wild* (1903) by Jack London. And yet none of these are quite as uncompromisingly ecological as Jefferies imperfect narratives (which are undoubtedly flawed as fiction), offering salutary warnings of when 'activism' overshadows art—not that Jefferies was really trying to persuade anyone; he seemed more interested in playing out his own rather misanthropic fantasies of a rewilded England. In Melville's magnum opus, whale-hunting is merely the context for an extended morality tale about hubris and obsession. In Conrad's novella, the jungle provides a wilder version of the archetypal Forest Perilous as an arena for colonialist 'Godgames' (to use Clute's term, 1999: 414–415). And in *The Call of the Wild*, the tension is between the domesticated canine (Buck, a St Bernard/shepherd dog cross) and its wilder huskie cousins—the millennia old dialectic between nature and culture, the natural world and civilisation, first seen in *The Epic of Gilgamesh*. At one point early in his new career as a trail dog, Buck lay near the fire, 'eyes blinking dreamily at the flames', (1903: 57) faintly remembering his former life and the comforts of domestication in the 'sun-kissed Santa Clara Valley' (ibid.: 58). And yet such memories 'had no power over him': 'Far more potent were the memories of his heredity that gave things he had never seen before a seeming familiarity; the instincts (which were but the memories of his ancestors become habits) which had lapsed in later days, and still later, in him, quickened and became alive again' (ibid.). This re-emergence of the natural self is a Rousseauian trope, which manifested in popular fiction such as *Peter Pan in Kensington Gardens* (1906); *Puck of Pook's Hill* (1906); *The Wind in the Willows* (1908); and *Tarzan of the Apes* (1912).

A surprising manifestation of this is the commonly urban and urbane literature of the Modernists. Although claims have been made for the ecological credentials of the writings of the Woolf, Eliot, and Joyce (Diaper 2023)—claims which perhaps over-project current concerns onto earlier writers, it is certainly tangible in the work of DH Lawrence, both his poems (*Birds, Beasts, and Flowers* 1923), stories (e.g. 'The Virgin and the Gipsy', 1926), and novels, chiefly *Lady Chatterley's Lover* (1928), which evokes a transgressive prelapsarian communion with nature, and a bold unmasking of the civilised self, beneath which a proto-Adam and Eve await, shed of societal constraints.

A contemporary of the Modernists, but perhaps better thought of as an anti-Modernist is John Cowper Powys (1872–1963), who shamelessly used his gargantuan novels as soapboxes for his peccadilloes and predilections, such as anti-vivisection, most notably in *Weymouth Sands* (1934), in which the main character rails against a local facility where experiments on animals take place. As a person, Powys was most vocal about his antipathy to the practice, declaring: 'No excuse, make it as plausible as you please, justifies vivisection.' He emphasised (as he was wont to do in his typically hyperbolic way): 'the only morality that is worth a fig, a crime committed not only against animals, but against everything that is noblest in ourselves' (cited in Krisdottir 2017).

Richard Adams took this one step further, in his anthropomorphic Childrens' Fantasies, *Watership Down* (1972) and *Plague Dogs* (1977), which not only gave voice to the more-than-human, but also included the destruction of their habitats and themselves (through hunting, disease, and experimentation) in scenes of emotional power. Young audiences expecting a Disney-like adventure were caught out by the haunting power of the animated adaptations, which left some mildly traumatised, according to anecdotal accounts.

Watership Down was to have a profound effect on two contemporary British nature writers, Nicola Chester and Melissa Harrison. In her memoir on place, protest, and belonging, *On Gallows Down* (2021), Chester describes how living within walking distance of the Berkshire landscape that had inspired Adams attuned her to literature's potent reframing of nature. And for Harrison, she was to turn to both adult (2015, 2018) and children's fiction (2021) as a way of exploring environmental themes.

There are many more novels that feature environmental issues, but what of novels that steer into the skid of activism more fully? Two striking examples both came out in the same year, 1975, when the first wave of the environmental movement had reached something of a generational peak, thirty years on from the dropping of the atom bombs on Japanese soil.

First published in 1975, but more relevant now than ever, Callenbach's novel, *Ecotopia*, is a flawed but important book. Using an epistolary form the novel purports to be the 'notebooks and reports of William Weston', an American journalist who undertakes a long assignment in the country of Ecotopia—formerly the western states of the USA, which have broken off from the union to follow a Green agenda and achieve an aspirational 'stable state' eco-economy. Chapter by chapter, Weston's despatches methodically chart Ecotopian society, technology, culture, and morality—Callenbach's expositional device for working through virtually aspect of modern life and reimagining it in an environmental, sustainable way. Although serious thought and research has clearly gone into the wide-ranging solutions, the ficto-critical framing device feels a bit thinly-veiled and unconvincing at times—a creaky means for stringing together a series of essays. There *is* a character arc, though, and even a 'shift'—a moment of gnosis—when the professional cynical, 'hard-nosed' Weston finally sees the light. As the querulous everyman Weston articulates the scepticism of the average reader, circumventing any criticism. Yet the exhaustive listing of eco-techno lifestyle fixes comes across a bit like a *Whole Earth Catalog* more than a novel. The introduction of Marissa, a forthright Ecotopian woman, does help to create some emotion in an otherwise concept-driven narrative. As the protagonist's 'object of desire' she animates Weston and is instrumental in his Damascus-like experience. Weston's dilated attempts to meet with the President of Ecotopia, and his desire to return home provide rather underpowered narrative traction otherwise. Yet one suspects a gripping thriller is not what Callenbach was attempting here—but without that quality, it makes the 'novel' less appealing to a wider audience. It is the kind of thing read by the 'converted'. How persuasive it would be at winning over eco-sceptics (or these days, climate change deniers) is negligible, despite his claims that 'without these alternate visions, we get stuck on dead center. And we'd better get ready. We need to know where we'd like to go.' (cited by Timberg, 2008)

Writing utopia is a challenge. It has produced some impressive, and certainly interesting (if not effective) novels: Thomas More's *Utopia* (1516); *Erewhon* (1872) by Samuel Butler; William Morris' *News from Nowhere* (1890); and Aldous Huxley's *Island* (1960) among others. Perhaps the most accomplished eco-novel of recent years is *The Overstory* (2018) by Richard Powers (although its bleak assessment of humanity is hardly utopian). In terms of the kind of interrogation of every aspect of society that Callenbach attempts Ursula K. Le Guin does it better—in *The Dispossessed* (1974) and *The Left Hand of Darkness* (1969) supremely so. But Callenbach's 'novel' is undoubtedly a very timely book—one that dares to challenge (almost) every aspect of modern life in an accessible and practicable way (i.e. in its reimagining of the education system it seems to have devised the prototype of Forest Schools). In this sense it is 'novel'—it offers something new (for its time). Now over forty years ago, technology has obviously moved on, and the challenges that the Climate Emergency presents us are far more challenging. The tragedy is that we were aware of the danger signals, *and* knew what to do, all those decades ago and failed to act. And now it may be too late. Yet perhaps more than ever we stories of hope in the face of such a far-reaching crisis—Solnit's 'literature of hope', because 'the revolution that counts is the one that takes place in the imagination' (2016: 26).

The other significant ecofiction that saw publication that year was Edward Abbey's *The Monkey Wrench Gang* (2000 [1975]). This iconic, influential novel inspired a whole generation of environmental campaigners—in particular Earth First!, but also the 'Pixie' road-protesters of the 90s—and in the light of the recent wave of protests by Extinction Rebellion, Culture Declares Emergency, and Climate Strikes/ #FridaysforFuture (started by the inspiring 16-year schoolgirl from Sweden, Greta Thunberg), and the wave of more recent protests (e.g. Earth Strike, 27th September, 2019), it seems timely to revisit it. Although this more interventionist early Twenty First century activity is impressive and impactful, it is good to remember environmental campaigning has been going on for a long time. Yes, it may be argued that it hasn't been effective enough/gone far enough; that it is imperative to declare a Climate Emergency and take immediate action—absolutely. But the awareness we have now is largely due to careful, time-consuming science, and the tireless campaigning of numerous NGOs, grassroots initiatives, and individuals—often unsung, under the radar, but all adding the long-term effort. This latest spike in activity and media coverage hasn't come from nowhere, and current eco-protesters stand on the shoulders of giants: Henry David Thoreau, Rachel Carson, Aldo Leopold, Annie Dillard, John Muir, Peter

5 Activism versus Art

Scott, Roger Deakin, and many, many more. One of these, it could be argued, is Edward Abbey, whose book—a mere novel—has cast a long shadow.

A rip-roaring, anti-establishment satire, and edgy eco-thriller, Abbey's cult classic seems wantonly disreputable in comparison with such esteemed company. It relates the triumphs, tribulations, and misadventures of a group of four self-elected eco-protesters (the wayward Dr Sarvis; his sometime companion, the Jewish New Yorker, Ms Azzbug; explosive Vietnam veteran George Hayduke; and wilderness guide and Jack Mormon, Seldom Seen Smith), who, over the course of a boat trip, hatch a (rough) plan to cause as much havoc as possible to disrupt the decimation of the epic canyon country of the American West. What begins as a series of relatively minor symbolic protests (the torching of billboards, the damaging of engines) quickly escalate into some spectacular destruction (the mass wrecking of whole road building operations; factories; and bridges). We may not condone any of the miscreant behaviour—it goes way beyond non-violent direct action when guns and bombs are deployed—but we can thrill to read of the colourful escapades of this modern-day outlaw gang. Abbey clearly draws upon the Western genre, as well as the chase thriller (e.g. John Buchan; Geoffrey Household), but his punchy, over-packed prose has more in common with Hunter S. Thompson and Chuck Palahniuk. Purists would no doubt dismiss the gang outright for, among other eco-crimes, littering—calling them hypocrites. But they are not *meant* to be E.C. (ecologically correct), but fully-rounded, deeply flawed characters. Abbey was not trying to write a manual for budding eco-warriors, signalling his virtue to the world—but write an entertaining novel which makes a point. It certainly crackles with an angry fire at the destruction of the remaining American wilderness, but it seems intent to be more provocative than coercive or corrective. It does not seek to offer a blueprint for a better way of living—but its wild energy and excoriating critique of the 'System', still can inspire to this day. But don't follow it literally. As Abbey, the sardonic trickster, himself warns: 'Anyone who takes this book seriously will be shot. Anyone who does not take it seriously will be buried alive by a Mitsubishi bulldozer.' (2000 [1975], xxiv)

Other novels have included activism as a key plot element, but have taken a more critical approach. The 'eco-terrorist' is a common plot-trope of hard-boiled tech-thrillers (which Michael Crichton led the market in) that like to portray any kind of environmentalism as extremist, unscientific, and misanthropic. Such portrayals are more indicative of the beliefs and political sympathies of the authors in question, rather than anything truly representative (white, male, so-called incels, media moguls, multinationals, corrupt governments, and wild card presidents could be said to have done more collateral damage on populations, resources, and the dominant techno-industrialist paradigm than any outlier eco-activist).

Frank Schätzing's bestselling eco-thriller, *Der Schwarm/The Swarm* (2004) seems at first to be using the Michael Crichton playbook—a pacy, multi-linear narrative restlessly crisscrossing the globe, featuring a range of earnest experts sharing their info-dumps of specialist knowledge as they combat a growing threat from the world's oceans, it has the inevitable irrational eco- 'terrorist', a wannabe Native American Sea Shepherd calling himself 'Greyowl', throwing a spanner in the works of the serious efforts of the scientists. And yet Greyowl's attention-grabbing chaos energy becomes co-opted in the fight against the aquatic antagonists; and the impact of eco-tourism, deep sea mining, and unsustainable lifestyles is fully acknowledged. The protagonists are compromised by the corporations that employ them and conflicted as individuals. No one is 'spotless', and the co-ordinated attacks from the depths, although extra-terrestrial in origin, are clearly a form of eco-karma for humanity's mistreatment of the biosphere.

In 2023 an 8-episode adaptation of *The Swarm* was released to mixed reviews. The risk with such a slick, maximalist approach is that, by masquerading as a techno-thriller, it quickly becomes assimilated into the mainstream as just more pop culture fodder.

Another approach is the well-informed but sardonic one, which is how the American novelist, TC Boyle, often approaches his subjects: usually cranky, maverick individuals who know a lot about one thing, but not perhaps lack in other areas, such as social skills. In novels like the prescient, *A Friend of the Earth* (2000), which imagined a West Coast of America ravaged by Climate Chaos, Boyle depicts a catholic cross-section of paradigms, from the earnest, well-meaning, but myopic 'green' to the cynical denier. In a large body of work, Boyle has explored many iterations of environmental issues, including self-driving cars in his short story, 'Asleep at the Wheel' (*The New Yorker* 2019).

He has recently returned to the Climate Crisis in *Blue Skies* (2023), which explores similar territory to *A Friend of the Earth*, but with the benefit of twenty-plus years more experience and knowledge of Climate Change. Dramatising what Rupert Read called a 'thrutopia', *Blue Skies*, 'unfold[s] in the uncertain present and work[s] through several even more uncertain years down the line. It deals with how regular people like you and me will live with the new normal and what it might mean in the larger context of our tenuous animal existence on this big hurtling rock we call home. It is, of course, a comedy, but a mighty grim one' (Boyle 2023). Boyle's potent gumbo of exhaustive research, engaging characters, vivid settings, deadpan humour, and sobering appraisal of the human condition has won him many fans in both North America and Europe, although his work has been critiqued for being too obsessed with the minutiae of the lives of his dysfunctional protagonists than the bigger picture (Margini 2017), a sardonic schadenfreude tilting things towards the comedic, and the culpability of the individual rather than the institutional.

Novels such as Richard Power's *The Overstory* (2018) and Michael Christie's *Greenwood* (2020) explore similar issues as Abbey's and Boyle's, but without the leavening effect of black comedy. They have other merits of course, but humour is a technique that should not be discredited in exploring environmental issues. An inability to see the funny side of any situation, to self-mock one's own earnestness and obsessions, hypocrisy, culpability and compromise, can be fatal. By deploying procatalepsis, the author of ecofiction circumvents a lot of criticism. Be your own worst heckler through characters who forcefully articulate any possible critiques to one's cherished thesis.

Another rhetorical strategy—the power of the personal testimony—is deployed in Octavia E. Butler's *Parable of the Sower* (1993), in which the main character unequivocally declaims her core beliefs, and challenges anyone to criticise them—backed up by the raw experience of surviving a transapocalyptic event.

Beyond the deployment of prolepsis or anecdote within the discourse of the narrative, some novels use the strategy of the unravelling denouement and imagine scenarios where the climate apocalypse has happened and the action is chiefly about surviving the aftermath on a day-to-day basis. Novels such as Ben Smith's *Doggerland* (2019) and Diane Cook's *The New Wilderness* (2020) portray unrelentingly bleak scenarios in which the challenge is not to prevent the 'bad thing' from happening, but to deal with its fallout—the new normal that must be habituated to. There is a shock value to these portraits of burnt and broken worlds—although one of diminishing returns as we become desensitised to them. Do any of them have the impact of John Martin's 1853 painting, 'The Great Day of His Wrath', when it first went on display and drew large crowds; or the final iconic scene from the first *Planet of the Apes* (1968) movie, when the surviving astronaut, George Taylor, played by Charlton Heston, stumbles upon the Ozymandian ruins of the Statue of Liberty, and realises that the planet he is on is in fact, a future primitive Earth where simians have evolved to become the dominant species? Pounding the sand, Taylor cries out: 'You bastards! You finally did it! You blew it up! Damn you all to hell!'.

These days there seems to be more shock value in portraying the 'bad thing' happening before our eyes, as in Jessie Greengrass' thrutopian novel, *The High*

House (2021), in which the matriarch, an environmental scientist, foresees what is to come and failing to prevent world governments from acting decisively and swiftly enough, prepares a domestic ark for her surviving family. The plight of the majority is clearly acknowledged by the narrator:

> Half the country is under water, as far as I can tell. The Thames has burst its banks above the barrier and god knows how many people drowned. They say it's worse in the Netherlands – Belgium and Germany, too. Switzerland has closed its borders. The French government say that they have suffered their own damages and don't have the resources to send aid. People have nowhere to go. Some of them were sitting on roofs, making videos of the water rising. Some of them were waiting to die. (2021: 83)

Acknowledging their awareness of this escalating crisis, and carbon-complicity, the narrator

> —We should have done something,
>   I said,
>   —we should have tried—
>   —Tried what?
>   (ibid.)

A former holiday home fortuitously elevated above the surrounding flooded East Anglian countryside, the 'ark' in *The High House* is the kind of refuge not available to the Global South. It has been prepared, with professional foresight by Francesca, an environmental scientist, who sees all too clearly the accelerating climate catastrophe, for her step-daughter, Caro, and son, Paul(y). Stewards of this Noah-esque home are the local handyman, Grandy, and his grand-daughter Sally. Greengrass sustains a tight focus throughout, alternating the viewpoint characters and dramatising the devastation in microcosm through the impact upon this social unit. It is well-crafted, and written with a poetic minimalism—speech marks pared down to Emily Dickinson dashes. And yet this is a very bourgeois apocalypse, which shows how white, middle-class privilege provides buffer zones in extremis that billions of others would not have the luxury of. It is best at depicting the incremental breakdown of civilisation; the slow-slow-rapid transformation of the everyday as tipping points are reached and transcended. And at dramatising how complicit we all are in making it happen:

> After years of incremental alteration you stand, surrounded by your accommodations, and wonder for the first time at the fact that everything should, somehow, have come to this. (2021: 84)

Arguably, the novel itself is a kind of ark, in which we include all the things we feel are worth saving or celebrating—defiant acts of pre-emptive salvage, restoration, and re-evaluation. As Atwood suggests, 'Writing is always an act of hope, because it assumes a reader. It assumes a reader in the future. The act of writing and the person reading it are separated by time and space' (interviewed by Erica Wagner 2022 [2019]).

And so, whatever approach one takes—pre-, trans-, or post-; defiant; denialist; delayist; survivalist; or quixotic—how does one go about writing such fiction?

Polonius Must Die: Practical Strategies

In Shakespeare's *Hamlet*, the young malcontent Prince of Denmark runs rings around his old tutor, Polonius, who is fond of declaiming hoary maxims, such as 'This above all, as the night follows day, to thine own self be true' (Act 1, Scene 3). In a play about authenticity, deceit, self-knowledge, and self-deception, this has ironic resonance, especially when the audience knows Hamlet is inhabiting the role of a sensitive son whose mental health has been severely disrupted by grief (which it, in fact, has—and he is less in control than he realises). And yet Polonius' old saws are not enough to deal with the complex, volatile situation at hand. To survive and thrive in the dangerous hall of mirrors of Elsinore, where the conceit of the court masques the ugly truth (that Claudius, Hamlet's uncle, murdered his father to freely marry his mother) Hamlet needs to cut through the etiquette and hypocrisy by transgressing social norms of accepted behaviour—to be unreasonable. To hack the system, or throw a spanner in the works. In the current Climate Emergency we have seen that role taken up by Greta Thunberg and her fellow youth activists, and by Extinction Rebellion. But in terms of ecofiction, how do we play the agent provocateur version of Hamlet? Well, on one level, with 'words, words, words'. With daring, ludic, polysemous wordplay—which dazzles, deceives, reveals, disturbs, and astonishes. On another level, we need to 'murder Polonius', (in the spirit of Arthur Quiller-Couch's much-quoted maxim, 'murder your darlings'): that didactic tendency to download knowledge in tedious expositional monologues, or 'info dumps'—the toxic landfill of prose fiction where unexpurgated facts are dumped on the reader.

As the writer channel Hamlet, but not Polonius, and you will stun your readers with your bold wit, rather than send them to sleep with your pre-Socratic lecturing. In the way that Socrates questioned and interrogated his peers, we need to be willing to hack the discourse, challenge every shibboleth, and be prepared to be the heretic and the sceptic—including of our own most cherished beliefs. As Yevgeny Zamyatin said, 'If we have no heretics we must invent them, for heresy is essential to health and growth'.

So, how to write fiction that explores important issues while avoiding the spectre of the preacher? I will focus here on a few suggestions: stealth exposition; the democracy of character; (don't) bend the plot; trust the reader; and make the reader trust you; and avoid solutionism.

Stealth Exposition

The classic advice of creative writing workshops is 'show, don't tell', but sometimes telling—using expositional methods—*is* the best strategy. It all depends how it is done. At its worst the use of exposition within prose fiction can read like the afore-mentioned 'info-dump', as though the action has freeze-framed and the author downloads some important information for the reader. It is like that moment in a 1950s B-movie when the 'boffin' scientist explains what is going on, using various pseudo-scientific techno-babble. Exposition in prose fiction can often feel like these pipe-jabbing moments. It can seem like the writer has done some research and they are keen to share it. Indubitably, do you your research, but avoid *showing* your research: unexpurgated, it can kill the narrative flow—so much expositional cholesterol blocking the story-arteries, and causing, at worst, narrative thrombosis. Some writers have deployed this tactic deliberately, as though offering a challenge to the reader: the narrator in Bret Easton Ellis' *American Psycho* (1991), Patrick Bateman, spends whole chapters expounding upon his music tastes in extreme examples of narcissistic 'mansplaining'. The obsessive materialist monomania of the collector fits well with the sociopathic serial killer, but the critique is aimed at *us*, the reader: how willing are we to be complicit in this, to indulge his obsessions for our own vicarious pleasure, to keep reading his tedious exhaustive recounting of the minutiae of his record collection or the recording of a particular middle-of-the-road artist? When will we be willing to press pause, stop, or even delete?

In terms of ecofiction, Kim Stanley Robinson is equally bold in his use of exposition in *The Ministry for the Future* (2020), in which Robinson stops the narrative flow to offer what seem like mini-essays on aspects of the multiple challenges of the Climate Emergency. It is as though he has stopped pretending to write a novel, when in fact he wants to offer a stark warning: a sobering audit of what we know, and what needs to be done. And, ultimately, he seems to be saying—doesn't that trump everything?

Surely, the conceit of fiction is only a thin veneer, a sticking plaster for what we face, at best? When fundamentally we need to *act*, and act *fast*.

Robinson's novel risked being just as complicit in this—what could be called the sideshow of literature—if not for the fact that the novel was featured prominently at COP26 in Glasgow, where an international cohort of policymakers and leaders had gathered: people with the power to change the world. Greta Thunberg challenged the 'blah blah blah' (2021) of even this high-profile gathering, but the event *did* have the attention of the world's media, and showed the seriousness of the problem, and scales of commitment from our governments. Robinson's strategy may not have created great literature, but it created impactful literature—speaking directly to those who needed to listen.

And yet these extreme examples aside, the best strategy in general for fiction writers is to deploy what I call 'stealth exposition': to find ways to sneak in the essential information in a way that *doesn't* disrupt the diegetic world of the novel. In short, to dramatise it in some way. This can be done through a range of techniques: by dialogic means, using various characters to relate the information in a way in that is faithful to the respective character and to the story world. Mentor figures can often be useful for this—the Nestors, Merlins, Gandalfs, Dumbledores, Obi-Wan Kenobis, Yodas, and Tenars who impart wisdom. Sometimes false mentors throw the protagonist a googly. Allies turn out to be enemies. Friends, rivals. But, critically, information is divulged—true, false, misleading—dialogically.

Another approach is through expositional devices such as letters, telegrams, emails, cryptic codes, newspaper reports, radio broadcasts, holographic recordings stored by a rogue droid, a treasure map, the transcript of an interrogation or interview, speech or surveillance recording, and so forth. Slip it in so that the reader does not notice, that it becomes an enjoyable part of the plot, and it adds texture to the text through the deployment of paratext, docemes, or the heteroglossic. Docemes are Lund's suggestion for additional textual elements, such as archives, newspaper clippings, birth certificates, shipping logbook, police report: 'Inspired by the verb *doceo*, [to show] I suggest the word DOCEME to describe any part of a document, which can be identified and analytically isolated, thus being a partial result of the documentation process' (2004).

In terms of paratext it could be in the use of footnotes, which may or may not contain accurate information. Sometimes footnotes are used to convey a faux-historicity or academic gravity to the main text, as in Susanna Clarke's *Jonathan Strange and Mr Norrell* (2004). Docemes, or found documents— real or fictional—can again be used to create a sense of verisimilitude, and sometimes the destabilising presence of counter-narratives, as in Mark Z. Danielewski's *House of Leaves* (2000)—a novel haunting itself with various texts erupting through the surface of the page at divergent angles, simultaneously interrupting the textual plane and the main plot. The heteroglossic can be deployed by having multiple viewpoint characters, with wildly differing voices—most boldly Richard Powers, in *The Overstory* (2018), which includes the Redwoods themselves as a tangible more-than-human perspective alongside that of the human cast resulting in a polyphonic affect akin to the dawn chorus. This cross-sectional approach we will consider in more detail next.

The Democracy of Character

Another effective way to avoid the deadening effect of dogma in fiction is to create a healthy cross-section of characters who between them represent a spectrum of beliefs, stances, and modalities. It is perfectly fine to have one mouth-piece character who aligns closely with your *own* views and values—as long as you have other characters robustly challenge, critique, mock, mimic, and dismiss those views and values. Let your novel dramatise a healthy debate between positions—otherwise you risk biasing one particular stance, or not fairly representing the cross-section of opinions and lifestyle choices available (and possibly alienating your reader). So, for example, you could have a main character who is a dedicated environmental protester and campaigner—well-intentioned, but perhaps a little evangelical in their beliefs. They want the world to live the way they do. But surrounding this character who have a climate denier dad, an ambivalent boyfriend, a supportive best friend, a fiercely critical teacher or boss, a nihilistic peer group who would rather just get wasted than think about it all, and a virtue-signalling green neighbour or colleague who likes to be seen doing the right thing but has actually got some unhealthy carbon habits such as astro-turf, a weakness for long-haul holidays to exotic climes, and so on. Let them all articulate or embody their position in relation to the main issue and give space for the reader to decide who they agree and disagree with, who they relate to and who they do not. Creating this negative space for the reader to inhabit credits them with discernment and draws them in—while as a didactic approach can push them away. Ensure each is fairly represented, even if you vehemently disagree with them. This avoids what Shawl and Ward call 'liberal perception fallacy' (2005). The act of compassionate imagination that writing a novel requires can often make us understand worlds very different from our own. Even if we do not agree with or condone them, we can understand them better—and that adds to the positive sum of humanity. A highly accomplished example of this polyvocality is Stephen Markley's immense thrutopian ecofiction, *The Deluge* (2023), which uses a vivid spectrum of characters to dramatise the complex positionalities of those impacted from different strata of society: eco-warrior firebrand, Kate Morris, and her high-level lobby group, A Fierce Blue Fire; the violent, anarchistic ecoterrorists, 6Degrees; environmental scientist, Dr Tony Pietrus; a struggling drug-addict; an actor turned religious zealot who builds a huge following preaching intolerance; a high-functioning climate model analyst; and a whole raft of Republican and Democrat politicians and lackeys out to climb the greasy pole to power while the world burns. Markley shows how virtually all are compromised and complicit, and leaves the reader to decide on the best way through this moral and existential maze.

(Don't) Bend the Plot

Unless you are Thomas Hardy it is best not to bend the plot of your novel to illustrate your own deterministic view of humanity. When it feels characters no longer have agency, and the illusion at least of multi-facetedness, but are merely pawns and cyphers, the reader can stop believing in them (or suspending their disbelief), and therefore stop caring for them. Without that emotional investment, narrative traction is lost, and the reader may simply put down the book and walk away. Plot should ideally emerge *out* of character and develop in what appears at least to be an organic way. Causality and continuity should be contingent upon the actions of the characters; rather than have them forced out of character to fit with the plot. Creaking plots can be avoided by giving characters time to make decisions, to reach their tipping point through what has been called by John Cowper Powys a 'concatenation of imperatives' (2007: 210). Hollywood screenwriters like to refer to this as the 'Fear/Desire Axis'. Imagine a set of scales. One end is weighed with enticing desires; the other with stifling fears—the desire to meet a new partner, to move to a new town, find a new job, experience something different; the fear of rejection, of loneliness, of failure, of unpleasantness. When the desire/s outweigh the fear/s the character will move 'forward', will act. If, however, the fear/s outweigh the desire/s then the character will freeze or retreat. This is simplified push/pull motivation—human psychology is more complex than that, than a simplistic seesaw diagram; but it gives a good indicator of how 'plot' should happen: how a character is forced out of their comfort zone; forced to act. The tipping point—when a character is teetering on the fulcrum—is the point of maximum dramatic tension. Shakespeare epitomised it in Hamlet's famous soliloquy: 'To be or not to be, that is the question'. If the Prince of Denmark had not suffered from procrastination—his 'fatal flaw'—then the play would have been over a lot quicker, but with far less impact. Because Shakespeare has his protagonist teeter on this knife edge for almost the entire five acts we have a masterpiece of tension, suspense, and psychological realism. The plot emerges from the behaviour of the character, or so it seems to the audience. Of course, for the writer it may feel the other way around. The story or play may start with an idea, a scene, an image, and then one has to work out how characters would act within that mise-en-scène. And yet the good stuff—the most gripping writing—occurs when the characters seem to come alive (to the writer), stray from the 'path' allotted them, and go rogue. The plot even be contingent upon the protagonists railing against their apparent 'lot', but it must seem like they have some kind of choice, and that not everything is predetermined, locked down, and not pliable to the application of will. Like Neo Anderson in *The Matrix* (1999), we hope eventually the protagonist will see through the apparent prison they are in and transcend it with daring boldness. That the protagonist has agency and can act upon the plasticity of their circumstances is far more satisfying for most readers, than having one who has no choice, no 'free-range'—a factory-farmed protagonist restricted to a cage of the writer's wishes.

Trust the Reader

It is important to trust the reader. Let them step forward and work out what is going on as you proceed. You don't need to spoonfeed them. Provide incremental 'breadcrumb' clues by all means. This will draw them through the narrative. But don't spell everything out. Use subtext and inference to leave space for the reader to consider the implications and quantum possibilities of every scene. Make each scene an equivalent to the Schrödinger's Cat experiment—vibrating between different states. As soon as you 'open' it as a writer and pin down one state, one meaning, one 'reading' of something, the scene stops having dramatic potentiality. The cat dies; or lives—and neither is interesting, dramatically. Only the uncertainty that lies between.

And Make the Reader Trust You

Equally, it is important to earn and retain the reader's trust—what has been called the Writer/Reader Contract established by the title, the blurb, and the opening few pages. If the novel is set up (by marketing, interviews, and the back cover blurb) as being a gritty, hard-boiled eco-thriller, but actually turns out to be a sentimental historical romance (or vice versa) then the reader will be probably disappointed, irritated, or enraged. If it is sold as being cutting edge, when it is in fact hackneyed, then you have cheated the reader. And you win the reader's trust by also taking care with the text on a micro-level: punctuation, presentation, consistency good editing. Ensure the reader receives a quality experience.

Avoid Solutionism

Finally, it is vital that your novel doesn't present glib solutions to the complex problems we face. There is certainly no single 'silver bullet' that will fix the multiplicity of challenges we face. As the protester placards say: 'Systems Change, Not Climate Change'. We need radical rethinking of all aspect of our lives. One single technofix, for example, everyone adopting solar power, will not solve everything. Ensure there are complications—because there will be. Kim Stanley Robinson's *Ministry* novel is good at imagining these in a convincingly robust and intelligent way. Narrative compression sometimes forces us into a resolution when life is seldom so neat. Deploying open endings, or ambivalence, messy compromises, and ongoing large-scale effort—rather than the closed, single note, neat, and singular.

An open ending will sustain the realism and present the reader with the choice—which is ultimately more empowering. It may disquiet, disturb, or even catalyse them into action.

The bottom line is: there is no one 'right way' of tackling ecofiction. There are too many variables in play. In the next chapter we consider how to address 'shaping a world in flux'.

MYCELIA: Connections to Writers, Texts, and Resources

- Buckland, David, ed. 2006. *Burning Ice: Art and Climate Change*. Dorchester: Cape Farewell.
- Cape Farewell: https://www.capefarewell.com/.
- Catton, Eleanor, 2023. *Birnam Wood*. London: Granta.
- Climate Fiction Writers League: https://climate-fiction.org/.

- Culture Declares Emergency: https://www.culturedeclares.org/.
- Emergence Magazine: https://emergencemagazine.org/.
- Griffiths, Jay. 2021. *Why Rebel?* London: Penguin.
- Hardisty, Paul E., 2023. *The Forcing*. London: Orena.
- Jamie, Kathleen, ed. 2021. *Antlers of Water: Writing on the Nature and Environment of Scotland*. Edinburgh: Canongate.
- Markley, Stephen, 2024. *The Deluge*. New York: Simon & Schuster.
- McMahon, Linden Katherine, ed. *We Are a Many-bodied Singing Thing*. RSPB. 2020: https://naturebftb.co.uk/2020/03/27/we-are-a-many-bodied-singing-thing/.
- Norbury, Katherine, ed. 2023. *Women on Nature: 100 + Voices on Place, Landscape & the Natural World*. London: Unbound.
- Porrit, Jonathan (2013) *The World We Made: Alex McKay's Story from 2050*. London: Phaidon.
- Scott, Manda, 2024. *Any Human Power*. London: September Books.
- Shahwar, Durre, & Nasia Sarwar-Skuse. 2024. *Gathering*. Edinburgh: 404 Ink.
- Solnit, Rebecca. 2016 [2004]. *Hope in the Dark: Untold Histories, Wild Possibilities*. London: Haymarket.
- The Dark Mountain Project: https://dark-mountain.net/.
- The Lost Words: https://www.thelostwords.org/.
- Thunberg, Greta. 2019. *No One is Too Small to Make a Difference*. London: Penguin.
- Williams, Heathcote. 1988. *Whale Nation*. New York, NY: Harmony.
- Williams, Heathcote. 1991. *Autogeddon*. London: Jonathan Cape.
- XR Writers Rebel: https://writersrebel.com/.

SPORES: Writing Activities

- Manifesto—write a manifesto: either a personal one, articulating your core beliefs and artistic vision; and/or from the point of view of one of your characters, in which you could adopt an extreme position (NB this could be used ironically within the text to highlight their failings, and to create dramatic irony). If the former, then consider what steps you will take to manifest this. Print it off and circulate it, or share it freely on the Internet to disseminate your ideas.
- The Angry Letter—write a letter in the voice of the Disgruntled Other, someone resisting the favoured rhetorical position of the novel/main protagonist, e.g. if the main character is an eco-activist, write it from the POV of a climate denier, sceptic, or advocate of Quietism or Doomism.

- Nomadic Emergence—drawing upon what Dr Harry Whitehead (University of Leicester) called 'nomadic emergence' (2013), consider how this approach can serve the writers of ecofiction. An alternative title for this would be what I call 'Wild Writing'. Go for a walk with a notebook and pen. Open your senses. Sit somewhere peaceful and notice the details of your surroundings through all of your multi-sensory awareness. How does it feel to sit there? Can you imagine what it was like before you arrived? Did you startle anything with your arrival? Or does your peacefulness attract the interest of the more-than-human? Be guided by the micro-details of the moment. Let these suggest writing prompts; keep the pen moving on the page in an extended freewrite. Don't even look at what you are writing. Let it flow out. If nature prompts you to move, then move. Explore your immediate surroundings with all your senses. Experience the environment in a more-than-human way.
- Permeable Structures—in *The Book of Trespass* (2021), Nick Hayes has pointed out how 'the notion that a perimeter should be impenetrable is a human contrivance alone'. With that in mind, explore how writing that trespasses and transgresses form and genre expectations often results in the best kind, the black swans and sui generis works. Write a piece of hybrid prose that wanders freely between forms, e.g. novel-writing; nature writing; travel-writing; memoir; diary. Weave in journal entries; eavesdropped dialogue; found poems; lists; prose-poetry—anything. Let the natural world suggest organic structures and patterning, to give the free-range piece some kind of shape.
- Time-specific project—conceptualise a time-specific project, e.g. over a season or a year, one that allows for a close observation of the subtle changes of nature (look at various classic and modern nature writing for examples e.g. *The Natural History of Selborne; The Journals of Dorothy Wordsworth; Pilgrim at Tinker Creek; The Living Mountain; Diary of a Young Naturalist*). On a large sheet of paper using Post-its and felt tips to map out the idea. Identify key themes and brainstorm around those. Consider stakeholders. Any connections between the different nodes of the project. Then start to identify the aims or goals of the project. Next, how to achieve them—your objectives, or outcomes. What resources do you need? Support? When and where will this take place? Avoid being too ambitious. Close observation of a single tree, pond, hedgerow, field, or species will be more productive than anything too broad in scope. Consider using nature-journaling as a way of capturing the changes over a year—weaving in sketches, field-notes, found objects, photos, quotes, etc. Create a Gantt chart to manage your project, or whatever system works for you.

References

Abbey, Edward. 2000 [1975]. *The Monkey Wrench Gang*. New York, NY: Harper Perennials.
Abram, David. 2017 [1997]. *The Spell of the Sensuous: Perception and Language in a More-Than-Human World*. New York, NY: Vintage Books.
Adams, Richard. 1972. *Watership Down*. London: Rex Collings.
Adams, Richard. 1977. *Plague Dogs*. London: Allen Lane.
Austen, Jane. 1817. *Northanger Abbey*. London: John Murray.
Barrie, J.M. 1906. *Peter Pan in Kensington Gardens*. London: Hodder & Stoughton.
Boyle, T.C. 2000. *A Friend of the Earth*. New York, NY: Viking.
Boyle, T.C. 2019. Asleep at the Wheel, February 4. *The New Yorker*. https://www.newyorker.com/magazine/2019/02/11/asleep-at-the-wheel (Accessed 5 July 2023).
Boyle, T.C. 2023. *Blue Skies*. London: Bloomsbury.
Burroughs, Edgar Rice. 1912. *Tarzan of the Apes*. New York, NY: A.C. McClurg.
Butler, Octavia E. 2019 [1993]. *Parable of the Sower*. London: Headline.
Butler, Samuel. 1872. *Erewhon, or Over the Range*. London: Trübner and Ballantyne.
Catton, Eleanor. 2023. *Birnam Wood*. London: Granta.
Chabon, Michael. 1995. *Wonder Boys*. London: Fourth Estate.
Chester, Nicola. 2021. *On Gallows Down: Place, protest, and belonging*. London: Chelsea Green.
Christie, Michael. 2020. *Greenwood*. Brunswick, Victoria: Scribe.
Clarke, Susanna. 2004. *Jonathan Strange and Mr Norrell*. London: Bloomsbury.
Clare, John. 1820. *Poems Descriptive of Rural Life and Scenery*. Stamford: Taylor and Hessey.
Clare, John. 1996 [1827]. *The Shepherd's Calendar*. London: Orion Publishing.
Clark, Alex. 2017, March 11. Writers Unite! The Return of the Protest Novel. *Guardian*. https://www.theguardian.com/books/2017/mar/11/fiction-as-political-protest-can-a-novel-change-the-world (Accessed 18 February 2023).
Clute, John, and John Grant. 1999. *The Encyclopedia of Fantasy*. London: Orbit.
Cook, Diane. 2020. *The New Wilderness*. London: One World.
Crace, John. 2013. *Harvest*. London: Picador.
Danielewski, Mark Z. 2000. *House of Leaves*. New York: Pantheon.
Diaper, Jeffrey. 2023. *Eco-Modernism: Ecology, Environment and Nature in Literary Modernism*. Clemson, SC: Clemson University Press.
Flaherty, Alice W. 2005. *The Midnight Disease: The Drive to Write, Writer's Block, and the Creative Brain*. Boston, MA: Houghton Mifflin/Mariner Books.
Flanagan, Richard. 2021. *The Living Sea of Waking Dreams*. London: Chatto & Windus.
Foulds, Adam. 2009. *The Quickening Maze*. London: Jonathan Cape.
Fowles, John. 1998. *Wormholes: Essays and Occasional Writing*. London: Random House.

Fuller, Peter. 1990, Autumn. Art and the Spiritual. Peter Fuller's Journey. *Modern Painters* 3 (3): 45–49.
Fuller, Peter. 1990, June 17. Crisis of Faith in Modern Art. *Sunday Telegraph*, p. 11.
Grahame, Kenneth. 1908. *The Wind in the Willows*. London: Methuen.
Greengrass, Jessie. 2021. *The High House*. London: Swift Press.
Haraway, Donna J. 2016. *Staying with the Trouble: Making Kin with the Chthulucene*. Durham and London: Duke University Press.
Hardy, Thomas. 2004 [1878]. *The Return of the Native*. London: Dover Editions.
Hardy, Thomas. 2004 [1887]. *The Woodlanders*. London: Dover Editions.
Harrison, Melissa. 2015. *At Hawthorn Time*. London: Bloomsbury Circus.
Harrison, Melissa. 2018. *All Among the Barley*. London: Bloomsbury.
Harrison, Melissa. 2021. *By Oak, Ash, and Thorn*. London: Chicken House.
Haskell, David George. 2022. *Sounds Wild and Broken: Sonic Marvels, Evolution's Creativity, and the Crisis of Sensory Extinction*. London: Faber and Faber.
Hayes, Nick. 2021. *The Book of Trespass: Crossing the Lines that Divide Us*. London: Bloomsbury.
Huxley, Aldous. 1960. *Island*. London: Penguin.
Kipling, Rudyard. 1906. *Puck of Pook's Hill*. London: Macmillan.
Kleon, Austin. 2020, June 29. Behold Octavia Butler's Motivational Notes to Self. *Open Culture*. https://www.openculture.com/2020/06/behold-octavia-butlers-motivational-notes-to-self.html (Accessed 6 June 2023).
Krisdottir, Morine. 2017. *Descents of Memory: The Life of John Cowper Powys*. New York, NY: Overlook Press.
Lanone, Catherine. 2022. Of Furtive Hedgehogs and Steam Machines: An Ecofeminist Reading of Thomas Hardy. *Fathom.* 7: 2022. https://doi.org/10.4000/fathom.2316.
Lawrence, D.H. 1923. *Birds, Beasts, and Flowers*. London: Martin Secker.
Lawrence, D.H. 1926. *The Virgin and the Gipsy*. London: Martin Secker.
Lawrence, D.H. 1960 [1928] *Lady Chatterley's Lover*. London: Penguin.
Le Guin, Ursula K. 1969. *The Left Hand of Darkness*. New York, NY: Ace Books.
Le Guin, Ursula K. 1974. *The Dispossessed*. New York, NY: Harper & Row.
Lincoln, Abraham. 1861, March 4. 'First Inaugural Address'. Washington, D.C.. Abraham Lincoln Online. Available from: https://web.archive.org/web/20100427035224/http://showcase.netins.net/web/creative/lincoln/speeches/1inaug.htm (Accessed 4 July 2024).
Lodge, David. 2003. *Consciousness and the Novel*. London: Penguin.
Lund, Niels Windfeld. 2004. Documentation in a Complementary Perspective. https://www.academia.edu/980627/Documentation_in_a_complementary_perspective (Accessed 5 July 2023).
Lupton, Hugh. 2010. *The Ballad of John Clare*. Dublin: Dedalus Press.
Mackenna, Kohn. 1993. *Clare*. Belfast: Blackstaff Press.
Maitland, Sara. 2012. *Gossip from the Forest: Tangled Roots of Our Forests and Fairytale*. London: Granta.

Manwaring, Kevan. 2023. 'Many Paths Through the Forest: Exploring Arborescence and Ecological Themes in Digital Interactive Narrative'. *Gothic Nature Journal*, iv. Available from: https://gothicnaturejournal.com/issue-iv/ (Accessed 4 July 2024).

Margini, Matt. 2017, December 27. T.C. Boyle's Fictions of Catastrophe. *The Atlantic*. https://www.scribd.com/article/367987426/T-C-Boyle-s-Fictions-Of-Catastrophe (Accessed 5 July 2023).

McCarthy, Cormac. 2006. *The Road*. London: Picador.

More, Thomas. n.d. [1516]. *Utopia: A Dialogue of Comfort*. London: Heron Books.

Morris, William. 1890. *News from Nowhere*. Oxford: Kelmscott Press.

Nakate, Vanessa. 2022. Interview. *UN Women*. https://www.un.org/africarenewal/magazine/march-2022/you-cant-have-climate-justice-without-gender-equality#:~:text=%E2%80%94%20Vanessa%20Nakate%2C%20Ugandan%20climate%20activist (Accessed 4 July 2023).

Nanson, Anthony. 2021. *Storytelling and Ecology: Empathy, Enchantment and Emergence in the Use of Oral Narratives*. London: Bloomsbury.

Orwell, George. 2019 [1949]. *Nineteen Eighty-Four*. London: Penguin.

Power, Kevin. 2023, March 3. Birnam Wood by Eleanor Catton Review—Hippies v Billionaires. *Guardian*. https://www.theguardian.com/books/2023/mar/03/birnam-wood-by-eleanor-catton-review-hippies-v-billionaires (Accessed 4 July 2023).

Powers, Richard. 2018. *The Overstory*. London: William Heinemann.

Powys, John Cowper. 2000 [1935]. *Weymouth Sands*. London: Penguin.

Powys, John Cowper. 2007. *Porius*. New York, NY: Overlook Press.

Raworth, Kate. 2017. *Doughnut Economics: Seven Ways to Think Like a 21st-Century Economist*. London: Cornerstone.

Schätzing, Frank. 2004. *Der Schwarm/The Swarm*. New York: ReganBooks.

Scott, Manda. 2023. The Blog. Available from: https://mandascott.co.uk/blog/ (Accessed 4 July 2024).

Shawl, Nisi, and Cynthia Ward. 2005. *Writing the Other: A Practical Approach*. n.p.: Aqueduct Press.

Sheridan, Richard Brinsey. 1775. *The Rivals*. n.p.

Smith, Ben. 2019. *Doggerland*. London: Fourth Estate.

Solnit, Rebecca. 2016 [2004]. *Hope in the Dark: Untold Histories, Wild Possibilities*. London: Haymarket.

Tolkien, J.R.R. 1997. *The Monsters and the Critics: And other essays*. London: HarperCollins.

Thunberg, Greta. 2021. Greta Thunberg Mocks World Leaders in 'Blah, Blah, Blah' Speech—BBC News. https://www.youtube.com/watch?v=ZwD1kG4PI0w (Accessed 5 July 2023).

Timberg, Scott. 2008, December 14. 'The Novel That Predicted Portland'. *The New York Times*. Available from: https://www.nytimes.com/2008/12/14/fashion/14ecotopia.html (Accessed 4 July 2024).

Wagner, Erica. 2022, September 18. "Writing is always an act of hope": Margaret Atwood on The Testaments. *The New Statesmen*, updated 28 March 2022. https://www.newstatesman.com/culture/2019/09/writing-is-always-an-act-of-hope-margaret-atwood-on-the-testaments (Accessed 5 July 2023).

Whitehead, H. 2013. Nomadic Emergence: Creative Writing Theory and Practice-Led Research. *New Ideas in the Writing Arts: Practice, Culture Literature*, ed. Graeme Harper. Cambridge: CSP.

Wodehouse, P.G. 2008. *Jeeves in the Offing*. London: Arrow Books.

6

Shaping a World in Flux

In a 'time of polycrisis' when 'the shocks are disparate, but they interact so that the whole is even more overwhelming than the sum of the parts' (Tooze 2022) how can our ecofiction reflect that apocalyptic gestalt while remaining readable, even enjoyable? In an age of increasing inequality, geopolitical tension, and 'shifting baseline syndrome' (Pauly's term, cited by Pearce 2020), when we have to habituate ourselves to cascading levels of air, soil and water quality, diversity, food and energy security, and basic levels of living standards and wellbeing, is this even possible? What has also been termed the 'meta-crisis' (Scott, 2024) shapes us all, whether we acknowledge its existence or not, impacting every aspect of the world we live in—and yet we can still choose, as writers, to formulate a narrative response to this to raise awareness, criticality, motivate, and empower. In this chapter we consider the challenges of *shaping* your material. We'll consider form, with an especial emphasis on 'found structure' and bio-mimicry—finding inherent forms in nature, thereby creating a marriage of form and content in writing that seeks to robustly engage with environmental issues and ecological concepts in an aesthetically-synchronous way. We will focus on specific geographical features—rivers, hills, archipelagos—as well as topographical approaches in general. We will look at temporal approaches also. We will also consider how we can use different kinds of text—intertextual, paratextual, and heteroglossic approaches comprising docemes from old and new media (e.g. text messages; news reports; tweets; adverts; AI-generated content) to provide 'texture' and a healthy range of voices.

In a 2017 *Guardian* article about the resurgence of the 'protest novel' during the turbulent period of the Trump administration, Alex Clarke asked:

How to swim, though, if your preferred stroke is made with a pen? Or: how to respond to a time of extreme political and social uncertainty, a time when language itself is contested at every turn, and when urgency seems the order of the day? What can fiction writers make of the shifting ground beneath their feet, and how does their participation in – or withdrawal from – public life affect our view of them? (Clarke 2017)

This is the challenge all writers face, but especially writers of ecofiction, which more than any other form seeks to address the 'polycrisis' we face in a committed, informed way. With the 'ground [shifting] beneath [our] feet', as Clarke suggests, is it even possible to formulate a single, static methodology? In short, no. But this chapter looks at a range of approaches which would allow for protean responses attentive to the continually changing variables we face—a multimodal feedback loop.

Key Aspects of Form

There are key aspects that will help most pieces of writing avoid shapelessness. I consider these to be length, form, structure, pace, and rhythm.

Sometimes the length and form of a piece of writing are dictated by the particular market or platform: a flash fiction or short story competition, magazine with specific submission guidelines, a radio or podcast slot, or genre of book. Ecofiction is a type of literary fiction and is not normally bound by the certain expectations of length one may find in, say, Fantasy or Historical fiction; however, in the development of the project and their career writers of ecofiction may well have to engage with the restrictive considerations listed above. Any experience of professional writing, e.g. in an academic or business capacity, can serve the writer well. Certainly, novelists who have had to learn their craft as journalists and press officers, such Neil Gaiman and Terry Pratchett, to name but two, have found the skillset useful. Whether this is the case or not, it is certainly wise to consider the general length of one's project—not in the precise word count, but in the broadest possible terms: will it be a one-off book, or a series? A short story, novella, or a full-length novel? This should be influenced by the nature of the material, of the story you want to tell: is it story that requires a large, sweeping novel format to relate? or would it work better as a short story or novella? Of course, sometimes one does not quite know until deep in the process—I will discuss this emergent approach below.

Structure is intrinsic to a successful narrative. Again, this can arise organically, but having a sense of shape in a piece of fiction, of any length, is essential. It shows you have made conscious decisions about where the story starts, how it progresses, and how it ends. In an extended narrative as complex as a novel, careful planning is vital: it is like building a cathedral—everything in the endeavour should contribute to its stability and aspiration: to reach towards the 'spire' of its climax. Every element of the novel supports this: the flying buttress of a flashback, the chancel of chapters, the nave of climax, the cloisters of a framing narrative, the crypt of subtext, and so forth. Alternatively, one could see the spire as the key theme or spirit of the novel—a certain intangible quality such as, say, immanence, in which you convey the inherent sanctity of nature. We have to start at ground level—with a character, minor or major, arriving into a scene, perhaps on the fringes of the main event—but as the cathedral-builder novelist, we need to see the bigger picture. Everything sentence should contribute towards the whole. To help provide stability we may choose to use tried-and-tested structural schemas, such as the triadic arc, or a five-act structure. We may wish to draw upon patterns and motifs from nature to embed within the novel an affinity with the subject matter—a marriage of form and content, as discussed above. We may wish to give our novel mythic resonance by drawing upon Larkin's 'myth-kitty' (1955)—world myths and legends. Adopting a comparative mythology approach, we may choose to draw upon models such as The Hero's Journey (Campbell 1993 [1949]) or Heroine's Journey (Murdock 1990), with the caveats mentioned above. Whatever one's approach, there should be sense of patterning and shaping—at least in later drafts. This creates a narrative elegance which is satisfying to read, as though we are in the audience of a world-class symphonic orchestra conducted by a world-class conductor.

So, bearing in mind the length, form, and structure of a narrative, one must pace it accordingly. A flash fiction will require a different level of pacing to a 'doorstep' novel, or series. Genre governs pacing too: a high-octane techno-thriller will be paced differently to a slow-burn epic. Pace relates to what T.C. Boyle calls the 'beat' (see **Interviews**)—the key component of good writing in his mind. This can be an instinctive quality one develops over time. And it relates to the final aspect: rhythm. This can be reflective of the metabolism of the writer: staccato; lyrical; frenetic, or meditative—one's embodied *beingness* in the world. By drawing upon this, one hones the unique DNA of one's writing: a voice as distinctive as your fingerprints. Of course, one can ventriloquise, mimicking the voices of others. This may be required in a multi-linear novel with contrasting voices or perspectives. The writing of BIPOC authors, especially those not writing in their native language, can sometimes be inflected by mother tongues and cultures refreshingly different to the white, western, and anglophonic hegemonies of much of what has been published and lauded until relatively recently, when many publishers have actively diversified their lists. This can influence not only distinctive vocabulary, syntax, turns of phrase, and the life-ways depicted, but also permeate through the structure, pace, and rhythm of the whole narrative.

And when we draw upon the more-than-human as our aesthetic and ethical lodestone, then a plethora of new life-worlds and narrative voices present themselves to us. This is beautifully demonstrated in the polyphonic poetry of Alice Oswald.

A River Runs Through It

Devon-based poet, Alice Oswald, explores the polyphonic qualities of landscape through collections such as *A Sleepwalk on the Severn* (2009), and the TS Eliot Prize-winning, *Dart* (2002). Her research is grounded in her intimate relationship with the land as a gardener. For *Dart*, Alice undertook field research, recording conversations with people who live and work in the River Dart in Devon. Drawing upon these—not verbatim, but paraphrasing or ventriloquising—the poet wove together a riparine songline, tracing the Dart from its source high on Dartmoor, to the sea in the English Channel. Each stakeholder, including the more-than-human, is represented fairly. All are honoured as part of the river's narrative: the poacher, ferryman, sewage worker, dairy farmer, forester, swimmer, canoeist, walker, salmon, and otter. The mythical and the historical collapse in Alice's palimpsest. In intertwining textual nodes, different voices and life-worlds appear through the 'surface' of the page, as though glimpsed beneath the glittering current. The 'flow' of words swirl and eddy across the textual plane of the page, using differing margins and spaces in a controlled flood. Although a poetry sequence, the writer of ecofiction can draw upon Alice's techniques: her demarcation of the textual plane with discreet nodes of paratext; her use of the found form of the river itself as a controlling idea or ordering principle, helping to give the swirl of words a shape; the catholic sampling of different voices—human; more-than-human—along the river. This bold, sustained deployment of the heteroglossic aptly echoes Bakhtin's ideation: 'another's speech in another's language, serving to express authorial intentions but in a refracted way' (1934). This *refraction* is a way of avoiding writing that is too on-the-nose in its environmental agenda. It affords a reflective space for the reader to consider each voice, presence, and life-world alluded to. The interpretation is not forced. The reader is encouraged to make an ontological shift in perspective—to leap the gap of consciousness. By allowing space on the page for each of these voices—sometimes with the use of hanging indents and other kinds of negative space—we are encouraged to 'allow space' for the presence of the non-anthropocentric other in our lives, in this world we share—to not colonise, or assimilate into a homogenous metaverse dominated by a prevailing paradigm (such as late-stage capitalism desperately trying to justify its validity in a resource-depleted world), but to mind the gap.

Making a Heap

One approach to the challenges of shaping material is to draw upon the found forms of nature—or, in this case, the man-made within nature. In his memoir of place and formative years, *On Silbury Hill* (2014) the poet Adam Thorpe fixes upon a famous landmark within the Wiltshire landscape, close to his former boarding school of Marlborough College: Silbury Hill is the largest man-made mound in Europe. Raised during the Neolithic period, approximately 2400 BCE, it is comprised of layers of packed chalk. No one knows exactly what it was constructed for, but evidence of grain pollens in the strata of chalk suggests it was construction during periods of harvest at the dawn of the agrarian revolution, indicating (possibly) some kind of connection with the fertility of the land. The very fact of the absence of a definitive 'reading' of the landmark, along with the plethora of alternative theories about the site and surrounding Avebury landscape, creates an aura of mystery about it, which is magnetic to visitors from around the world, and was certainly fascinating to the young schoolboy, Adam Thorpe. Thorpe uses Silbury Hill as his axis mundi and circles it in his memory—writing his memoir from continental Europe. Adopting a customised Neolithic praxis, he 'builds' his memoir like the builders of Silbury Hill—in layers, with fragments (of memory; texture; details). He uses the found form of the hill to suggest the shape of his memoir: circling and circular in structure with the hill as the centre. Thorpe creates layers of prose consisting of poetic flights of fancy, archaeology, folklore, local history, and schooldays memoir—layers which he digs down into via a kind of 'personal excavation. The effect is idiosyncratic—a prose-poem memoir of place and rites-of-passage. It echoes the approach of fellow poet, David Jones, who in *The Anathemata* (1952) said: 'I have made a heap of all that I could find", alluding to Nennius, the 9th Century Welsh monk, author of *Historia Brittonum*, who wrote: 'coacervavi omne quod inveni' ('I have made a heap of everything I have found'). Thorpe articulates this methodology:

So a life builds up in layers, piecemeal, a kind of haphazard engineering that has elements of skill and cunning – the previous layers mostly hidden, as are the smaller mounds within, the clumps of different-coloured earth, the burnt offerings, the nodules of pain and the delight. The hard graft of the chopped-off antlers, picking and stabbing and scraping. The embers of old fires, old flames, in mute fragments of charcoal. (2014: 91)

Thorpe's approach might not be ideal for novelists whose long-form narratives often require meticulous planning, although there is often a feeling in the early exploratory stages of drafting that one *is* creating 'a heap of everything … found'—as though one is the Devils Tower-obsessed character, Roy Neary, played by Richard Dreyfuss in *Close Encounters of the Third Kind* (Spielberg 1977), creating simulacrum out of first mashed potato and then anything he can pile into his living room. This layering is echoed in another approach exemplified by the German, UK-based writer, WG Sebald.

Intertextuality

In *The Rings of Saturn* (Germany: 1995; UK: 1998) WG Sebald recounts a highly-fictionalised journey by foot through the liminal zones and hinterlands of coastal East Anglia. He deploys intertextuality elegantly to discuss a wide range of authors, texts, moments of history, and personal associations—turning the digression into an art-form. His peregrinations are deliberately discursive, quixotic non-sequiturs as idiosyncratic as the author, as though his intention is to portray the lateral synaptic activity of consciousness as much as the psychogeographical dimensionality of the landscape he walks through: a reclaimed land saturated with history. Sebald walks through terrain haunted by text, and other cultural artefacts, as Edward Parnell does in his memoir of ghost stories and place, *Ghostland: in search of a haunted country* (2019). A metanarrative, a story about stories, can work very successfully in a novel—as one of the very first, Cervantes' *Don Quixote* (1605–1615) showed. A contemporary example of this, with distinctive ecological qualities is *Cloud Cuckoo Land* (2021) by Anthony Doer, discussed in more detail in the previous chapter, which uses the Gothic device of the found manuscript to create historical gravitas and verisimilitude to a flight of fancy worthy of Baron Munchausen.

Archipelagic States

Another ordering principle for an extended narrative is the archipelagic—a form found in some of the earliest narratives. In the early Irish echtrai ('adventure tale') or immrama ('voyage tale') such as the Seventh/Eighth Century *Voyage of Bran*, and the Sixth Century *Navigatio Sancti Brendani Abbatis* (Voyage of St Brendan the Abbott), we find apocryphal tales of intrepid holy men visiting a series of islands, each containing remarkable treasures and wonders. These seem to mirror the Homeric tradition, as epitomised by *The Odyssey* (Eighth Century BCE), but also to be found in *The Voyage of Argo* by Apollonius of Rhodes, (Third Century BCE), and other tales of ocean-going heroes. By having the hero-protagonist and his crew visit a series of wonder-filled islands, the storyteller has a resilient, flexible format that can extended indefinitely. Gene Roddenberry applied this Homeric structure to televisual drama in his seminal science fiction series, *Star Trek* (1963–1969), which was originally going to be called *Wagon Trek to the Stars*.

In terms of ecofiction, we are closer to home in *The Earthsea Cycle* by Ursula K Le Guin (*A Wizard of Earthsea; The Tombs of Atuan; The Farthest Shore; Tehanu; Tales from Earthsea; The Other Wind*, collected as *The Books of Earthsea* in 2018) set in the archipelago of Earthsea, which although set in a Secondary World of dragons and magic, foregrounds ecological principles from the implied balance or tension of the title onwards. The daughter of an anthropologist, Le Guin was perhaps more sensitive to the subtle ecologies of both the human and more-than-human world than most, as she has explored in many of her later essays and stories. As she famously said: 'We live in capitalism. Its power seems inescapable. So did the divine right of kings. Any human power can be resisted and changed by human beings. Resistance and change often begin in art, and very often in our art, the art of words' (2014). Le Guin's narratives often look hard at cultural norms and carefully deconstructs them, suggesting vividly-realised alternatives—we will consider her utopias and dystopias in the next chapter. But island-hopping or equivalents (such as the planet-hopping of Saint-Exupéry's (2002) *The Little Prince*) provides the perfect narrative model for exploring different paradigms. It affords perspectival shift which encourages the consideration of different modalities.

To bring this back closer to familiar shores, I want to end this section by briefly considering a form usually outside the bailiwick of ecofiction: a travel memoir, because as we have seen, innovation and originality can emerge from widening the sphere of one's influence. In 'Three Ways of Looking at St Kilda' (2012) poet and nature writer Kathleen Jamie describes three visits to the remote Hebridean isle of St Kilda. With precise, terse language that deliberately eschews the romanticisation of both nature and nature writer in traditional work, Jamie described the three attempts to reach St Kilda, which is notoriously difficult to land on due to the rough seas surrounding it: in the first, she fails entirely; the second is very brief; and the third is slightly longer, thanks to securing a place on a survey. These three 'ways of looking at St Kilda' could be summed up as the romantic; the touristic; the ecological, and the triadic structure flagged up in the title. Brevity is part of the style—a hard, exacting terseness reflective of the austere beauty of the land- or seascape, and each section is like an 'island' of words, surrounded by the white of the page. Jamie deliberately jettisons a lot of the self-valorisation and hubristic baggage of old nature- and travel-writing. All that is unnecessary is left on the quayside; and what is left out is telling by its absence. The unspoken and the negative space of the page are Jamie's allies, as though she is keen to honour the spaciality and isolated situatedness of such places, and not to seek to colonise them with her words.

An archipelagic quality can be emulated in the form of a composite novel, comprising a series of linked short stories. David Mitchell was instrumental in making this neglected form popular through his bestseller, *Cloud Atlas* (2008)—although he had been fine-tuning it through his restlessly transnational earlier novels—and he continued to use it in *The Bone Clocks* (2014). Typical of Mitchell, he ranges widely across genres—convincing pastiches that obfuscate the authentic voice—but it is in the final section, set on the Sheep's Head Peninsular in southwest Ireland, that we find matter relevant to us. In what is arguably the most engaging and committed section of an otherwise tonally jarring and unsatisfying novel, Mitchell imagines a powered-down, Post-Peak Oil scenario, where a community struggles to survive in a liminal space at a liminal time of 'transition' (Hopkins 2008).

Temporal Approaches

Another approach to shaping one's material is to use temporal structures. A naturalistic approach would be to implement a diachronic treatment of events with the narrative unfolding over a period of time. This could be in a chronological or non-chronological order, but the span of time provides a broad canvas in which to dramatise the cause and effects of choices and factors, both human and non-human. The works of Kim Stanley Robinson commonly deploy this long view and bigger-picture approach. A synchronic approach would focus on a specific moment in time—a hyperfocalised and possibly hyper-localised 'snapshot'. This is an approach that Matt Margini suggests TC Boyle deploys. Discussing a story, 'Surtsey' in Boyle's collection, *The Relive Box and Other Stories* (2017), which features like much of his oeuvre since 2000, a foregrounding of environmental issues and their impact of specific lives, Margini observes the close-focus, (and possibly limited scope) of the story: 'it never expands to meet the size of its subject; it remains isolated, in terms of both geography and perspective' (*The Atlantic* 2017). For Margini this seems both the strength and weakness of much of Boyle's oeuvre—an anthropocentrism foregrounding self-centred characters and their foibles, and a refusal to zoom out.

The other extreme of this is the trope of 'eco-thrillers', which are fond of depicting multiple viewpoints presenting a cross-section of stakeholders and impacts. When done well this can create a worldly polyphonic authority. Frank Schätzing's blockbuster climate fiction, *The Swarm* (2006) is a typical example of this. However, it has become something of a cliché now and feels slightly dated—a technique that seemed cutting edge around the millennium, but in an increasingly divided world seems rather patronising and totalising: a Netflix of fiction where every possible kind of context is reduced to an identical format—a little block of content within a dominant consumerist frame. A single author attempting to represent any possible viewpoint with equal authority risks cultural appropriation and feels neo-colonialist—the equivalent of the hubristic Victorian attempts to categorise everything into Causubonesque 'key to all mythologies', such as Sir James Frazer's *The Golden Bough* (1994, 1922]). It may be attempted with good intentions—a gesture to multiculturalism, a sensitivity to the divergences of impact of different sections of the population, and an extended act of empathy—but can be summed up as the fallacy of omniscience, which is arguably part of the hubristic paradigm that has contributed to the Climate Emergency. As David Abram suggests (2017 [1997]), we can only know one place with a true depth of intimacy—by being fully present, senses attuned to the 'subtle logos of the land' (p. 268), a sentiment that Nan Shepherd, with her 'deep mapping' (2011 [1977]) would also sympathise with.

> We can know the needs of any particular region only by participating in its specificity—by becoming familiar with its cycles and styles, awake and attentive to its other inhabitants. (Abram, 2017 [1997]: 268)

That sustained act of attention on one place, instead of an ADHD-type shuffling through multiple life-worlds, is, arguably, a more convincing act of honouring. As the poet and author of *Autobiography of a Supertramp* (2013 [1908]), WH Davies, wrote in his most famous poem, 'Leisure': 'What is this life if, full of care,/we have not time to stand and stare?' (1934) In an attention-deficit age, one exacerbated by the dopamine-hits of algorithm-driven social media, the conscious act of undivided attention seems like a precious gift to bestow. It is one that conveys respect, and is ennobling for both bestower and recipient.

Novelists need to learn to 'stand and stare', and not just press fast forward on the remote control of fiction (exposition; a scene- or chapter-transition). Sometimes, we need to press pause or move through a scene frame-by-frame (detailed description; dramatisation). Punctuation, syntax, dialogue, and formatting are all micro-adjusters of this narrative flow.

As writers, we control the speed of the narrative. It seems many beginner writers are in a rush to tell their stories—cramming everything into opening chapters, rather than pacing their narratives accordingly.

A novel is a marathon, not a sprint, as marathon-running novelist, Haruki Murakami, articulates in his memoir on running and writing (2009): it is all about self-discipline, stamina—psychological, as much as physical—and learning to do a thing by doing it. But most of all, it is about pacing yourself. So to with writing a novel. Remember there are twenty-six miles to go, not one hundred metres.

Another naturalistic way of framing a narrative is to use the seasons—which in the west are traditionally four, although of course this is only one cultural paradigm; other cultures and ecosystems experience the seasons differently. And such a framing is increasingly unreliable and poignant, in a time when Climate Change continually disrupts meteorological patterns and records. The eschewing of the seasons throughout a novel can dramatise the shifting baseline syndrome of climate-challenged modern life—how the 'norms' of childhood are being constantly disrupted. A seasonal frame can suggest a four-act or two-act narrative, accordingly (such as Ali Smith's seasonal quartet, 2016, 2017, 2019, 2020). Or, if you wish to go more into the realms of the speculative, then anything goes: NK Jemisin played with this fundamental backdrop to our lives by deploying *five*, in *The Fifth Season* (2016), as part of her Broken Earth trilogy, which imagined an Earth shattered by vast tectonic upheavals.

Other time-based frames including using months, or moons; weeks; days; hours; minutes; or even seconds. For instance, one could draw upon the Doomsday Clock, a symbolic and salutary warning about how close the world is to annihilation, created in 1945 by Albert Einstein and members of The Manhattan Project aware of the part they played in creating the existential threat of Armageddon. In January 2023, the Science and Security Board of the Bulletin of the Atomic Scientists reset the clock to 90 seconds to midnight: 'largely (though not exclusively) because of the mounting dangers of the war in Ukraine. The Clock now stands at 90 seconds to midnight—the closest to global catastrophe it has ever been' (Bulletin of the Atomic Scientists 2023).

One could go in the other extreme and create a narrative that seeks to dramatise Brian Eno's 1978 ideation of The Long Now: 'The Long Now is the recognition that the precise moment you're in grows out of the past and is a seed for the future. The longer your sense of Now, the more past and future it includes' (2003). Eno's idea has been taken up by The Long Now Foundation, which has designed a nuclear clock to keep count of time long into the future—ten thousand years in fact—the opposite of the Doomsday Clock, and a symbol of the long-term thinking the foundation seeks to advocate. Designed by Dannis Hillis, The Clock of the Long Now, has been created. A colleague of the Long Now Foundation, Stewart Brand, said:

> Such a clock, if sufficiently impressive and well engineered, would embody deep time for people. It should be charismatic to visit, interesting to think about, and famous enough to become iconic in the public discourse. Ideally, it would do for thinking about time what the photographs of Earth from space have done for thinking about the environment. Such icons reframe the way people think. (2000)

Deep Time—John McPhee's concept (1981) summarising the vast timescales of geological epochs first mooted by Scottish geologist James Hutton—is an important one for putting human activity into perspective, but also for catalysing the notion of our new geological epoch: the Anthropocene, can also be used to frame a narrative, as Anthony Nanson does in his 2015 novel.

An epic journey into the heart of Africa and the origins of life, essentially Nanson's novel is a quest narrative, but one in the tradition of the classics of Travel Literature, the accounts of early explorers, Marco Polo, Livingstone, and Nansen (whom the author has portrayed in a storytelling performance). Yet it is perhaps closest to Darwin's *Voyage of the Beagle* in its zoological and evolutionary concerns. In its exhaustive quest for the origins of life and even the source of time, the novel provides an arena for what have been called 'God Games' (Clute and Grant 1997). The team assembled by Merlie to conduct an ecological survey of a zone threatened by civil war (the ponderous, bookish Portia; the vulnerable, good Christian Vince, the rapacious Alpha-male Curtis, and the sublime, mysterious Salome) slowly get whittled down by the travails of their journey and the perils they face, until an archetypal struggle is enacted by the survivors, one which seems to play out the dynamic of the Garden of Eden: Adam and Eve and the Serpent. It will not be giving too much away to reveal that the team stumbles upon a refugium of 'deep time' (the various epochs of evolutionary cycles stretching over hundreds of millions of years, referred to as 'palaeomes'). As they transect these, they encounter increasingly primitive (or sophisticated in some senses) forms of life, until inevitably they find themselves walking with dinosaurs.

As a primer in palaeontology the 'novel' could be very useful; and it is a rattling yarn in the manner of classic adventure stories by Arthur Conan Doyle, H. Rider Haggard, and the like. If one embraces this apparent oppositional duality then the novel straddles the creative-critical divide in an interesting way, a K-T boundary which the reader must be bold enough to cross back and forth.

With the author being an experienced storyteller, a sense of orality informs the prose, giving it often a toothsome suppleness, most palpably in the action sequences, which are vivid and visceral. This storytelling quality emerges in different ways: on a macro-level, the very name of the viewpoint character, Brendan, alludes to the immrama tradition, the wonder voyages of Celtic saints, which this is a sophisticated riff on. On a micro-level, this manifests in a sequence around a tribal campfire (a scene which Nanson performed from memory at the launch in his hometown of Stroud, thus returning it, in effect, to the oral tradition); in the indigenous folklore; and in the Campbell-esque 'Road Back', when the surviving member of the expedition uses the knowledge acquired to ease their passage. As in countless tales, the return is a way of reminding the audience of key scenes and motifs, culmination combined with acceleration—that which first was struggled through is whizzed through in 'fast-forward', creating a sense of euphoric relief. The effortful becomes effortless. With the map of life in hand the soul can flourish. Hard-won wisdom becomes graceful skill. The protagonists are changed fundamentally by their experiences, and so, hopefully is the reader—Nanson returns us to the world with a cleansed perception and an imperative to save the planet's remaining resources.

Within these pages there is a profound, life-affirming humanity and a deep sensuality—not only the exotic but the natural is eroticised. Nanson channels elements of D.H. Lawrence in his protracted descriptions of the physical—an 'earthiness' in both senses—and he captures the crackle of sexual current between the sexes well. The novel's structure is multi-climactic— in epiphanic waves of sensation it appropriately ends on the shores of the primordial ocean, and the female, as the source of life, is honoured and emancipated from any prescriptive role man might give her. Similarly the tricky depiction of indigenous cultures is handled with sensitivity and skill, circumventing the quicksand of Colonialist rhetoric often embedded in Portal-quest (Mendlesohn 2008) narratives.

Ultimately, the novel's gaze of longing is turned towards the ineffable, as veiled by the fastness of the rainforest and the vastness of time. Nanson's protagonists walk into its mystery, taking up from where J.G. Ballard's *The Drowned World* (1981 [1963]) ends—with man stepping into the depthless jungle, relinquishing control and all trappings of civilisation to its green mind. *Deep Time* is a paean to Creation and to whatever sung it into being (the nature of which the author wisely leaves to the reader to decide).

Finally, in terms of structural devices, astronomical events, and demarcations could also suggest framings, such as the solstices, equinoxes, and eclipses. Eleanor Catton deploys this method to powerful effect in her novel *The Luminaries* (2013), which has chapters of decreasing size reflecting the waning of the moon, with characters based upon the occidental zodiac, and others based upon the planets. Catton described her lunar cycle approach as 'like a wheel, a huge cartwheel, creaky at the beginning and spinning faster and faster as it goes'. Such framing thus creates pace as well as structure. The novel becomes its own orrery, or one evocative of a mechanical medieval clock—archetypal figures paraded before the reader with clockwork precision.

The risk here is it becomes too mechanistic; too finely wrought to truly represent the messy reality of life, and characters become automata. Such was the critique of *The Luminaries* by Kevin Power:

> Take the novel's characters, each one carefully painted but nonetheless in thrall to Catton's great determining structures. The luminaries have personalities but not really that much in the way of life. Catton's marvellously imagined 19th-century world revolves, and the astrologically directed people go about their tricksy business, but it is difficult not to feel that the machinery underneath it all is the real star of the show. As with certain CGI blockbusters, you marvel at the spectacle and wonder about the vision. (2023)

Everything is *too* precise, *too* instrumentalist, to have that elusive spark of true life.

Characters should have mud on their shoes and dirt beneath their fingernails, or at least a sense of place, rather than *being placed* like so many chess pieces.

Topographical Approaches

A topographical approach offers the writer of ecofiction another palette of potential structuring and framing devices. One could use thresholds of various kinds as the ordering principle: borders, boundaries, crossings, bridges, portals, ports, terminals, and doors are all places of dramatic tension and potential. Each chapter could feature one, or the whole narrative could be set on or in one. Thresholds can also be evoked by the spaciality of the text, and by the various elements of paratext around it (see below).

Pathways and routes of various kinds could also be used to act as 'throughlines' for the narrative, as in Cormac McCarthy's dystopian novel, *The Road* (2006). For an erudite exploration of pathways Robert Macfarlane's *The Old Ways: a journey on foot* (2012) would be a great starting point.

One could also use the framing of human settlements: a hamlet, village, town, city, conurbation, oil rig, cruise ship, Antarctic survey base, a temporary hunter gatherer camp, farmstead, ranch, and so forth. The way human habitation impacts upon the natural world is brilliantly dramatised in *Cloud Cuckoo Land* (2021) by Anthony Doerr. One could adopt a contrasting approach—humans in nature, e.g. Ian Macpherson's post-apocalyptic *Cold Harbour,* (1936), which vividly depicting the travails of a pacifist couple who flee to the Scottish Highlands to escape the madness of humanity, and their struggles to find safe shelter. This is taken to even more of an extreme in Geoffrey Household's *Rogue Male* (1939), in which the protagonist is run to ground in a Dorset holloway after being pursued by Nazi agents, following a failed attempt to assassinate Adolf Hitler. The unnamed protagonist burrows into the side of the holloway to escape his enemies, but is eventually discovered, forcing him to take desperate measures. Ostensibly a chase thriller of exceptional quality, *Rogue Male* qualifies as ecofiction for its extraordinary sense of situatedness and attention to the natural world. The protagonist is unapologetically a hunter—a fact which means he can find common ground and begrudging respect from his pursuant—but he has a sense of ecological balance, natural resourcefulness, and a touching affection for a cat which discovers and befriends him. His survival is contingent on 'becoming animal' in a sense, as the layers of civilisation are stripped back to Darwinian survival of the fittest, in Herbert Spencer's original ideation of the phrase, that is being 'the most appropriate to its environment'.

There are a plethora of other topographical forms one could draw upon to help shape a narrative: caves, mountains, deserts, savannah, canyons, plains, plateaus, calderas, and so forth. Any can have metaphoric potential and suggest structural elements: topographical nodes and delineations of narrative, suggesting extent, terroir, and focus.

Sometimes the shape or form is imposed on nature, but can also provide a focalising aspect for the novel, as in Sarah Hall's *The Wolf Border* (2015), and John Lanchester's *The Wall* (2019). In the latter, Britain's coastline has been changed beyond recognition due to the creation of a National Coastal Defence Structure, known colloquially as the titular wall. This seems designed to keep out climate refugees and rising sea levels, as much as the population in, and as such serves as an extended metaphor for Brexit, and the tabloid scare stories of 'marauding mobs' of asylum seekers, attempting to make the perilous crossing of the English Channel in the hope of a better life. Geography, as ever, is political, and the source of much contention. It can serve as an effective frame for a narrative and also the generator of plot.

Yet one has to be wary of reductive symbolism, which forecloses on the polysemous potentiality of prose fiction. A novel should open a space for discourse, not railroad it into narrow readings.

Now let us consider some textual elements which can help give a narrative texture and shape.

Docemes

A doceme is perhaps not typical in a novel, or at least in a typical novel, but the most interesting work happens when writers push boundaries and innovate. Danielewski's *House of Leaves* (2000) is a great example of this—the very epitome of the postmodern novel when it was published at the millennium, it presented a novel haunted by itself in the embers of a century haunted by itself. The novel presents itself as a documentary, in pseudo-archival format with various academic embellishments, such as footnotes, as well as transcripts, news reports, letters, diary entries, and other docemes which help to convey a sense of faux-historicity. It is the classic strategy of the Gothic narrative—the found manuscript, yet in a way that creates a disquieting sense of unreliable reality, as Baker suggests, in his discussion of the found manuscript in Scottish Literature: 'The trope of the found manuscript is often used to highlight the problematic relationship between text, language, and the past' (Baker 2014: 55). As both the Gothic novel, and earlier iterations of the novel—*Don Quixote* (1605); *The Life and Opinions of Tristram Shandy* (1759); *Frankenstein, or The Modern Prometheus* (1818); *Dracula* (1897) attest, the use of docemes is not as daringly innovative as it may seem in Danielewski's Twentieth Century swansong. But what are they precisely, and where did the term originate? Niels Windfeld Lund suggested the term in a 2004 paper: 'Inspired by the verb *doceo*, [to show] I suggest the word DOCEME to describe any part of a document, which can be identified and analytically isolated, thus being a partial result of the documentation process'. Lund epitomises it as: 'Documentation in a complementary perspective' (ibid). It can be a useful device, especially if drawing upon real-life material, although one always has to ask: is this enhancing the narrative, or detracting from it? If your docemes are just visual clutter then consider cutting them. The writing should stand on its own merits, and only the most discerning use of docemes (e.g. an intrinsic plot element) should be countenanced.

Paratext

Another bricoleur approach to constructing a text is to consider paratext, which is strictly-speaking material associated with but distinct from the main body of a book, film, game, etc., typically produced by someone other than the original author or creator. This usually includes front matter (peri-text) and end-matter (epitext) like endorsements; contents; introduction; dedication; foreword; endword; accompanying notes; appendices; acknowledgements, etc., but can also include matter created *by* the author, including glossaries, dramatis personae, and marginalia. It is any text that sits alongside the main text. Philippe Lejeune emphasises its significance when he describes it as 'a fringe of the printed text which in reality controls one's whole reading of the text' (cited in Genette, 1991). And Gérard Genette suggests it is, 'more than a boundary or a sealed border, the paratext is, rather, a threshold'. (ibid) It is 'a zone between text and off-text, a zone not only of transition but also of transaction: a privileged place of pragmatics and a strategy, of an influence on the public, an influence that … is at the service of a better reception for the text and a more pertinent reading of it' (ibid). As well as an ontological zone of transition, it may be useful to think of paratext architecturally—the way it prepares the reader is akin to the vestibule of a church. As Brujin suggests in his analysis of the materiality of literature in written and printed forms in the space of a book, 'This *is* Architecture (and Alchemy)' (Brujin 2010: 48). The pages of endorsements one finds at the front of a new book are like the stern statuary, icons, and architectural coding that primes the pilgrim and the worshipper as they enter their holy place. It creates a deliberate shift of consciousness. This use of the threshold is seen in the earliest temples, such as the 'henge' of Stonehenge—a bank-and-ditch enclosure delineating mundane space from sacred space. The positioning of paratext is phenomenological—the flipping of the pages, the white space increasingly filled with text like an orchestra tuning up (the endpapers; blank page left for inscriptions and bookplates; the minor title page; other works; the main title page; the verso filled with publishing information; bionote; dedication; contents page; another blank page—the dramatic pause before the orchestra begins; an epigraph; then, finally, chapter one, page one) seduces the reader into the trance of the text. Subliminally, it instructs us to treat the text with respect, in the way there is a certain etiquette to observe when entering a place of worship. Paratext puts a 'spell' on us. As David Abram suggests (2017 [1997]), our engagement with alphabetic language in the form of the printed word is a kind of animistic one. We read the signs and interpret their meaning, but also respond to them synaesthetically: we start to see voices, hear colours, smell sounds in a subtle, mercurial way. Suddenly there are ghosts or spirits in the room. The seance has worked. The Ouija board of the paratext, with its hex of language, has done the trick.

Epistolary Devices

Margaret Drabble tells us that, 'the epistolary novel [is] a story written in the form of letters, or letters with journals, and usually presented by an anonymous author masquerading as "editor"' (1985: 332). It reached an early apotheosis in the works of Samuel Richardson, notably *Pamela* (1740), although its popularity quickly led to pastiche, as in Fielding's *Shamela* (1741). It once conveyed immediacy and a sense of Pepysian eavesdropping, although the modern-day rarity of letter-writing, especially longhand (which has taken on a charming, old-fashioned quality) means the form has somewhat been overtaken by social media, where blogs, vlogs, podcasts, tweets, Facebook and Instagram posts, and TikTok videos perform a relentless daily version of the epistolary novel—vast, ever renewing, and ephemeral. However, such forms are not to be dismissed. Nor is the epistolary novel, which can draw upon these elements to give it a contemporary (although rapidly out-of-date) feel, or even deploy more archaic forms of communication to create a sense of historicity, testimonial, and confession. And the two are not mutually exclusive, but can create a poignant tonal counterpoint, especially effective in dual-narrative novels, as exemplified by John Fowles' *The French Lieutenant's Woman* (1969), and AS Byatt's *Possession* (1990). Perhaps more appositely to ecofiction, the epistolary novel can take the form of journalistic dispatches, as in Ernest Callenbach's *Ecotopia* (1975) already discussed.

However, the letter seems to have been subsumed by other emergent forms facilitated by digital technology, though a narrative constructed of 'snailmail' letters might be a way of foreshadowing a Post-Peak Oil, post-collapse, or future primitive world, as for instance imagined in *The Postman* (1985) or *Station Eleven* (2014).

New Media

New media presents us with a range of options with which to embellish our narratives. We could create social media profiles for our characters, generate 'minority world' content (Germaine's subversive inversion of the hegemonic paradigm, 2023), and then insert them into our novels. We could write digital manifestos, ventriloquising their voices, beliefs, and agendas. We could create fake news bulletins, which we weave into the narrative, or use epigraphically to create (hopefully ironic) counterpoints to the accompanying drama. And, we could even mimic the 'voice' of an Artificial Intelligence; or throwing ethical and aesthetic considerations aside (and possible legality, resulting in publishing issues), even use AI to write, or co-write the book. Since the advent of AI-content generators like ChatGPT, many commentators have discussed its implications, with some advocating an engagement with it; although the expectation that one simply *must* engage with it, basically 'adapt or die' (LinkedIn, February 2022), is a form of digital Fascism. Nothing is compulsory in creativity, and nothing is ruled out. AI is simply another tool that some of us may choose to engage with, although the virtual sphere is only really a thin slither of the available reality of the world—despite its noisy, cyclopean demands to the contrary.

The Non-linear and Biomimetic Structuring

The natural world offers a far richer, deeper, 'thicker' pool of available reality to draw upon, which someone who has never ventured beyond their screen into an *actual* rainforest, moor, desert, mountain range, glacial field, barrier reef, etc., will rarely understand. A flat screen is just a flat screen however pretty the pictures, numerous the pixels, flashy the computer animation, or fast the Wi-Fi connection. As ecofiction is contingent upon the 'environment', these real-world sites should be our primary source material. Go outside. Feel the air move around you, the sun on your skin. Get wet, cold, muddy—it doesn't matter. It is precious visceral experience, embodied actuality that will stay with you: prima materia as muscle memory, which will help you evoke a vivid authenticity in your narrative—a lived experience, however analogous, will create what Morton calls 'truthiness', which is about as good as we're going to get, in real life or fiction. Inspired by the vast (but not infinite) variety and inventiveness of nature we can mirror its forms via biomimicry—this can manifest in character or scene design, structural design, themes, and motifs. An example of this is Michael Christie's novel, *Greenwood* (2020), which is structured like the cross-section of a tree—starting in the near future on the outer edge, then progressing back in time towards the 'centre', then in reverse order out again, ending back in the future.

As I have argued elsewhere (Manwaring 2023) arborescence can suggest narrative structures, especially effective for ergodic fiction (Aarseth 1997). The complex interconnectedness of a novel's characters, themes, and ideas can suggest mycelial structures, which I'll explore in more detail in the last chapter (**The Rhizomatic Writer**). One example of this is Intan Paramaditha's novel, *The Wandering* (discussed in **Voices of the Global Majority**). The myceliality in this novel feels slight, however. A diagram of the narrative pathways would suggest more 'railroad' than 'branchiness' (Manwaring 2023). A novel with not only a deeper engagement with biomimesis structurally but also thematically would be Robert Holdstock's *Mythago Wood* (1985), the patterning of which I have also discussed elsewhere (2010).

Other biomimetic frames could draw upon the bacterial, insectoid, reptilian, geological, and so forth. The Book of Life is open access to all—a vast (but not endless) repository of ideas, forms, cycles, and ways of being in the world.

The novel can be a fragment, a ruin, a microcosm, a petri dish, a Rorschach inkblot test. In short, it should be its own world. Even if it purports to be a mirror of the world, it needs to be its own shape, as mirrors are—a finite frame, as limited and as precious as the Earth.

MYCELIA: Connections to Other Writers, Texts, and Resources
- Hergenrader, Trent. 2018. *Collaborative Worldbuilding for Writers and Gamers*. London: Bloomsbury Academic.
- McKee, Robert. 1999. *Story: Substance, Structure, Style, and the Principles of Screenwriting*. London: Methuen.
- Murdock, Maureen J., 1990. *The Heroine's Journey: Woman's Quest for Wholeness*. Boulder, CO: Shambhala.

- VanderMeer, Jeff. 2013. *WonderBook: The Illustrated Guide to Creating Imaginative Fiction*. New York, NY: Abram Image.
- Vogler, Christopher. 1999. *The Hero's Journey: Mythic Structure in Screenwriting*. London: Pan.

SPORES: Writing Activities

- Site-specific project—conceptualise a site-specific project with an environmental aspect, e.g. a poetry trail in a public park; a podcast recorded in situ celebrating local distinctiveness; an interactive story of foodways using a locative mapping app. What are the challenges and opportunities? Who are the stakeholders? Who do you need to ask permission from? Are there any key organisations you could work with? Draft a proposal and research funding streams and other opportunities. Make it happen.
- Wild Writing—in this exercise you are encouraged to jettison a structured, linear, 'left-brained' approach, and write whatever emerges in the moment, using a combination of close observation and movement. In a natural, peaceful, outdoor space—a park, woodland, beach, meadow, hillside, lakeside, etc.—start by arriving in your body. Be aware of your posture, noticing any tension, aches, or awkwardness; become mindful of your breathing, letting each out-breath relax each part of your body. Then, focus on each of your five senses (sight; sound; taste; touch; smell), noticing a few things with each. Then, notice what have been called the sixth and seventh senses: proprioception (the awareness of your body in space); and enteroception (the awareness of your inner space—internal physical sensations and feelings). Now, slowly and mindfully start to move through your chosen space, sensitive to where and how you tread. If you feel adventurous, try to move like a particular local species. Imagine being them: how do they experience the world? What is important to them? What impacts on the quality of *their* life? After a few minutes doing this, sit somewhere quiet and write down some reflections. Start by writing in the voice of the species you have just embodied—in first person, let them speak through you. Adjust the way you write, hold your pen, make marks, and use language accordingly. Rewild your writing!
- Make Fake News—write a few environmentally-themed fake news tweets, press release from a bogus government agency, or a blog. Invent quotes from fake experts and fictionalised academic citations. Make them as convincing as possible. These could be along the lines of the oil lobby-funded climate denier or delayer camp, disseminating misinformation and uncertainty; or they

could perhaps be wildly optimistic about the success of positive climate solutions, 'talking up' such initiatives and encouraging more optimistic visions of the future. Be mindful how you use these! Within the fictional context of a novel such an approach is perfectly fine; on social media, used un-ironically, can be unconscionable.

- Finding the Form—draw upon a natural form or ordering principle, such as the Fibonacci sequence of Nautilus shells, the Linnaean system of classification, or the seasonal cycles. Make some notes about how that could inform the structure of your narrative, representation of characters, and rendering of scenes. Aspire to a marriage of form and content.

References

Aarseth, Espen. 1997. *Cybertext: Perspectives on Ergodic Literature*. Baltimore and London: The John Hopkins University Press.

Abram, David. 2017 [1997]. *The Spell of the Sensuous: perception and language in a more-than-human world*. New York, NY: Vintage Books.

Baker, TC. 2014. Authentic Inauthenticity: The Found Manuscript. in *Contemporary Scottish Gothic: Mourning, Authenticity, and Tradition*. Palgrave Gothic, Palgrave Macmillan, pp. 54–88. https://doi.org/10.1057/9781137457202_3.

Bakhtin, Mikhail. 1934. Discourse in the Novel. *Literary Theory: An Anthology* 2 (1934): 674–685.

Ballard, J.G. 1981 [1963]. *The Drowned World*. London: Dragon's Dream.

Boyle, T.C. 2017. *The Relive Box and Other Stories*. New York: NY, Ecco Press.

Brand, Stewart. n.d. *The Clock of the Long Now*. https://longnow.org/clock/ (Accessed 16 March 2023).

de Bruijn, Willem, A.C. 2010. *Book-Building: A Historical and Theoretical Investigation into Architecture and Alchemy*. Doctoral Thesis. Bartlett School of Architecture, University College London, University of London.

Brin, David. 1985. *The Postman*. New York, NY: Bantam.

Bulletin of the Atomic Scientists. 2023, January 24. A time of unprecedented danger: It is 90 seconds to midnight. *Doomsday Clock*. https://thebulletin.org/doomsday-clock/ (Accessed 16 March 2023).

Byatt, A.S. 1990. *Possession*. London: Chatto & Windus.

Cervantes, Miguel de, 1605–1615. *Don Quixote*. Habsburg: Francisco de Robles.

Christie, Michael. 2020. *Greenwood*. London: Scribe.

Callenbach, Ernest. 2009 [1975]. *Ecotopia*. New York, NY.

Campbell, Joseph. 1993 [1949]. *The Hero with a Thousand Faces*. London: Fontana Press.

Catton, Eleanor. 2013. *The Luminaries*. London: Granta.

Clarke, Alex. 2017, March 11. Writers Unite! The Return of the Protest Novel. *Guardian.* https://www.ft.com/content/498398e7-11b1-494b-9cd3-6d669dc3de33 (Accessed 16 March 2023).
Clute, John, and John Grant, 1997. *The Encyclopedia of Fantasy.* London: Orbit.
Danielewski, Mark Z. 2000. *House of Leaves.* St Louis, MI: Turtleback Books.
Davies, W.H. 2013 [1908]. *Autobiography of a Supertramp.* Cardigan: Parthian.
Davies, W.H. 1934. *The Poems of W.H. Davies.* London: Jonathan Cape.
Doerr, Anthony. 2021. *Cloud Cuckoo Land.* London: Fourth Estate.
Drabble, Margaret. 1985. *The Oxford Companion to English Literature.* London: Guild Publishing.
Eno, Brian. 2003, November 14. The Big Here and The Long Now. *The Long Now Foundation.* https://longnow.org/essays/big-here-long-now/ (Accessed 16 March 2023).
Fielding, Henry. 1741. *Shamela: An Apology for the Life of Mrs. Shamela Andrews.* London: A. Dodd.
Fowles, John. 1969. *The French Lieutenant's Woman.* London: Jonathan Cape.
Frazer, James. 1994 [1922 abridged]. *The Golden Bough: A History of Myth and Religion.* London: Chancellor Press.
Genette, Gérard, and Marie Maclean. "Introduction to the Paratext." *New literary history 22,* no. 2 (1991): 261–272.
Germaine, Chloe. (2023). Dark forests and doomed adventurers: an ecocritical reading of horror roleplaying games. In: *Generation Analog: the Tabletop Games and Education Conference* 2021, 27 July 2021 - 28 July 2021, Online.
Hall, Sarah. 2015. *The Wolf Border.* London: Faber.
Hopkins, Rob. 2008. *The Transition Handbook: From oil dependency to local resilience.* Totnes: Green Books.
Household, Geoffrey. 2013 [1939]. *Rogue Male.* London: Orion.
Jamie, Kathleen, 2012. *Sightlines.* London: Sort of Books.
Jemisin, N.K. 2016. *The Fifth Season.* London: Orbit.
Jones, David. 1952. *The Anathemata.* London: Faber.
Lanchester, John. 2019. *The Wall.* London: Faber.
Larkin, Philip. 1955. cited in Enright, D.J. editor, *Poetry of the 1950s: An Anthology of New English Verse.* Tokyo: Kenyusha Ltd.
Le Guin, Ursula K. 2018. *The Books of Earthsea.* London: Gollancz.
Lund, Niels Windfeld. 2004. Documentation in a Complementary Perspective. https://www.academia.edu/980627/Documentation_in_a_complementary_perspective (Accessed 5 July 2023).
McCarthy, Cormac. 2006. *The Road.* London: Picador.
Macfarlane, Robert. 2012. *The Old Ways: A journey on foot.* London: Hamish Hamilton.
Macpherson, Ian. 1989 [1936]. *Cold Harbour.* Edinburgh: Canongate.

Manwaring, Kevan. 2010. Ways Through the Wood: The Rogue Cartographies of Robert Holdstock's Mythago Wood Cycle as a Cognitive Map for Creative Process in Fiction. *Writing in Practice*, Vol. 8. https://www.nawe.co.uk/DB/wip editions/articles/ways-through-the-wood-the-rogue-cartographies-of-robert-hol dstocks-mythago-wood-cycle-as-a-cognitive-mapfor-creative-process-in-fiction. html (Accessed 16 Marcg 2023).

Manwaring, Kevan. 2023. Many Paths Through the Forest: Exploring Arborescence and Ecological Themes in Digital Interactive Narrative. *Gothic Nature*, Vol 4. https://gothicnaturejournal.com/issue-iv/ (Accessed 10 July 2023).

Margini, Matt. 2017, December 27. T.C. Boyle's Fictions of Catastrophe. *The Atlantic*. https://www.theatlantic.com/entertainment/archive/2017/12/tc-boyles-fictions-of-catastrophe/549173/ (Accessed 16 March 2023).

Mendlesohn, Farah. 2008. *Rhetorics of Fantasy*. Middletown: Wesleyan University Press.

Murakami, Haruki. 2009. *What I Talk About When I Talk About Running*. London: Vintage.

Le Guin, Ursula K. 2014, November 20. Ursula K Le Guin's Speech at National Book Awards: 'Books Aren't Just Commodities'. *Guardian*. https://www.theguardian.com/books/2014/nov/20/ursula-k-le-guin-national-book-awards-speech (Accessed 10 July 2023).

McPhee, John. 1981. *Basin and Range*. Straus and Giroux: Farrar.

Mitchell, David. 2008. *Cloud Atlas*. London: Random House.

Mitchell, David. 2014. *The Bone Clocks*. London: Hatchette.

Murdock, Maureen. 1990. *The Heroine's Journey: woman's quest for wholeness*, Boulder, CO: Shambhala.

Nanson, Anthony. 2015. *Deep Time*. Stroud: Hawthorn.

Oswald, Alice. 2002. *Dart*. London: Faber.

Oswald, Alice. 2009. *A Sleepwalk on the Severn*. London: Faber.

Parnell, Edward. 2019. *Ghostland: In Search of a Haunted Country*. London: William Collins.

Pearce, Reagan. 2020. Are You Suffering From Shifting Baseline Syndrome? Earth.org. https://earth.org/shifting-baseline-syndrome/ (Accessed 16 March 2023).

Power, Kevin. 2023, March 3. Birnam Wood by Eleanor Catton Review—Hippies v Billionaires. *Guardian*. https://www.theguardian.com/books/2023/mar/03/birnam-wood-by-eleanor-catton-review-hippies-v-billionaires (Accessed 10 July 2023).

Richardson, Samuel, 1740. *Pamela: or Virtue Rewarded*. London: Rivington and Osborn.

Saint-Exupéry, Antoine de. 2002 [1945]. *The Little Prince*. London: Egmont.

Schätzing, Franz. 2006. *The Swarm*. London: Hodder.

Scott, Manda. 2024. 'THRUTOPIAN WRITING: Crafting route maps through to a future we'd be proud to leave behind.' Writing the Earth Guest Talk for Earth Day 2024. Arts University Bournemouth. 24 April 2024.

Sebald, W.G. 1998. *The Rings of Saturn*. London: Granta.
Shepherd, Nan. 2011 [1977]. *The Living Mountain*. Edinburgh: Canongate.
Smith, Ali. 2016. *Autumn*. London: Penguin.
Smith, Ali. 2017. *Winter*. London: Penguin.
Smith, Ali. 2019. *Spring*. London: Penguin.
Smith, Ali. 2020. *Summer*. London: Penguin.
Spielberg, Steven, director. 1977. *Close Encounters of the Third Kind*. Paramount. https://www.imdb.com/title/tt0075860/
St John Mandel, Emily. 2014. *Station Eleven*. New York, NY: David Knopf.
Thorpe, Adam. 2014. *On Silbury Hill*. Beaminster: Little Toller.
Tooze, Adam. 2022, October 28. Welcome to a world of the polycrisis. *Financial Times*. https://www.ft.com/content/498398e7-11b1-494b-9cd3-6d669dc3de33 (Accessed 16 March 2023).

7

One Man's Heaven

Narrative fiction can be a valuable tool for imagining other modalities. In a kind of willed hallucination the novel-writer can envision lives and times far removed from their own. The most imaginative conceptualise and dramatise other worlds, while some, other ways of being in *this* world (which can be more challenging, but also more rewarding, than the tabula rasa of a Secondary World). This aligns with the writer of ecofiction who wishes to present corrective or cautionary, inspiring or salutary modalities to the reader. Such writing blurs into speculative fiction, and some writers may simply wish to write about the present day (which can often seem like some of the worst-case scenarios imagined by earlier writers anyway; side by side with dazzling innovations and solutions). But let us consider the main options presented to writers wishing to explore brave new worlds: utopia, dystopia, ustopia, and thrutopia.

Utopias

Sir Thomas More (1477–1535) was an English lawyer, writer, and statesman. He was one of Henry VIII's most trusted civil servants, becoming Chancellor of England in 1529, although due to his strong Catholic convictions he was eventually executed and martyred. More's book, *Utopia* (1516) imagines a complex, self-contained community set on an island, in which people share a common culture and way of life. He coined the word 'utopia' from the Greek *ou-topos* meaning 'no-place' or 'nowhere'. It was a pun—the almost identical Greek word *eu-topos* means 'a good place'. So at the very heart of the word is a vital question: can a perfect world ever be realised, or is it unattainable? It is unclear as to whether the book is a serious projection of a better way of life, or a satire that gave More a platform from which to discuss the chaos of European politics. It is possibly both.

More's Utopia seems to be functioning in a similar way to Plato's Atlantis, as a fictional device used to critique a certain model of society, or to ennoble the existing one. More, as a Catholic in Henry Tudor's England would certainly have been desirous of a better paradigm, but as the King's chancellor he was painfully aware of the expedient compromises in a negotiated reality. Although, of course, he ultimately decided to prioritise his faith over his life—the ultimate form of utopianism, as he translated himself to 'no place' with his martyrdom, thus becoming another one of history's 'nowhere men'.

The principal sources for the legend of More's ur-utopia Atlantis are two of Plato's dialogues, *Timaeus* and *Critias* (360 BCE). In the former, Plato describes how Egyptian priests, in conversation with the Athenian lawgiver Solon, described Atlantis as an island larger than Asia Minor and Libya combined, and situated just beyond the Pillars of Hercules (the Strait of Gibraltar). About 9000 years before the birth of Solon, the priests said, Atlantis was a rich island whose powerful princes conquered many of the lands of the Mediterranean until they were finally defeated by the Athenians and the latter's allies. The Atlanteans eventually became wicked and impious, and their island was swallowed up by the sea as a result of earthquakes. In the *Critias*, Plato supplied a history of the ideal commonwealth of the Atlanteans. Considering the eco-catastrophe that results in its demise, Plato's *Atlantis* (which went on to inform is conception of the Republic) could be seen as an early ecofiction.

Once the idea of utopia—formulated by Plato and given a focalising linguistic frame by More—was circulated, like the bag of winds gifted to Odysseus by Aeolus, the Hellenic God of Winds, then there was no putting it back. It has swept writers off their feet ever since.

A classic of utopian fiction is William Morris' *News from Nowhere, or An Epoch of Rest, Being Some Chapters from a Utopian Romance* (2003 [1890]). *News from Nowhere* is an iconic 'fantasy' novel from the Arts and Crafts visionary and polymath William Morris. Although it is an important work for its lucid dramatisation of Morris' Socialist ideals, on the surface it appears to be a work of the Fantastic (a timeslip narrative with a loose science fictional device): a man called William Guest (a thinly-veiled alter ego of the author) goes for a swim in the River Thames in the late Nineteenth Century and emerges in the early Twenty-first Century, to see a vision of

England transformed into a place of restored beauty, craftsmanship, and co-operation. Guest explores this land, with the Thames providing the common link, as he slowly wends his way upriver. The novel's extent is demarcated by his two homes: in Hammersmith and Kelmscott, and focuses on a stretch of the river that Morris knew well. In this sense the novel is geographically unambitious, but in many other ways, it was thinking big—certainly beyond the consensus reality of his day. Morris reimagines reality according to his principles, providing a blueprint to aspire to, for some at least. Morris' utopia is vividly imagined and alluring on the surface, as pleasant to dip into a wild swim in a glittering river on a summer's day: an aesthetic and harmonious Arts and Crafts utopia, with an emphasis on 'work for pleasure', common ownership, co-operation, and liberty to choose where one lives, one's profession, and one's morality. The self-governing anarchists live in beautiful houses, wear beautiful clothes, and make beautiful things. It is perhaps all too good to be true, and in most fictional utopias this is when the protagonist discovers the ugly truth, the mask slips, and they find themselves trapped in some nightmare.

Well, for some, Morris' utopia undoubtedly would be. It is perhaps a bit like living in a Tolkienesque Shire—a bucolic aesthetic that belies some worrying subtexts. For a start, it is completely Anglocentric—Morris depicts a very English utopia: what has happened to the rest of the world is not discussed, except for a brief, disparaging reference to America being reduced to a 'wasteland'. There is a worrying emphasis on women being pretty—every female Guest meets is assessed in this way (as a potential 'stunner'). The novel is clearly written from a male gaze. There is nothing 'wrong', per se, about appreciating female beauty—but when it becomes the chief characteristic, the defining trait, that is problematic; in addition, the women are on the whole portrayed as being content in domestic roles, or being a bit 'empty-headed' (except for the stonemason and the free-spirited Ellen, who is inquisitive and seems to know more than she lets on—a portrait of Jane Morris, similarly 'snatched' from the working classes; in the way Guest is clearly Morris himself). Also, according to presentist sensibilities, *New from Nowhere* is very white, cis-gendered, and straight, but Morris was writing from his time (late Nineteenth Century) even though he was imagining the early Twenty-first Century. His imagine didn't stretch far enough to imagine alterity. His vision seems impossibly idealistic, and relies upon the common decency and common sense of the masses—everyone being nice and abiding by agreed values—which, as we can see in contemporary life, is very unlikely, even when laws are enforced. There is the odd crime of passion, but these are forgiven by society as the perpetrator is left to come to terms with their actions. Yet human nature doesn't tend to be that enlightened. Even if one society achieves this level, there will always be other groups wishing either to seize its resources or simply destroy it (as Aldous Huxley imagines in his heartbreaking utopia, *Island* [1960]).

Yet, Morris's 'utopian romance' is a hopeful act of positive visualisation—a thought experiment for the world the Socialist Morris wish to see manifest. For him it was a vision much longed for; and one he tried to implement with his restless energy and huge output. He perhaps achieved in at Kelmscott and the other centres of Arts and Crafts activity.

Now there is an appreciation of artisan skills, of the hand-made, the hand-crafted, the home-grown—farmers' markets and craft markets are very popular; Transition Town schemes and similar initiatives are skilling people up for the 'power down'. Alternative currencies such as LETS and Timeshare have been trialled, but the lack of money seems the least convincing of Morris' notions—though with the devastation caused by Neoliberalism, perhaps the one that needs addressing as urgently as the environmental one. We need to replace the false economy of venture capitalism, of 'progress' and 'growth' (based upon finite, dwindling resources and catastrophically damaged biosphere) with the more sustainable one of Deep Ecology.

Morris' vision is a message in a bottle cast in time's stream, and although it has many alluring qualities, perhaps it is not radical enough, as it clings to some medieval paradise that never was, yet these thought experiments are worth undertaking. Morris throws down the gauntlet for us all to imagine the world we would like to live in.

Morris' vision was grounded in the principles of the Arts and Crafts Movement, a cluster of groups and initiatives which emerged out of the Arts and Crafts Exhibition Society, founded in London in1887:

> The birth of the Arts and Crafts movement in Britain in the late 19th century marked the beginning of a change in the value society placed on how things were made. This was a reaction to not only the damaging effects of industrialisation but also the relatively low status of the decorative arts. Arts and Crafts reformed the design and manufacture of everything from buildings to jewellery (V&A).

The polymath Morris was at the forefront of this movement, and turned his indefatigable talents to not only transforming the home and every aspect of production, but also society. Morris was inspired by the writings of the renowned art critic John Ruskin, who could be seen as a protoenvironmentalist in his early warnings about the impact of the Industrial Revolution on the natural world.

The Arts and Crafts Movement was only one of the several utopian socialist programmes to emerge from the second half of the Nineteenth Century. One of the most significant is referred to as Fourierism, after French social theorist, Charles Fourier (1772–1837), who advocated a reimagining of society based on an egalitarian ethos. He suggested a societal restructuring founded upon communal associations known as 'phalanges' (phalanxes). Based on an agrarian-handicraft economy, the phalanx consisted of about 1500 people. Work was voluntary and goods produced were the property of the phalanx. But members were paid an hourly wage (the scale escalating according to the disagreeableness of the task), and private property and inheritance were permitted. Fourier's premise was that people could live harmoniously in a state of nature, free of government intervention. Transcendentalists found much to admire in Fourierism, and true believers predicted that eventually the entire world would be organised into phalanxes. However doomed Fourier's optimistic vision was—due to the vested interests of the dominant Capitalist ruling class—it is an inspiring thought experiment, and one that could provide the solid foundation for utopian ecofiction. There are many other good models one could draw upon to give one's vision of a better world substance, such as sociocracy, mutual aid networks, ecovillages, and *Buen Vivir*—the South American socialist reform principle of 'good living' or 'well living', although it is not a wellbeing movement in the Western individualistic sense of self-care, as one of its proponents, Eduardo Gudynas, emphasises:

> These are not equivalents at all. With buen vivir, the subject of wellbeing is not [about the] individual, but the individual in the social context of their community and in a unique environmental situation. (cited in Balch, 2013)

Yet one has to be mindful of the potential pitfalls of a utopian approach, as China Miéville emphasises in his essay, 'The Limits of Utopia': 'Utopias are necessary. But not only are they insufficient: they can be part of the system, the bad totality that organises us, warms the skies, and condemns millions to peonage on garbage scree' (2018). The road to Hell, as the saying goes, is paved with good intentions. One man's Heaven can be another woman's Hell. And one's own attitude can transform one into the other. John Milton, via his anti-hero, the rebel angel, Lucifer—the ultimate contrarian refusenik— summed this up perfectly: 'The mind is its own place, and in itself can make a heaven of hell, a hell of heaven' (Milton, 2003 [1667] Book I, lines 234–235).

Dystopias

The antithesis of utopia is dystopia: 'an imaginary place or society in which everything is bad' (OED, concise). The dramatic potency and resonance of dystopia has attracted some of our greatest writers, producing some of literature's most powerful and prophetic pieces of writing: *We* (1921); *Nineteen-Eighty-Four* (1949); *Brave New World* (1932); *The Handmaid's Tale* (1985); *The Road* (2006). However, such writers were not necessarily looking ahead, but reflecting upon the present: Aldous Huxley imagined the endgame of the eugenics of the 1930s in his novel, *Brave New World*. George Orwell merely re-arranged the year he started work on his famous dystopia, 1948, to imagine where post-war geopolitics could lead. Margaret Atwood emphasised she only drew upon examples from the real world in her nightmarish vision of an ultra-right wing theocracy Gilead, and wryly observing current trends in the USA has said that her novel was 'not an instruction manual' (2017). All of these works have cast a long shadow and remain disturbingly relevant, but let us look at a more recent example, one with a strong environmental focus.

Diane Cook's short story collection, *Man V. Nature* (2015), explored a similar schism to that in her Booker Prize shortlisted novel, *The New Wilderness* (2020), but in the latter the focus is very much 'woman versus nature', or rather, women working *with* nature. As such, it could be seen as a significant example of ecofeminist fiction. The story, set in an indeterminate, depleted near future America, involves a mother, Bea(trice) and her daughter, Agnes, who leave the 'City' (an unnamed and unhealthy urban centre) due to the effect it is having on the daughter's health (a serious lung condition). Bea decides to take part in an experiment in the 'Wilderness State' with her current partner, the academic Glen: a small group of people will live in the state as hunter-gatherers—forced by bullish Rangers to continually roam, leaving no trace. As the accoutrements, sensibilities, and needs of 'civilisation' fall away, the majority of the group find themselves adapting and attuning to their environment—hunting game, skinning and preparing hides, gathering berries and herbs, living and travelling lightly. Yet the outer world catastrophically disrupts this neo-arcadia—first with news of Bea's mother's death; and then with the arrival of 'Newcomers' and rule-breaking 'Mavericks'. The apparently pristine aspect of the Wilderness State becomes compromised with tell-tale traces of the human invasive species—litter, truckers, the occasional corpse, and then eventually refugees escaping the increasingly brutal City. Unnamed 'Administrations' come and go and with each regime change, the rules change, and the 'Originalists', as they self-define, are forced out of their comfort zone routine, range, and habitus again and again. Alongside these external pressures, internal tensions within the group threaten to split it apart. Alpha males and females jockey for power and control. Bea is ostensibly the epitome of the 'bad mother'—abandoning her daughter; sleeping with the enemy—but Cook is careful to deconstruct this, and the backbone of the novel is the problematic mother/daughter relationship and how no one is perfect. The precocious daughter, Agnes, comes of age in the wilderness and adapts to it better than anyone. She is a skilled tracker and guide but is not the 'leader' she thinks she is. We are repeatedly shown how her knowledge of the world is flawed—she is continually wrongfooted and infuriated by her mother. The complexity of the love/hate between them is convincingly dramatised. Cook brings alive the liminal existence of the group in the Wilderness State in a visceral, embodied way. Here, nature is no mere backdrop. It is centre stage, and far from picturesque 'landscape'. An explicitly ecological novel, living in 'harmony' with nature is not seen as a pretty thing—but messy and smelly, unsentimental and unforgiving. Nature—both the human and more-than-human kind—is red in tooth and claw. Unlike so many dystopian narratives, the shock and awe are not evoked by images of ruined and rewilded cities, but by a kind of crumbling of social mores and shibboleths—like so many overwhelmed coastal cities. The true 'apocalypse' or revelation here is the 'wilderness in us', which emerges, as in Richard Jefferies' *After London, or Wild England* (1980 [1885]), after the implosion of civilisation. It is a study of what we 'truly are', when the veneer has been stripped away—part adult *Lord of the Flies*, part nature documentary in which we are the subjects. It is a grim read at times, but it is electrified by by Cook's prose and deep insight into human nature.

Cook's dystopia is an uncompromising, and often challenging read, but it vividly dramatises a worst-case scenario, and imagines a way of surviving it, and so perhaps offers its own gleam of hope: a chiaroscuro effect articulated more fully by Margaret Atwood's blended approach.

Ustopias

Margaret Atwood, a writer who knows this territory better than most, has advocated a more realistic, blended approach to the utopia/dystopia dialectic in her ideation of 'ustopias':

> Ustopia is a world I made up by combining utopia and dystopia—the imagined perfect society and its opposite—because, in my view, each contains a latent version of the other. In addition to being, almost always, a mapped location,

Ustopia is also a state of mind, as is every place in literature of whatever kind. (2011)

This has the ring of truth to it, for as Charles Dickens pointed out, 'It was the best of times; it was the worst of times'. And when has it ever been otherwise? For one person, it is the best day of their life, for another, their worst. Even in the totalling 'polycrisis' we live in there are daily moments of happiness. Rebecca Solnit, in her exploration of this existential paradox, *Hope in the Dark* (2016 [2004]), would agree.

Unfortunately, the prevailing tendency, especially over the last twenty-five years, has been towards dystopia: they crowd our bookshelves, our streaming platforms, our computer games, news, politics, and popular/populist discourse.

Mark Fisher, paraphrasing Frederick Jameson said, 'It's easier to imagine the end of the world than the end of capitalism' (2012). Jameson wryly responded to his own adage: 'Someone once said that it is easier to imagine the end of the world than to imagine the end of capitalism. We can now revise that and witness the attempt to imagine capitalism by way of imagining the end of the world' (2003). Many dystopias do just that: thrombotic freeways clogged with abandoned vehicles, rewilded shopping malls, deserted metropolises, brutalised suburbs, and desecrated homes. This kind of apocalypse-porn evokes an Albrechtian solastalgia, but not for the death of nature, which often reclaims these posthuman spaces, but for the death of capitalism. The shock and awe of such vistas—tropes rehashed in countless TV dramas, films, computer games, and comics—is that 'business as usual' is no more. We are made to shudder in our consumerist comfort bubbles, chilled at the very thought we could no longer order anything we wanted from the infantilising room service of the internet, whatever the ecological cost—the unconscionable, clickable fuck of 'buy now', which should be 'buy tomorrow', as we pass on the environmental impact to future generations, or rather 'goodbye tomorrow'. Our daily actions and lifestyle choices help to bring dystopia a little bit closer, so it is small wonder it dominates our imaginations.

Dr. Elizabeth Sawin flagged up the tendency of the hegemonic bias towards dystopia: 'The current powers have convinced millions that what is merely practical (following the instructions for thriving on an interdependent planet) is utopian. What's more, they assert that what is actually dystopian (acting out of domination & separation) is merely practical' (Twitter, 12 February 2022). Untangling this is critical for forging a path for protecting a liveable planet. And for those of us who, by accidents of birth, end up at least some of the time in the position to dominate, it's critical for our humanity.

A powerful example of an ustopia is from Atwood's long-time friend and fellow writer, Ursula K. Le Guin: *The Word for World is Forest* (2015[1972]). Le Guin believed, 'As a fiction writer, I don't speak message, I speak story…' This is something she remained resolute about, even towards the end of her long and distinguished career. The statement was partly in exasperated response to school librarians and teachers asking her for books with the 'message' front-loaded. Philip Pullman, a writer very different in tone than Le Guin but no less ambitious in his grappling with big ideas about the human condition and the nature of reality, has experienced a similar problem. In discussing avoiding didacticism in *his* writing Pullman said: 'Ideas are best conveyed by making them look not like ideas at all, but events' (2010). Le Guin, in this slim novel first published at the height of the Vietnam War, has tried to do just that—not by offering a polemic, but by dramatising the problem—the wearily familiar dynamic of an aggressively Capitalist colonial power subjugating and exploiting the indigenous inhabitants for the purposes of extracting the maximum amount of wealth (resources, either in the form of slave labour or mineral wealth, or both), no matter the cost to the ecosystem, its biodiversity, and the lives of the aboriginal dwellers. This rapacious pattern (the inevitable manifestation of 'progress without limits', and 'free trade', the mantra of late Capitalism, Neoliberalism) has played out throughout humanity history—although that should not make it normative. We come to think of it as the only game in town, and 'the way things are', when, with enough willpower, other ways are possible and other worlds. In Le Guin's story—set within the archipelago of novels exploring the Hainish universe (an advanced intellectual race who may or may not be the progenitors of humankind)—the author transposes this pattern onto a distant planet. Although it is forgivable to see the echoes of the Vietnam conflict, by setting the action on a richly Tropical planet the human colonists call 'New Tahiti' Le Guin creates the cognitive estrangement which defamiliarises us and makes us see the situation anew. Here, *both* sides are flawed, moral dualisms become enmeshed in complexity, and the obvious empathic leap, identifying with the diminutive hirsute natives (the Athsheans as the literal 'underdogs') starts to feel uncomfortable when we see them enacting 'war crimes' against the Colonist just as heinous as those they have endured. The cycle of violence seems inexorable until the arrival of a passing ship from Earth, the *Shackleton*, conveying Hainish and Cetian ambassadors and an 'ansible' (interplanetary communicator) changes the rules of the game. Le Guin's father was an anthropologist, and her exposure to his discipline and careful methodology informs not only this, but much of her work—yet here it is foregrounded in the figure of Raj Lyubov, a 'spesh' (specialist) who has deep sympathies for the Athsheans after learning their language and studying their sophisticated dream-praxis. Yet although Lyubov's frustrated attempts to ameliorate the brutish treatment of the 'Creechies' (as the inhabitants are dehumanised), and wanton destruction of the sylvan biome (the extraction of the incredibly valuable timber drives the 'annexing' of the planet) are for a while the main line of desire, ultimately Lyubov is seen as an emasculated protagonist, amid the ultra-machismo of the military endeavour (which Le Guin darkly satirises: the staccato jargon, testosterone-pumped behaviour, and self-destructing madness mirroring Heller's *Catch-22*). As the viewpoint shifts to Selver, the Athshean rebel figurehead 'god', it is easy to assume we are going to fall into a classic rebellion narrative—Robin Hood in space; but Le Guin has more sophisticated fish to fry. To say more than that would involve spoilers; but the whole, brief novel (practically a novella) is familiar to movie-goers across the world, for James Cameron *Avatar* (2009) feels like a very loose, unofficial 'revisioning' of it. However, those expecting things to play out in a similar way will be deeply surprised. Le Guin is not one to go for the crowdpleasing payoffs. Her universe is more complex than that. In such a short 'novel' it is perhaps inevitable that the characters will seem (relatively) thinly sketched: Captain Davidson, the violent, indignant antagonist, is the least convincing; although there is nothing simple about Mr Lepennon, the Hainish visitor, or the troubled reluctant messiah, Selver. What comes across most authentically amid the ambitious thought experiment of it all (the logical endgame of infinite growth on a galactic stage) is Le Guin's cri-de-coeur for the protection of precious habitats, the biodiversity of life they contain, and the autonomous rights of those who dwell among them. Environmental awareness was developing when she wrote the book, but it feels increasingly prescient in an age of Climate Chaos and the latest IPCC report urging governments to act now before it is too late. As such, Le Guin's book is a message in a bottle from the future—but one that interweaves that 'message' very skilfully into the texture of the narrative, challenging us as readers: confronting us with our assumptions and complicities. But that is to make it sound abstract and intellectual, when in essence it is an adventure story told at a cracking pace. To let Le Guin have the last word: 'The complex meanings of a serious story or novel can be understood only by participation in the language of the story itself. To translate them into a message or reduce them to a sermon distorts, betrays, and destroys them'.

This blended approach Mohsin Hamid describes as 'critically optimistic', in a discussion on his 2017 slipstream novel, *Exit West* (BBC Radio 4, Open Book, Sunday 30 June 2024), in which he uses the classic Fantasy trope of portals to imagine other ways of being in the world, while never losing sight of the grim realities we face in the present.

Now let us turn to a new alternative, in which 'ways through' become the dramatic fulcrum of the entire narrative, and not just a convenient plot device.

Thrutopias

In a blog for the *Huffington Post,* the philosopher Rupert Read mooted the speculative neologism, 'thrutopia':

> What are desperately needed, but as yet barely exist, are what I term thrutopias. Thrutopias would be about how to get from here to there, where "there" is far far away in time. How to live and love and vision and carve out a future, through pressed times that will endure. The climate crisis is going to be a long emergency, probably lasting hundreds of years. It is useless to fantasise a shining sheer escape from it to utopia. But it's similarly useless, dangerously defeatist, to wallow around in dystopias. We need ways of seeing, understanding, inhabiting, creating what will be needed for the very long haul. Visioning the politics and ecology of getting through. (2017)

Read suggests the 'nearest' we have to fictional dramatisation of a thrutopia is Le Guin's *The Dispossessed* (2002[1974])—a fine early example of the proposed subgenre, but one that is firmly within the realm of science fiction, however convincing its anthropological and political observations. Recent and more relevant (for our purposes) examples of thrutopia include *The New Wilderness* (2020), *The High House* (2021), *Doggerland* (2019), and *The Ministry for the Future* (2020), although Octavia E. Butler wrote one of the earliest, *Parable of the Sower* (2019 [1993]) and one could argue that George Stewart's *Earth Abides* (1949) got there even earlier. These stories have a voyeuristic car crash quality to them—transfixed by witnessing the destruction of all that we know, we cannot turn away. Seeing the impact of the dreaded apocalypse on ordinary lives, we imagine what we will do. Forewarned by the hindsight of another's narrative, we would like to imagine we would fare better. At the very least, thrutopias encourage us to spot the early warning signs and to act accordingly—to start filling the bath as soon as the lights across the city go out, as does the nameless father in McCarthy's *The Road* (2006)—or, even better, do all that we can to prevent the 'big bad' from happening in the first place.

Such territory has already been explored, arguably, in transapocalypse narratives such as Stephen King's *The Stand* (2011 [1978]), and the many multi-linear speculative bio-horror thrillers that have followed in his wake, or even earlier by Richard Jefferies' *After London: or Wild England* (1885). And yet Read's concept is a useful one, and has been seized by novelist, Manda Scott, who has set up a training programme to nurture writers of thrutopia: 'We need to write Thrutopias: clear, engaging routes through to a world we'd all be proud to bequeath to future generations' (Scott 2022).

Scott's notion of thrutopia is slightly different from Read's. She defines it as dramatising the: 'crucial steps of how we get to where we need to be to bequeath a functioning, flourishing future to the generations that come after us' (interview, 2023).

Thrutopia can not only contain practical 'crucial steps', but as a *form* can offer a promising, grounded approach to tackling the challenges of the Climate Crisis through fiction for writers of ecofiction. For Rupert Read, Stephen Markley's 900-page novel, *The Deluge*, articulates all that the form can achieve: 'This is the finest example we have yet of actually imagining our future. Imagining A FUTURE' (@GreenRupertRead, X, 28 October, 2023). Read found it more 'realistic' than Kim Stanley Robinson's *The Ministry for the Future*, which perhaps imagines humanity at its best, than at its worst, whileas Markley's novel does not hold back from showing the nightmare of neoliberalism's endgame as it struggles to not only survive, but thrive in the face of the metacrisis.

The final option we will consider here chooses to *not* focus on the 'big bad', even if it is the elephant in the room, but what could be called the 'big good'.

Solarpunk, Hopepunk, Green Stories

'Solarpunk' was coined in an anonymous blog, 'From Steampunk to Solarpunk', in 2008, as an ecoconscious alternative to Cyberpunk, Bruce Bethke's term from 1983 for a school of writers exploring emergent technology in hard-boiled dystopias, epitomised by the works of William Gibson, the so-called Godfather of Cyberpunk. His *Neuromancer* (1984) definitely established the aesthetic—a variation of the tech-noir and hyper-urbanisation of *Blade Runner* (Scott, dir. 1982) with an emphasis on virtual reality and the posthuman. Grafted onto these cybernetic speculations, the 'punk' part highlighted the pervading tone of estrangement, alienation, and anti-establishment anger. Peter Nicholls observes: 'A punk disillusion, often multiple—with progressive layers of illusion being peeled away—is a major component of these works' (1999: 288). The slippery ontologies and late capitalism of Cyberpunk emerged, in part, as a hacking of the hard materialism of Reaganomics and Thatcherism. Since then, several other subgenres have claimed the 'punk' suffix with decreasing credibility like so many Nth-generation xeroxes. The most successful, commercially at least, has been Steampunk—a form of retro-science fiction imagining counter-factual Victorian paradigms with airships, rocketships, pith helmets, and blunderbusses—resurrecting the vintage storyworlds of Jules Verne and H.G. Wells. The fan culture that has emerged—cosplay festivals, music, and the plethora of Steampunk ephemera, props, accessories, and 'merch'—shows creative brio and skill. The celebration of the analogue is an understandable reaction to the overly technologised world of the Twenty-first Century, where the digital dominates, permeating every aspect of our lives; but the largely uncritical celebration of the Colonial and Imperial is problematic, as is the rejoicing in a resource-plenty, carbon-heavy Industrial Revolution aesthetic where Climate Change is not a concern. As a mode of Fantastika it perpetuates a form of nostalgism and political quietism.

A potentially more radical spinoff of Cyberpunk, Solarpunk, seeks to offer positive near future alternatives, drawing on existing and hypothetical sustainable technology. Brazil has been cited as the seedbed for the movement, largely due to the influential anthology, *Solarpunk: Histórias Ecológicas e Fantásticas em um Mundo Sustenavel* (Lodi-Ribeiro, Gerson, and Spindler, Roberta 2013). Whether that's the case, Solarpunk has certainly gained traction in Latin American countries, as the Solarise2022 online festival showcased (https://www.youtube.com/watch?v=U20OFV-M8V0) which featured a strong element of Latinx artists and writers.

Numerous anthologies have sought to promote Solarpunk as a viable literary subgenre, and in 2022 the *Solarpunk Magazine* was launched with the same intent, but there is yet to be written a Solarpunk novel with real impact—one that fully embodies the 'hopeful' ethos of the movement. Certainly there have been some successful novels that have incorporated Solarpunk elements in their storyworlds—first and foremost being Paolo Baciagalupi's *The Wind-up Girl* (2010), which imagines a post-Peak Oil world where genetically mutated elephants power giant turbines. And yet this is closer to Cyberpunk in its gritty tone, and conceptually more 'Biopunk' (fitting alongside works such as Lauren Beukes' *Zoo City*). The inherent problem with the central tenet of Solarpunk is a dramatic one: how does one write a dramatically engaging narrative when the problems of the world have been solved and an optimistic tone must pervade? *Solarpunk Magazine* challenges this, stating:

> Not all solarpunk stories take place in idealistic utopias. Many tales are rife with compelling conflict among people and communities optimistically striving to reach that ideal while still struggling to solve some existing challenges. But all solarpunk stories do have things in common such as future or near-future settings, optimistic perspectives, and looking toward a better future with at least a growing harmony between nature, technology, and humanity. In short, solarpunk stories are decidedly not dystopias. (2020)

Whether such tales are 'rife with compelling conflict' maybe a matter of taste, but many Solarpunk tales read a bit flat: well-intentioned, but insipid. Certainly conflict does not have to be the driver of *all* fiction, and narrative traction can be created by simply bringing to life vivid, convincing characters and their life-worlds. Or by the sheer quality of the writing. And this perhaps is easier to achieve (or sustain) in a short story than a full-length novel, as can be seen in the short stories of Vandana Singh (2018), as well as other anthologies which actively promote BIPOC voices: *New Sun: Original Speculative Fiction by People of Color* (2018); *Multispecies Cities: Solarpunk Urban Futures* (2021b); *Revenge of Gaia: Contemporary Vietnamese Ecofiction* (2021); *This All Come Back Now: An Anthology of First Nations Speculative Fiction* (2021a); *Africa Risen: A New Era of Speculative Fiction* (2022), are among the most recent.

There are numerous small-scale projects too—self-funded, crowd-funded, or funded through an environmental charity such as RSPB's anthology, *We Are a Many Bodied Singing Thing* (2020), which encouraged writing that celebrated a list of endangered British species and ancient oaks. One of the most successful initiatives of this type is Green Stories—a range of free writing competitions across multiple formats that 'showcase what a sustainable society might look like', the brainchild of Dr Denise Baden, Professor of Sustainable Business at the University of Southampton and author of the ecofiction novel, *Habitat Man* (2021). Baden explains the aim of 'Green Stories': 'Our mission is to create a cultural body of work that entertains and informs about green solutions, inspires green behaviour and raises awareness of the necessary transformations towards a sustainable economy'. So far, the competitions have included the novel, short stories, graphic novels, children's writing, and scripts.

Based at York St John University, Dr Catherine Heinemeyer, is Lecturer in Arts and Ecological Justice. For the Writing the Earth programme—convened by the author at Arts University Bournemouth—Dr Heinemeyer ran a workshop on 'It's Not the End of the World: rewriting the eco-apocalypse' (Writing the Earth, Arts University Bournemouth, April 2021), in which she emphasised the societal links (climate refugees; resource wars; mental health impact) and systemic causes of Climate Change (Capitalism and the massive inequalities it creates). Starting by getting participants to create a character living in a co-operative based on a real-world example (https://cooperationjackson.org/), she then encouraged them to imagine a scenario in 30 years' time, extrapolating on 'current global-scale trends'. The 'rules' she set down for this future scenario were:

- People are no better or worse than they are right now
- But circumstances can be radically different and people respond to that
- Change tends to look impossible until it is inevitable
- People may be aware of global/national issues but are primarily concerned with what's happening around them in the local present (Heinemeyer 2021).

This positive, empowering approach dovetails into what has been called 'imagineering'.

Imagineering and Thinking Outside of the Box

'Imagineering' emerged out of the West Coast of America in the 1970s, but humankind has been using its imagination to problem-solve and conceptualise other modalities for as long as it has been around. Today, imagineering has been taken out of the hands of tech-pioneers and theme-park designers, and is being used by those seeking to implement a paradigm shift into a more sustainable and just society. One of these is Rob Hopkins, founder of the Transition Town movement. In his book, *From What If to What Is: Unleashing the Power of Imagination to Create the Future We Want* (2019) he advocates the use of play as an important tool:

> …play is key to brain development. It is as natural as learning how to walk, breathe or speak. It teaches social skills, cooperation, creativity and conflict resolution. It builds resilience and produces adults who are better at finding solutions.

Hopkins also emphasises the importance of story, which 'unlocks new possibility':

We need to become better storytellers in such a way that we can, through a variety of media, give people a visceral sense of what a positive future would sound, taste, feel and look like.

Another key proponent of this radical rethinking of our collective frame—the consensual reality that is far more malleable than most people realise, and can be reimagined by an act of collective will—is Roman Krznaric, who advocates a longer view on things to counter the short-termism which is hardwired into our political systems and is contributory to so many of the problems we face. In his non-fiction book, *The Good Ancestor* (2021), Krznaric offers six ways to think long-term: Deep-Time Humility: 'We must accept the reality that our personal stories from birth to death, and all the achievements and tragedies of human civilisation will barely register in the annals of cosmological time'; Cathedral Thinking (instigating projects that may not see fruition for several generations); Legacy Mindset (shifting our priorities to what we will leave behind); Holistic Forecasting (usually a variety of indices, not just the reductive ones like GDP); Intergenerational Justice (sometimes called 'Seventh Generation Thinking'—prioritising the impact of future generations beyond our immediate descendants); and Transcendental Goal (aligning our actions towards something greater than the individual or even their immediate community, e.g. Gaia-consciousness). These are useful criteria for systemic change on all levels, but also as guidelines for ecofiction—for writers wishing to think big, beyond the mere charting of the local or global impact of Climate Change.

For those wishing to engage more fully with the idea of systems thinking and societal change, then MOOCs (Mass Open Online Course) such as 'Towards Co-operative Commonwealth: transition in a perilous century' (2023) run by the Synergia Institute with support from Athabasca University and the Canadian CED Network, are recommended. There are many such initiatives on a local, regional, and sometimes national level happening in the world right now, which can provide practical, real-world models for writers of ecofiction to work with. One can 'stress test' such scenarios through a fictional lens and imagine things going right (utopia), wrong (dystopia), some blended in-between (ustopia), or even just the process of attempting to transition from one paradigm to another (thrutopia). The choice is yours.

Mycelia: Connections to Other Writers, Texts, and Resources

- Asubel, Kenny. 2012. *Dreaming the Future: Reimagining Civilization in the Age of Nature*. London: Chelsea Green Publishing.
- Centre for Alternative Technology: https://cat.org.uk/.
- Eden Project: https://www.edenproject.com/.

- Green Stories: http://www.greenstories.org.uk/.
- Hopkins, Rob. 2019. *From What Is to What If: Unleashing the Power of Imagination to Create the Future We Want*. London: Chelsea Green Publishing.
- Krenak, Alton. 2020. *Ideas to Postpone the End of the World*. Portland, OR: House of Anansi Press.
- Krznaric, Roman. 2021. *The Good Ancestor: how to think long term in a short-term world*. London: WH Allen.
- [Re]starting the Future: a collaboration between Icarus Complex, Where the Leaves Fall, and Emergence. 20 May 2021. https://emergencemagazine.org/event/restarting-the-future/ (Accessed 27 March 2023).
- Robinson, Kim Stanley. 2021, July 16. The Novel Solutions of Utopian Fiction. *The Nation*. https://www.thenation.com/article/culture/utopian-fiction-climate-literature/ (Accessed 19 July 2023).
- Science Fiction and Ecological Thinking, BBC Sounds: https://www.bbc.co.uk/sounds/play/m000h6yw.
- Solarpunk: http://solarpunkfestival.com/history/.
- The Alternative: https://www.thealternative.org.uk/.
- Towards Co-operative Commonwealth: https://synergiainstitute.org/toward-co-operative-common-wealth-transition-in-a-perilous-century/.

Spores: Writing Activities

- Imagining Nowhere—imagine a utopia (literally 'no-place'), an ideal society, which, in this instance is living in harmony with nature. What kind of dwellings do the inhabitants live in? How is energy generated? What transport is used, and how is this powered? What do people wear? What do they eat? How do they produce, store, transport, and distribute their food? What is the economic system? The organisational system? What do people do to relax? What are the laws and customs of this place? Try to imagine every aspect. Describe a day there as a first-time visitor. Focus on the senses. First impressions.
- The Imaginary Dust Jacket—visualise a hypothetical dust jacket with your name (or pen name) on. This is the book you have dreamed into being. It is an ecofiction novel, or collection of short stories. What's the title? Describe the cover or even create a mock one. Write a promotional blurb to grab the prospective reader and summarise the contents. And, finally, write a biographical note in third person, imagining yourself as a successful author in 5 years' time.
- Being the Voice of the Critic—in this exercise you are asked to circumvent criticism (a rhetorical technique called prolepsis) by playing the Devil's

Advocate with your own writing: what are the elephants in the room, the blind spots, the epistemological weaknesses? Is there something you are not addressing? What words or phrases are you fond of repeating? Any clichés? Or sections you know are under par? Identify several valid criticisms, and write a robust, convincing response to each, as though fielding questions from a formidable interviewer.

References

Atwood, Margaret. 2010 [1985]. *The Handmaid's Tale*. London: Vintage.
Atwood, Margaret. 2011, October 14. Margaret Atwood: The Road to Ustopia. *Guardian*. https://www.theguardian.com/books/2011/oct/14/margaret-atwood-road-to-ustopia (Accessed 27 March 2023).
Atwood, Margaret. 2017. Margaret Atwood on What 'The Handmaid's Tale' Means in the Age of Trump. *The New York Times*. https://www.nytimes.com/2017/03/10/books/review/margaret-atwood-handmaids-tale-age-of-trump.html (Accessed 11 November 2023).
Bacigalupi, Paolo. 2010. *The Wind-up Girl*. London: Orbit.
Balch, Oliver. 2013, February 4. Buen Vivir: The Social Philosophy Inspiring Movements in South America. *Guardian*. https://www.theguardian.com/sustainable-business/blog/buen-vivir-philosophy-south-america-eduardo-gudynas (Accessed 8 June 2023).
Baden, Denise. 2021. *Habitat Man*. Southampton: Habitat Press.
Butler, Octavia E. 2019 [1993]. *Parable of the Sower*. London: Headline.
Cameron, James, director. 2009. *Avatar*. 20th Century Studios. https://www.imdb.com/title/tt0499549/?ref_=nv_sr_srsg_3_tt_8_nm_0_q_Avatar
Cook, Diane. 2020. *Parable of the Sower*. London: Headline.
Fisher, Mark. 2012. *Capitalist Realism: Is There No Alternative?* Portland, OR: Zero Books.
Gibson, William. 1984. *Neuromancer*. New York, NY: Ace.
Greengrass, Jessie. 2021. *The High House*. London: Swift Press.
Heinemeyer, Catherine. 2021, April. It's Not the End of the World: Rewriting the Eco-apocalypse. Writing the Earth programme, Arts University Bournemouth.
Hopkins, Rob. 2008. *The Transition Handbook*. Totnes: Green Books.
Hopkins, Rob. 2019. *From What Is to What If: Unleashing the Power of Imagination to Create the Future We Want*. London: Chelsea Green Publishing.
Huxley, Aldous. 1968 [1932]. *Brave New World*. London: Heron Books.
Huxley, Aldous. 1976 [1960]. *Island*. London: Granada.
Jameson, Fredric. n.d. Future City. Available from: https://newleftreview.org/issues/ii21/articles/fredric-jameson-future-city (Accessed 11 July 2023).

Jefferies, Richard. 1980 [1885]. *After London, or Wild England*. Oxford University Press.
King, Stephen. 2011 [1978]. *The Stand*. London: Hodder.
Krznaric, Roman. 2021. *The Good Ancestor: How to Think Long Term in a Short-term World*. London: WH Allen.
Le Guin, Ursula K., 2015[1972]. *The Word for World is Forest*. S.F. Masterworks. London: Gollancz.
Le Guin, Ursula K., 2002[1974]. *The Dispossessed*. London: Gollancz.
Le Guin, Ursula K. (n.d.) A Message About Messages. https://www.ursulakle guin.com/message-about-messages#:~:text=As%20a%20fiction%20writer%2C%20I,in%20terms%20appropriate%20to%20storytelling (Accessed 11 July 2023).
Lodi-Ribeiro, Gerson, and Roberta Spindler. 2018 [2013]. *Solarpunk: Ecological and Fantastical Stories in a Sustainable World*. n.p.: World Weaver.
McCarthy, Cormac. 2006. *The Road*. London: Picador.
McMahon, Linden Katherine, ed. 2020. *We Are a Many-bodied Singing Thing*. RSPB. https://naturebftb.co.uk/2020/03/27/we-are-a-many-bodied-singing-thing/
Miéville, China. 2018, March 2. APOCATOPIA? UTOPALYPSE? China Miéville: The Limits of Utopia. https://climateandcapitalism.com/2018/03/02/china-Miéville-the-limits-of-utopia/ (Accessed 27 March 2023).
More, Thomas. n.d. [1516]. *Utopia: A Dialogue of Comfort*. London: Heron Books.
Milton, John. 2003 [1667]. *Paradise Lost*. London: Penguin Classics.
Morris, William. 2003[1890]. *News from Nowhere, or An Epoch of Rest, Being Some Chapters from a Utopian Romance*. Peterborough, Ontario: Broadview Literary Texts.
Nicholls, Peter, and John Clute. 1999. *The Encyclopedia of Science Fiction*. London: Orbit.
Orwell, George. 2019 [1949]. *Nineteen-Eighty-Four*. London: Penguin Classics.
Pham, Chi, and Chitra Sankaran, eds. 2021. *Revenge of Gaia: Contemporary Vietnamese Ecofiction*. London: Penguin Random House.
Plato. 1977 [360 BCE]. *Timaeus and Critias*. London: Penguin Classics.
Pullman, Philip. 2010, April 1. *On Freedom of Speech*. Sheldonian Theatre. https://www.youtube.com/watch?v=QnMW9sLTQfI (Accessed 8 June 2023).
Read, Rupert. 2017, November 6. THRUTOPIA: Why Neither Dystopias Nor Utopias Are Enough To Get Us Through The Climate Crisis, And How A 'Thrutopia' Could Be. *Huffington Post*. https://www.huffingtonpost.co.uk/rupert-read/thrutopia-why-neither-dys_b_18372090.html (Accessed 27 March 2023).
Robinson, Kim Stanley. 2020. *The Ministry for the Future*. London: Orbit.
Rupprecht, Christoph, Deborah Cleland, et al. (eds.). 2021a. *This All Come Back Now: An Anthology of First Nations Speculative Fiction*. n.p.: World Weaver Press.
Rupprecht, Christoph, Deborah Cleland, et al. (eds.). 2021b. *Multispecies Cities: Solarpunk Urban Futures*. n.p: World Weaver Press.
Scott, Manda, 2022. *The Thrutopian Masterclass*. Available from: https://thrutopia.life/ [accessed: 6 July 2024]

Shawl, Nisi, ed. 2018. *New Sun: Original Speculative Fiction by People of Color*. Oxford: Solaris.
Singh, Vandana, 2018. *Ambiguity Machines and Other Stories*. Easthampton, MA: Small Beer Press.
Smith, Ben. 2019. *Doggerland*. London: Fourth Estate.
Solnit, Rebecca. 2016 [2004]. *Hope in the Dark: Untold Histories, Wild Possibilities*. London: Haymarket.
Stewart, George. 1999 [1949]. *Earth Abides*. London: Millennium/Gollancz SF Masterworks.
Synergia Institute. 2023. Just Transition Framework infographic. 'Toward Co-operative Commonwealth: Transition in a Perilous Century'. Synergia Institute 2023 MOOC.
Thomas, Sheree Renée, Oghenechovwe Donald Ekpeki, and Zelda Knight, eds. 2022. *Africa Risen: A New Era of Speculative Fiction*. New York, NW: St Martin's Press.
V&A (n.d.) Arts & Crafts: An Introduction. https://www.vam.ac.uk/articles/arts-and-crafts-an-introduction (Accessed 11 July 2023).
Zamyatin, Yevgeny. 2007 [1921]. *We*. London: Vintage.

8

The Rhizomatic Writer

The modern writer of ecofiction cannot thrive in a vacuum. They need to be able situate themselves within their relevant 'ecosystem', find their niche, connect with fellow creatives and industry professionals—and, like a mycelial network—share 'nutrients' and information. The secret of thriving is not by being competitive (part of the mindset that has created the Climate Crisis), but by being co-operative: by forging networks, supporting one another, sharing opportunities and advice. By keeping things flowing and always passing on the luck. This more generous paradigm is intrinsic in many cultures—the tradition of hospitality to strangers. The historian Bettany Hughes identifies a 'prehistoric word-idea' that acted as a catalyst for civilisation:

> This Proto-Indo-European term *ghosti* (from which we get the words guest, host and ghost) referred to a kind of unspoken etiquette, a notion that on seeing strangers on the horizon, rather than choose to fell them with spears or sling-shots, instead we should take the risk of welcoming them across our threshold – on the chance that they might bring new notions, new goods, fresh blood with them. Over time this word-idea evolved into the Greek *xenia* – ritualised guest-host friendship, an understanding that stitched together the ancient Mediterranean and Near Eastern worlds.
>
> (Hughes 2017: 5)

By welcoming ideas and different paradigms across our thresholds we are enriched. The Twenty-first Century writer cannot, in all conscience, shut the door on the world for, in sending our words out into the public sphere are we not seeking the same gift of hospitality, the same generosity of spirit? Do we all not wish for our books to be welcomed into people's homes and hearts?

In Saharan Africa, if someone asks for water you give them some of yours, however little you have—this is the custom of the desert, and essential for survival—as vividly brought to life in the migration documentary, *Tenere* (dir. Söylemez, 2020). Lewis Hyde explores the culture of the 'economy of the creative spirit' in his book, *The Gift* (2006 [1983]), in which he advocates a circular economy, where acts of generosity are never directly reciprocal—the zero sum of linear transactions ('I give you this so that I benefit', or so 'you give me something back of equal worth'), but are 'paid forward', benefitting others you may never know, but enriching the community as a whole as they too 'pay it forward'. This is like nutrients passing around an ecosystem in a mycelial network—trees absorb sunlight and carbon and exchange this for nutrients from the soil, producing precious oxygen and fruit, seed, leaf and other biomass that supports a myriad of life-forms All benefit.

Rhizomatic Thinking

Rhizomes are 'a continuously growing horizontal underground stem with lateral shoots and adventitious roots at intervals' (Oxford Concise). The philosopher Deleuze and psycho-analyst, Guattari, in their influential collaboration, *A Thousand Plateaus* (1988), use the extended metaphor of the rhizome in their wish to encourage a non-hierarchical, non-linear way of thinking and being. Through five 'plateaus' they pursue this approach through epistemology, ontology, anthropology, ethics, and politics. Post-structuralists arising out of the ashes of the Paris uprising of 1968, Deleuze and Guattari composed their collaboration (a cross-fertilisation fed by a rich nutrient soup of their respective disciplines and major influences—Marx and Trotsky, Derrida and Lacan—which epitomises their rhizomatic methodology) like jazz-musicians, disrupting linearity with their artful digressions and improvisations. These plateaus can be read in any order, pushing against the bourgeois construct of the book. Like a textual version of the Paris Commune, the authors wanted their work to emulate, in microcosm, one of their key tenets: chaosmos—the cosmos is self-organising. They suggest: 'modes of organisation emerge from matter immanently instead of being opposed from above as a form of law' (1988: 24–25). This autochthonous anarchy foreshadows Hakim Bey's Temporary Autonomous Zone (1985). Nodes of meaning emerge organically and authority—or authorship—are shared. This approach is summed up by their term 'deterritorialization'. The rhizome is the resilient, rooted analogy that grounds all of this. It 'enables us to think **with** the world rather than thinking about the world' (1988: 24–25). For Deleuze and Guattari it provides a fertile metaphor for their modus operandi: 'Make rhizomes, not roots, never plant! Don't sow, grow offshoots!... Run lines, never plot a point!... Have short-term ideas. Make maps, not photos...' (ibid.).

Mycological research in recent years has confirmed much of what Deleuze and Guattari intuited. In the 1990s, Professor Alan Rayner, a biologist at the University of Bath, observed how the organisational principles of fungi challenged discreetist thinking (1997), through his notion of 'dynamic boundaries' (2006). In his book, *Entangled Life* (2020), mycologist Merlin Sheldrake delved into the endlessly fascinating world of mycelia—showing how these sometimes vast underground networks that exist beneath forest floors, connecting through their hyphae fungus with the roots of shrubs and trees, share nutrients and information, challenging notions of selfhood, gender, and anthropocentric intelligence.

Applying a mycelial frame to world mythologies, Sophie Strand showed how it can deconstruct outmoded patriarchal thinking and regenerate toxic masculinities into something more playful, life-affirming, and ecologically harmonious (2022). Discussing the honey fungus found in Malheur National Forest, Oregon—more than 2.4 miles wide and at two to seven thousand years old, one of the largest and oldest living beings on the planet—Strand said, with her poetic wit, 'Each mushroom is a poem of a certain place, an eruption suited to a specific patch of moss, distribution of sulfur, supply of sugar from symbiotic plant, and forest-floor detritus' (2022: 57).

One could argue that every novel is like this too—a honey fungus of consciousness arising out of the mulch of influences, the 'terroir' of one's life and times.

Sheldrake talks about how his studies of mycelial expanded the 'grammar of animacy' (2020: 46) for him. Strand concurs, seeing within the mycelial world a dissolution of dualism, which is at the very heart of the problem. At pains to dismiss binary thinking (matriarchy/patriarchy; civilisation/wilderness; human/more-than-human), she says: 'The opposite of our current predicament—climate collapse, social unrest, extinction, mass migrations, solastalgia, genocide—is, in fact, the disintegration of opposites altogether' (2022: 113). Preferring the term *Animacy* to notions of the 'Divine Feminine' and 'Sacred Masculine', Strand says 'Animacy is plushier. Springier. More mosslike. It seems a soft spot to rest on while I try to understand and explain how very sentient the world is to me these days' (ibid.). The bryologist, Robin Wall Kimmerer would perhaps sympathise with this perspective, finding within her study of moss and her own indigenous wisdom tradition as an enrolled member of the Citizen Potawatomi Nation (2003; 2013), powerful 'medicine' about how to be in the world:

> We need acts of restoration, not only for polluted waters and degraded lands, but also for our relationship to the world. We need to restore honor to the way we live, so that when we walk through the world we don't have to avert our eyes with shame, so that we can hold our heads up high and receive the respectful acknowledgment of the rest of the earth's beings.

By not only honouring the more-than-human, but also aligning creative-critical practice to ecological principles—in 'relationship' with the world—the writer of ecofiction expands their vocabulary of being, the available reality accessible to their imagination. At the same time, a regular, immersive connection with nature nurtures resilience and a healthy perspectival shift from the solipsism of human 'beingness'.

The rhizomatic writer probes the pockets and hollows of their practice, their *field*, finding ingenious ways to thrive—by making serendipitous links, and finding unexpected sources of 'nutrients': inspiration, support, resources, etc. They do this not by waiting for official approval or guidelines—but by going below the radar of the hegemonic; by adopting a grassroots, guerrilla, eco-punk approach. Like a tenacious root slowly splitting a rock, interstices of opportunities are *created*, by being pro-active and determined—not by waiting passively for them to drop into your lap.

Taking a leaf from William Blake's (self-illustrated; self-printed) book, the rhizomatic writer embodies his dictum: 'I must Create a System, or be enslav'd by another Mans/I will not Reason & Compare: my business is to Create' (1804–1820). Each ecofiction writer's manifesto and modus operandi is as unique as their artistic DNA, but could perhaps be customised from the following principles: explore; innovate; deconstruct; challenge; and collaborate.

These meta-concepts will serve the budding writer of ecofiction far better than any prescriptive craft advice. A healthy DIY attitude of lateral-thinking, problem-solving, and project management will achieve your goal beyond the saws of creative writing manuals. Like a pioneering mountain man or woman, we need to strike out into the wilderness with a few essential tools and a lot of common sense, resourcefulness, and grit. And like those who flourished in such environments, the best learnt to read the land, or learnt from those who could. Armed with a humility and sensitive eco-literacy anything is possible.

The writer David James Duncan, author of the epic ecofiction, *Sun House* (2023) perhaps embodies the spirit of the 'mountain man' in his embodied situatedness more than most, living amidst wildneress on a little trout stream in Montana (following the advice of his late friend Jim Harrison's advice to 'finish his life disguised as a creek'). Talking of his home state, Duncan said: 'I love Montana. I love it in a physical way that's very outdoorsy. You know, backpacking, fly fishing, just spending time standing in rivers, birding—there are so many wonderful hikes available right outside this studio around Missoula, Montana. It's just ever present. And so I wanted to combine the landscape that comes out in this secretive mountain culture, the Lûmi people.' (interview, *Emergence Magazine*, 2024). We do not have to be so outward bound (although that comes with enormous benefits to one's well-being), but adopting a creatively pioneering approach can reap benefits.

Whether we use mycelia, moss, trees, or another kind of natural form as our guide, by doing so our practice will have a resilient, grounded quality—one that is rooted, pun intended, in the real world.

Emergent Forms

Another way the writer of ecofiction can disrupt the restrictions of a traditional print novel is by exploring different media. These are not necessarily mutually exclusive, and one could author a print novel, and then, according to contractual terms if publisher's consent is required, manifest it in different formats too. Sometimes this is part of the publishing 'package': print, audio, e-book; but sometimes the author has to take it upon themselves to manifest their narrative in different ways. Could it become a digital interactive fiction? Or an audio drama? Or how about a role-playing game? Some of these forms have been around for a while, but others are emerging as technology develops. No doubt Virtual Reality and Artificial Intelligence will provide new narrative opportunities (with the caveat that content largely contingent upon Generative-AI may facilitate the 'death of the author', in terms of it being a viable profession), although one has to ask exactly how ecological such technology will be—and will its carbon-heavy footprint be in contradiction to any kind of ecological message of the narrative? In New Materialism no object is in isolation, without its footprint and intersection of cultural and socio-economic forces:

> In new materialist ontology there are no structures, systems or mechanisms at work; instead there are innumerable 'events' comprising the material effects of both nature and culture, which together produce the world and human history. (Fox, n.d.)

These 'events' have consequences. Nevertheless, while current technological levels continue nothing is off the table. How long this will last is contingent upon the solutions found to counter finite resources on a planet that already lives beyond its life-sustaining potential. Until humanity learns to live within its 'donut' (Raworth, 2017) we will always be on borrowed time—and the idea of infinite technological advancement is an illusion. And so an over-reliance upon the latest gimmicky device or platform is unwise. Far better to future-proof our narratives by creating forms that will outlast the disposable platforms of the present with their built-in obsolescence. No one wants their magnum opus to be stuck on the equivalent of a floppy disc or Betamax video in years to come. Printed books can of course disintegrate, but have a longer shelf life than the latest digital format—at least it could be still read in centuries to come compared to some inaccessible data file.

Also, narratives that rely upon the latest, often expensive, platforms do not acknowledge the reality of digital poverty and illiteracy for many (The British Academy 2022).

Nevertheless, one may still consider alternative narrative formats, or ways of interacting with the storyworld you have created. Sometimes the most satisfying is the most 'low tech', such a table-top role-playing game, or spoken word performance. One should consider one's narrative as a porous construct with an inherent plasticity—one that could manifest in any number of ways. It may indeed flourish better in another form, so it is best not to get too attached to one specific output. Aspire to the endless inventiveness of evolution that tries a myriad variations until finding the one that flourishes.

Multimodality

In her 2019 book, *The Multimodal Writer: creative writing across genres and media*, Josie Barnard advocates a fluid, multi-directional approach to writing in the Twenty-first Century. She says: 'For creative writers, whether established or aspiring, the task of embracing multimodality—its challenges and opportunities—is key today' (2019: 2). She elaborates upon what she means by multimodality:

> I define a multimodal writing practice as: a creative approach wherein the inter-relationships between and among a writer's decisions and different media and modes contribute to the production of meaning. A multimodal writer who has adopted a multimodal writing practice works to develop a personalised model of creativity robust enough to enable improvement of productivity and/or creativity in the face of fast-paced change (Barnard 2019: 6)

Barnard emphasises that 'creative flexibility is key' (2019: 42) and sets out key principles for the multimodal writer: remediating skills and experience (using existing knowledge, and applying it in new forms); code-switching (switching fluidly between different media and their respective 'codes', as a polyglot would be able to switch between different languages); flexibility (to be able to adapt to new circumstances and briefs in a mercurial fashion, and not to be ossified in one's practice, or too fixated on one's work being in a fixed mode); industry (one needs to be prolific, focused, motivated, and disciplined); and finally, effective writing strategies (the most efficient and effective writing practices, such as alternating between different projects at different stages of completion—e.g. a novel in the morning; a non-fiction book in the afternoon; a draft proposal; proofing a late-stage manuscript, etc.). To achieve this, one needs to carefully monitor one's energy and attention levels, and timetable one's day accordingly. When are you best at creating new content? When would you time be spent best on some light editing, critical reading, listening to a podcast, writing a review, or reading for pleasure? One can apply tried-and-tested modes of working such as the Pomodoro Technique (developed by Francesco Cirillo in the late 1980s), where you work in focused, 25-minute 'bursts', punctuated by 5-minute breaks. After four consecutive work intervals, one normally takes a longer break of 15 to 30 minutes. By contrasting these work intervals with other activity away from the desk and anything digital—offline activities such as gardening—one reconnects with the natural world, exercises, and gets pulled out of one's anthropocentric solipsism by engagement with the more-than-human—this can be as simple as spending time playing with the cat or dog, or feeding the ducks in the park.

On one memorable occasion I was working on a novel in a remote croft in Wester Ross, overlooking the body of water between the West Coast of Scotland and the Outer Hebrides, called The Minch. As I wrote in the conservatory, I would look up frequently to gaze over the lively waters of Gairloch Bay—deep blue waves topped with crests of white beneath the vast fortresses of cloud above. As I did so, at one point, I spotted the fins of porpoises and felt somehow plugged into the grid of creation—what I was beholding fed back directly into what I was writing (a description of an analogous biome): an electrifying feedback loop that gave my writing a spine-tingling vivacity and authenticity. This mode switching between the human and more-than-human, and between changes of scale, is most effective, and I would argue, essential, for the writer of ecofiction.

The Writer in the World

There is perhaps inevitably a lot of emphasis placed upon the novel as the culmination of a writer's ambitions—the focus of all their energies, and the validation of their craft. However, the printed book—or e-book, audio book, or other emergent format—is only *one* iteration of the writer's craft. And, as we have seen, our words can manifest in a myriad of ways. And yet, beyond the fixed form of the conventional novel, a writer can utilise their craft and promote their ideas in all kinds of context. Firstly, one needs to reframe the act of writing as something done in isolation. It can be a collaborative act, as in a community-based project such as an anthology, newsletter, or chronicle of a neighbourhood, much-loved natural resource, or the more-than-human (a collective celebration of distinctive flora and fauna). Writing can also be co-authored; be based in a shared-world; or be a wiki-style platform. Work can be anonymised, and shared freely, using the concept of 'copyleft'. We can choose to offer our writing as a gift, passing it forward to help and inspire others. For some this would be a step too far, depriving them of a potential livelihood, but as conscionable authors we should always think about what impact our words have on the world. We can choose to embody what we wish to advocate, and we can choose to create 'good works' for the benefit of the many, not just the author.

The writer of ecofiction can run creative writing workshops for community groups. All one needs is an accessible venue, such as the meeting room in a library. As an example—in 2003 I ran 'Creative Writing and the Environment'—a 10-week community writing class at Envolve, the environment centre in the city of Bath, Somerset. I applied for and won a small grant from the Reading Families Millennium Award, which helped pay for the venue hire and the creation of an anthology, which was co-edited by the participants. *Writing the Land: An Anthology of Natural Words* (2003) was launched at a local spoken word showcase, and profits went to the local Friends of the Earthgroup. I drafted a press release and managed to get the event featured in the local paper with a photograph. The group that started on my course, Natural Words, is still going, twenty odd years later, and have produced their own anthologies since. More recently, I have run a writing and walking wellbeing project called 'Green Words' in my home county of Dorset. Over Spring 2023 I ran a series of guided walks to local parks and nature reserves, accompanied by writing workshops. These generated poems and prose for an anthology, *Green Words: An Anthology of Natural Words from West Dorset* (2023) launched at a showcase that summer. I collaborated with the local arts centre to secure some funding from Dorset Council (Dorset Council Culture

Project Fund 22–23), which helped fund the sessions and the anthology. Such sessions are a pleasure to run, and deeply satisfying—combining many of my core interests and passions. The trick is to design a community project that is tailor-made for you.

Another option is to apply for a writing residency: these allow you time to focus on your writing often in inspiring locations. Depending on the residency, it may be catered, or self-catered, including a stipend or other perks and in-kind support, or involving participant expense. Certain expectations may be required: a talk or reading, workshop, or creative output. Residencies can be held in a wide range of venues: schools, libraries, prisons, tattoo parlours, sports centres, businesses, museums, galleries, visitor attractions, nature reserves, hotels, heritage properties, digital residencies in a virtual space (a website, blog, forum, etc.), and so forth. They can be highly competitive to apply for, but can provide valuable focused 'quality' writing time—although there may be attendant challenges around group dynamics of hosts and fellow residents, members of the public, pressure to 'create', and so forth. Some writers become very adept at applying for such residencies—and even spend a significant amount of time away from home, travelling from residency to residency. Where a residency does not already exist, one can sometimes create one—by suggesting it to the host organisation. If they are willing to provide you with a space to write they can receive the kudos of having a writer-in-residence, whose remit may be to raise awareness about their work. This is especially effective for NGOs such as charities—being the writer-in-residence for an environmental charity can be a profoundly motivating and validating, as one becomes a kind of ambassador for the chosen cause.

Alternatively, if you would prefer to avoid such a public role and simply want dedicated writing time away from the distractions of one's home, work, etc., then a Writing Retreat may be more appropriate—there are many host organisations around the world, and one simply needs to do a thorough search to find one that suits you and is within your means. Occasionally, such retreats offer bursaries, or one can apply for a grant through an art development agency to receive the support required.

If one is confident in public speaking (or willing to development these skills, perhaps through a mentorship programme) one can enter spoken word competitions such as poetry and short fiction 'slams', and modern eisteddfodau (creative competitions in many artforms, which take place across the Welsh diaspora and beyond). Winning one of these can provide a very empowering platform—a launchpad for a professional career, even. By becoming a 'City Laureate', or 'Bard' one is given the mandate to be the spokesperson for their chosen community and most heartfelt causes. The way one is expected to manifest this may be enshrined in the self-penned artistic 'manifesto' submitted as part of the contest, or in the terms and conditions of the role. It is a chance to engage with a wide cross-section of the public and to inspire up-and-coming talent and future generations.

A Potential Harvest

This book has discussed many different frames and guiding principles with the intention that diversity is far more resilient (and interesting) than a monoculture. There is no single way to write an ecofiction narrative, (as these chapters, and the following **Interviews** show) and the potential writer—having reflected upon the cross-section offered here and conducted their own explorations—can devise a methodology aligned to their specific ethical and aesthetic sensibilities.

To offer a final potential set of principles I would like to share these ergodic guidelines from games researcher, Chloé Germaine, who developed 'A framework for evaluating "nature" games' (2022) that draws upon the work of Sicart (2014) and the MDA framework (Hunicke et al. 2004). It offers some useful suggestions for writers of ecofiction too. One merely needs to change 'players' to 'readers:'

1. That they engage players with the moral considerability of more-than-human beings, inclusive of 'individual' organisms, however contingent that individuality, to whole ecosystems, without erasing difference.
2. That they extend concepts of sociality and agency beyond the human.
3. That they explore the ways that agency is distributed across networks and assemblages, rather than being a property held by an individual. Indeed, I contend that distributed agency is a necessary condition for solidarity between lifeforms.
4. That they disclose collaboration as a fundamental condition for the development of life.
5. That they complicate neat distinctions between human and 'natural' systems. (2022: 151)

Some may find such guidelines too prescriptive, but Germaine's criteria are all important factors to consider in works that seek to *genuinely* engage with ecological concepts, and aspire to permeate that thinking through every aspect of the novel—rather than just use 'nature' or the multifarious crises we face, as a merely scenic or topical backdrop.

By developing an organic creative practice—one in harmonious alignment with life-nourishing and regenerative principles, and mutually supportive systems the rhizomatic writer builds in resilience and sustainability into their writing and writing life. A key benefit of this methodology of mindfulness and eco-responsibility is to one's own wellbeing. And this ripples out into one's community and ecosystem. Collectively, this can have a positive influence on the biosphere as a whole. Writers, readers, agents, editors, booksellers, and all those involved in the production, dissemination, and consumption of ecofiction can have a positive impact. Together, our words can change the world.

MYCELIA: Connections to Other Writers, Texts, and Resources

- Accidental Gods podcast: https://accidentalgods.life/.
- Amazing Writing Residencies to Apply for in 2023 (INT): https://blog.kotobee.com/writing-residencies-2023/.
- Apples and Snakes: https://applesandsnakes.org/.
- Blue Moose small press: https://bluemoosebooks.com/.
- Bomb magazine quarterly round-up of residencies (mainly US): https://bombmagazine.org/articles/fellowships-residencies2023/.
- British Fantasy Society: https://britishfantasysociety.org/.
- British Science Fiction Association: https://www.bsfa.co.uk/.
- Bush Retreats for Eco-Writers (AUS): https://thebrewnetwork.org/.
- Chelsea Green: https://www.chelseagreen.com/.
- Dostoyevsky Wannabe: https://www.dostoyevskywannabe.com/.
- Earth Day: https://www.earthday.org/.
- Emergence podcast: https://emergencemagazine.org/podcast/.
- Fantastic Fungi: https://fantasticfungi.com/.
- Hawkwood College artist residencies: https://www.hawkwoodcollege.co.uk/artist-residency/.
- Hedgespoken small press: https://hedgespokenpress.com/.
- Literature Works: https://literatureworks.org.uk/.
- Little Toller small press: https://www.littletoller.co.uk/.
- National Association of Writers in Education: https://www.nawe.co.uk/.
- National Centre for Writing residency opportunities: https://nationalcentreforwriting.org.uk/residencies/residency-opportunities/.
- Peepal Tree small press: https://www.peepaltreepress.com/home.
- Unique and Inspiring International Writing Residencies (INT): https://aspiringauthor.com/resources/international-writing-residencies/.
- Valemon the Bear—myth in the age of the anthropocene—Martin Shaw: https://emergencemagazine.org/feature/valemon-the-bear/.

SPORES: Writing Activities

- Design a community project—start by creating a Venn diagram of your core interests/passions. Where these overlap is your USP as a writer. Design a project based upon these shared aspects. Consider the community it would serve: what would they get out of it? Look for a venue. Apply for a small community grant to help support it. Publicise it: create a poster, draft a press release, create a photo opportunity to launch it, etc. Spread the word on social media. Plan each session carefully, allowing time for spontaneity and the unexpected. Cater to the needs of your group—make them feel comfortable, welcome, and appreciated. Celebrate them.
- Hybrid forms—in this activity you are encouraged to consider hybrid forms, e.g. ficto-criticism (a blend of fiction and non-fiction exploring ideas in a critical, self-reflexive way); or a podcast/audio drama blending ecology and storytelling. Challenge yourself to create a piece of writing/an episode, etc., in this hybrid form. Perhaps you will have to research beyond your area of knowledge, or learn how to use a new piece of software. Look out for training opportunities and advice, e.g. there is a load of free information and guidance on how to set up and run a podcast. As with any form you are attempting, study a cross-section of successful examples. What works? What would you do differently?
- Creative ecosystems—start making a list of key organisations, websites, and initiatives. Join at least one subject-specific, or genre-specific organisation, or network. Reach out and make contact. Participate in forums; attend conferences; and contribute to journals or zines. Have a voice, a presence, volunteer, contribute, and enjoy feeling part of a community of intent.
- Finding your niche—after researching the above, see if you can identify any gaps in the 'ecosystem'. Is there a particular genre, issue, and/or demographic that is not being represented? Consider creating your own network, or platform for yourself and creative kindred spirits. This could be a Discord forum, a new website, a podcast, or some other platform. Promote through social media, make it friendly and welcoming, solicit submissions, post regular new content, and nurture it like a good gardener.

References

Barnard, Josie. 2019. *The Multimodal Writer: Creative Writing Across Genres and Media*. Red Globe Press.

Bey, Hakim, 1985. *Chaos: The Broadsheets of Ontological Anarchism*. Weehawken, New Jersey: Grim Reaper Press. Available from: https://theanarchistlibrary.org/library/hakim-bey-t-a-z-the-temporary-autonomous-zone-ontological-anarchy-poeticterrorism(Accessed 9 July 2024).

Blake, William. 1988. (1804–1820) Jerusalem, Plate 10, lines 2–21, cited in *Blake: The Complete Poetry & Prose*, ed. Erdman, David V. New York, NY: Anchor Books/Doubleday.

Cirillo, Francesco. n.d. *Pomodoro Technique*. https://francescocirillo.com/products/the-pomodoro-technique (Accessed 12 July 2023).

Deleuze, Gilles, and Félix. Guattari. 1988. *A Thousand Plateaus: Capitalism and schizophrenia*. London: Bloomsbury.

Duncan, David James, 2023. *Sun House*. New York: Little Brown.

Fox, Nick. n.d. *New Materialism*. https://globalsocialtheory.org/topics/new-materialism/ (Accessed 12 July 2023).

Germaine, Chloé. 2022. 'Nature' Games in a Time of Climate Crisis. In *Material Games Studies: A Philosophy of Analogue Play*, Germaine, Chloé and Paul Wake, eds. London: Bloomsbury.

Hughes, Bettany. 2017. *Istanbul: A Tale of Three Cities*. London: Weidenfeld & Nicolson.

Hunicke, Robin, Marc LeBlanc, and Robert Zubek. 2004. MDA: A Formal Approach to Game Design and Game Research. Northwestern University. https://users.cs.northwestern.edu/~hunicke/MDA.pdf (Accessed 19 July 2023).

Hyde, Lewis. 2006 [1983]. *The Gift: How the Creative Spirit Transforms the World*. London: Canongate.

Kimmerer, Robin Wall, 2003. *Gathering Moss: a natural and cultural history of mosses*. London: Penguin.

Kimmerer, Robin Wall. 2013. *Braiding Sweetgrass: Indigenous Wisdom, Scientific Knowledge and the Teachings of Plants*. London: Penguin.

Raworth, Kate. 2017. *Doughnut Economics: Seven Ways to Think Like a 21st-Century Economist*. London: Cornerstone.

Rayner, Alan. 1997. *Degrees of Freedom: Living in Dynamic Boundaries*. London: Imperial College Press.

Manwaring, Kevan, ed. 2003. *Writing the Land: An Anthology of Natural Words*. Bath: Awen Publications.

Manwaring, Kevan, ed. 2023. *Green Words: An Anthology of Natural Words from West Dorset*. Bridport: Salt House Press.

Rayner, Alan. 2006. Alan Rayner on Inclusionality, Boundaries and Space. Recorded by Jack Whitehead. *Youtube*. https://youtu.be/yVa7FUIA3W8 (Accessed 12 July 2023).

Sheldrake, Merlin. 2020. *Entangled Life: How Fungi Make Our Worlds, Change Our Minds, and Shape Our Futures*. London: Bodley Head.

Sicart, M. 2014. *Play Matters*. Cambridge, MA: The MIT Press.

Söylemez, Hasan, director. 2020. *Tenere*. n.p. https://www.waterbear.com/watch/tenere (Accessed 13 April 2023).

Strand, Sophie, 2022. *The Flowering Wand: Rewilding the Sacred Masculine: Lunar Kings, Trans-species Magicians, and Rhizomatic Harpists.* Rochester, Vermont: Inner Traditions.

The British Academy. 2022. *Understanding Digital Poverty and Inequality in the UK*. https://www.thebritishacademy.ac.uk/publications/understanding-digital-poverty-and-inequality-in-the-uk/ (Accessed 12 July 2023).

Vaughan-Lee, Emmanuel, 2024. Sun House: Interview with David James Duncan. *Emergence Magazine*. 27 June 2024. Available from: https://emergencemagazine.org/interview/sun-house/?utm_source=Emergence+Magazine&utm_campaign=9828a089e9-Emergence%E2%80%9420240707&utm_medium=email&utm_term=0_73186f6259-9828a089e9-41261777 (Accessed 9 July 2024).

Part III

Interview

9

Interviews

Adam Connor

Adam Connor is a former physicist and former child who likes writing stories and building unlikely, poorly thought through gadgets with his sons. He started his career as a physicist, building part of the Large Hadron Collider in CERN. He has also sold encyclopaedias in Chicago, worked for an investment bank, taught physics in Sudan, fitted emergency Wi-Fi in the refugee camps in Greece, and now works as an engineering manager in the Google Research team. He lives in Hertfordshire with his partner, two sons, and a dog named Rosie. FFI:

http://aconnors.com

How do you define your writing? Ecofiction? Solarpunk? Hopepunk? Or something else?

I personally like the term: Cli-Fi. But that's mostly because I like SciFi as a genre, but the publisher seemed to want to avoid the term SciFi so it became a "science inspired thriller", and Cli-Fi feels like a good compromise.

What examples of work have you written that explore environmental issues?

My debut YA thriller: *The Girl Who Broke The Sea*.

Do you decide to write about a particular issue first, or do you start with a character, a scene, an image, etc., and then the environmental issues emerge?

I started with the character and the situation, a parental break-up. It's happened to a few friends, where parents split up and this forces a house-move –/ a double-whammy of upheaval for kids. So then I looked for the worst possible place somebody would be forced to move to, and hit on a deep-sea mining rig. It was only when I started researching about the deep-sea in order to bring a bit more colour and depth to the story that I learned about the issues of deep-sea mining for the first time, and that shaped the whole dynamic (and ultimately the plot) of the book. I didn't realise I was writing Cli-Fi until I was a couple of drafts in, but when I did, it gave the book much more purpose.

Did you need to undertake research on environmental issues for your writing?

Yes. I started just with reading summaries and articles online. Deep-sea mining gets very little attention given the level of potential damage that might soon be caused, but there are plenty of good overviews online. As I got nearer to finishing I started to become aware of the gaps in my knowledge so I started searching for academic papers on the subject. A few names were coming up regularly so I reached out and a few individuals were kind enough to chat to me and let me pick their brains for a bit.

Do you think there are 'conflicts of interest' between didactics and aesthetics—between wanting to convey a message and wanting to tell a story—and if so, how do you navigate them as a writer?

A book needs to engage, and we do that through character and story. If a book fails to engage then you accomplish nothing. In earlier drafts I did the typical thing of putting in too much didactics, wanting to show-off all my hard research. But when I went back over it they stuck out and really jarred. Especially with my book being teen/YA you just can't get away with character's educating each other. There are few well-known tricks: you can get away with a bit more exposition if something else is happening at the same time. But mostly, you have to bake the message into the whole shape of the story, not have the characters spout wise words at just the right time.

Do the arts have a part to play in the Climate Crisis, and if so in what way?

Completely. Stories (books, films, but all forms of art) are important because they guide us in what is worthy of our attention in the world. It's not about "raising awareness", you can do that with a news article. It's about affecting the way people think and feel. I don't think any single piece does that in one go, but incrementally, once you've read a number of ecofiction stories you'll start to think differently. With the deep-sea it's especially important—we're land-dwelling, anthropocentric, fruit-eaters, the deep-sea is very hard for us to connect with. If all TV does is show the deep-sea as a dark void filled with fish with giant teeth, it's no wonder we don't emotionally connect with it, and that makes it hard to care when we talk about the destruction deep-sea mining might wreak. I wanted the deep-sea in my book to be a place of emotional discovery and connection, I hope that that's encouraging readers to feel closer to the deep-sea, more connected to it, and I hope that ultimately they'll care more about deep-sea mining as a result.

Who or what inspires you as a writer—people, places, publications, etc.?

I tend always to be drawn to the idea first. As a former physicist turned software engineer I tend to read a lot of technical documents, research papers, etc., and there's always germs of ideas buried in the most mundane of articles… They tend to swill around in my subconscious for a while until I can connect them with a particular setting or character and the whole thing starts to turn into a story.

Are you working on any new 'ecofiction' projects?

One of the arguments in favour of deep-sea mining (there are plenty of counter-arguments) is that land-based mining has both an environmental and *human* impact. So researching *The Girl Who Broke The Sea* I started to get interested in the human impact of mining. I've kind of an outline in my head out how that collides with a couple of other things and becomes a story, but I'm not very far through yet.

A. E. Copenhaver

A.E. Copenhaver is a writer, editor, climate interpreter, and science communicator. He was born in Bellevue, Washington, and has lived most of his life in Carmel, California. His debut novel, *My Days of Dark Green Euphoria*—winner of the Siskiyou Prize for New Environmental Literature—was published by Ashland Creek Press in 2022. You can find links to all his fiction and non-fiction writing and latest news at his website: www.aecopenhaver.com. You can also learn more about his work with the Study of Environmental Arctic Change by visiting SEARCHArcticScience.org.

How do you define your writing? Ecofiction? Solarpunk? Hopepunk? Or something else?

Most broadly I'd call my first novel eco-fiction, meaning ecological fiction, or a story that engages with ecological themes. Narrowing that I'd say the book explores climate grief and 'solastalgia,' a term created by environmental philosopher Glenn Albrecht. Solastalgia defines the feelings of sorrow, loss, and despair that come with witnessing (or imagining in the inevitable near-future) the negative changes to or destruction of one's home environment. Albrecht coined this term not only to acknowledge our current ecological crises, but also to suggest new linguistic pathways to help us bring into being the world we all need. My first novel, *My Days of Dark Green Euphoria*, references a number of Albrecht's proposed words and phrases (or versions of those words) as a nod to Albrecht's work and as a means of recognizing that even as we are crippled with despair, we can hearten ourselves with visions of a just, compassionate, and symbiotic existence on Earth. Albrecht refers to our future world unfettered by ecological crises as the 'Symbiocene,' to mark the era when humans learn to live in true symbiosis with the living world. For me, that transformation—from where we are now to where we want to be—begins with language.

To that end, some readers have asked me what the title of my book means, and I don't have a good (concise) answer! 'Dark green euphoria' is a permutation of Bruce Sterling's phrase, 'dark euphoria,' which first appeared in his 2009 address to the Reboot 11 Conference. Sterling describes dark euphoria as "what the twenty-teens feels like. Things are just falling apart, you can't believe the possibilities, it's like anything is possible, but you never realized you're going to have to dread it so much. It's like a leap into the unknown. You're falling toward earth at nine hundred kilometers an hour and then you realize there's no earth there. That's a dark euphoria feeling. It's the cultural temperament of the coming decade."

For the main character of my novel, Cara Foster, 'dark green euphoria' and her experience of that sensation could be, at least, some combination of two concepts: the feeling she has when she's plummeting deeper into her climate grief and, for inexplicable, unspeakable reasons, she relishes the chaos and despair of that hopelessness and apathy. And, two: the potent cocktail of hope-joy-courage Cara experiences when an unwavering vision comes through and reveals the peaceful, abundant, symbiotic world we have the power to create on Earth.

What examples of work have you written that explore environmental issues?

In my first job out of college I served as an editorial assistant with the former travel editor of NBC (Peter Greenberg, who currently is the CBS News Travel Editor) where I had the chance to research and ghostwrite a number of chapters for his *New York Times*-bestselling book, *Don't Go There! The Travel Detective's Guide to the Must Miss Places of the World*. My three chapters explored the 'stinkiest places' in the world, cities suffering from horrible traffic pollution, along with a number of other environmental concerns. In researching the places with the foulest stench, I had the privilege of engaging with community members who lived next to industrial agriculture operations–chicken and hog factories, specifically. I spoke with some incredible people who have been voicing their concerns for decades about the social, racial, and environmental injustices associated with factory farming—not to mention the smell. This environmental lens colors and informs my worldview.

Some years later I was hired as a staffer at Monterey Bay Aquarium, where I served alongside their field research science team for seven years. I had a dream job there: working with scientists and researchers to support operations while also sharing stories about their work and how, for example, young white sharks have a lot to say about our changing climate and warming ocean. I was beyond thrilled to have the chance to help share stories of really fascinating and important science about our global ocean, how we are all connected to it and the role that the living ocean plays as the heart of our climate system.

In my current position with the International Arctic Research Center at University of Alaska Fairbanks, I help bring together Indigenous Knowledge Holders, scientists, and policy- and decision makers to share understanding of the changing Arctic environment and how these changes affect people from local to global scales. Our organization, Study of Environmental Arctic Change (SEARCH), is funded by the National Science Foundation and works across the global Arctic. Our latest written exploration of environmental issues is called "Consequences of rapid environmental Arctic change for people" and was published as a chapter in the 2022 Arctic Report Card.

And while each component of my career might seem disparate from the creative realm of writing eco-fiction, I find each informs the others. In SEARCH we are always striving to understand when our worldviews overlap, intersect, connect, or completely diverge. What language do we use to describe and represent our understanding of the world? How can we understand each other better, in all aspects of our lives, and what stories might we tell—and in what ways—to encourage and illustrate this understanding? These are the questions that I aim to explore both in fiction and in my everyday work.

In a flash fiction piece entitled "Let Them Eat Trees," which I wrote in 2021 for the *Kirstofia Anthology*, the two main characters come from wildly different backgrounds but end up learning that seemingly forgotten stories have a way of returning, of finding new and better ways to be told.

Do you decide to write about a particular issue first, or do you start with a character, a scene, an image, etc., and then the environmental issues emerge?

My book, *My Days of Dark Green Euphoria*, started with the opening scene: the main character is spying on her boyfriend while he's in the bathroom, and she witnesses him kill a spider and then flush the spider's corpse. The hyperconscientious narrator, Cara Foster, struggling with climate grief, led the way from there—but not as I had expected. Her excoriating voice and searing judgments of everyone around her grew into satire almost immediately. So while the issues raised and explored in the book are serious realities our planet is facing in the 21st Century, Cara's characterization and response to these atrocities are often humorous or absurd (and not entirely inconsiderate to her suffering).

Did you need to undertake research on environmental issues for your writing?

Constantly. For everything. From equations that strive to describe consciousness in quantum mechanics, to how you say "I'm in love" in Portuguese, to the scientific name of every single domesticated apple variety sold in the United States in the 1860s. For my second (as yet unpublished) novel, I spent a week reading a fascinating publication from the National Park Service called "Fruitful Legacy: A Historic Context of Orchards in the United States, with Technical Information for Registering Orchards in the National Register of Historic Places." An enthralling read! As one of my dear uncles like to say, data sets you free. I'd add that data (and research) set our stories free—contrary to the idea that sticking to the facts might somehow constrain our stories, research and facts are the combusting agents I find necessary to ignite creativity. When the research begins to spill over into the life and voice of the character—that's pure delight.

Do you think there are 'conflicts of interest' between didactics and aesthetics—between wanting to convey a message and wanting to tell a story—and if so, how do you navigate them as a writer?

I recall Vladimir Nabokov being asked why he wrote *Lolita*. His response: "Why did I write *Lolita*? Why did I write any of my books, after all! For the sake of the pleasure, for the sake of the difficulty. See, I have no social purpose, no moral message. I am not a messenger, and I have no general ideas to exploit. But I like composing riddles; I like finding elegant solutions to my riddles—to those riddles that I have composed myself."

I agree with Nabokov in this sense: writing fiction is a pleasurable and satisfying enterprise for me as a writer. I always have a specific puzzle or problem that I set out to solve in the writing of any given piece, and my job is to realize that solution as elegantly as possible. If our stories are well written and fully realized, readers will engage and remember—for better or for worse. We might engage readers by thoroughly offending them, but if it's well written, then the riddle's point, purpose, and integrity remain long after those disgruntled readers slam the book shut. But if readers are slamming the book shut because the book is so poorly written they cannot bear to go on—then everyone loses, especially the reader and undoubtedly any 'message' we may or may not have hoped to get across. That said, it takes an astute and open reader to engage with a book that offers opposing or even abhorrent points of view, relative to their own. We need readers and critics to help determine whether and by how much a book fails or succeeds to meet expectations, and we need them to articulate this rationale in a meaningful way.

I dug into this concept a bit more in a recent essay published in the Climate Fiction Writers League newsletter. The essay is called, "A brief thread on 'sanctimony literature': Or, the risks and rewards of working on environmental issues while writing eco-fiction."

Do the arts have a part to play in the Climate Crisis, and if so in what way?

I've been attempting to remix the famous quotation about how people don't always remember what we say or do, but they always remember how we make them feel. Something like: People may not always remember the science or the statistics we share, but they are far more likely to remember how the stories we share make them feel...alright—it needs some work! But it's in this sense that the arts have a powerful role to play in the Climate Crisis.

How are we telling (showing) the Climate Crisis and beyond that, what can we do about it? How do the stories we choose to tell help or hinder understanding and action? Sometimes stories about shirking our responsibilities, devolving into the self-loathing of climate grief, or indulging a secret obsession to find relief from climate grief are the types of stories we need in that moment—to be reminded that we are suffering, that it's OK to suffer, and that there are better and worse ways to cope. Other stories are more triumphant, more galvanizing. Either way, we need art and storytelling as the scaffolding for our bearing witness, for finding solace, and for mustering the courage to contribute whatever we can to solutions.

Who or what inspires you as a writer—people, places, publications, etc.?

I find inspiration in nearly every kind of writing: fiction, non-fiction, poetry, criticism, academic, scientific. I always return to my first love, non-fiction, though, thanks to my Dad. Both my parents are lifelong and avid readers, so they've influenced my habits. I am also influenced and inspired by music (Enya, Grimes, Pogo, Beethoven, The Who, The Darkness), by art (Odilon Redon, Julie Heffernan, Eyvind Earle), by the scholarly journal *Ecological Citizen*, by the journal of politics and culture, *Liberties*, and anything and everything by Carol J. Adams, Vladimir Nabokov, Toni Morrison, and Richard Powers.

I am also a member of the Association for the Study of Literature and the Environment (ASLE), and I find their discussion boards thought-provoking.

In terms of non-fiction books, lately I have been making my way through the important, riveting, terrifying story of the 1921 Tulsa Race Massacre called *The Burning* by Tim Madigan.

Another epic non-fiction book I enjoyed—*The Big Burn: Teddy Roosevelt and the Fire that Saved America* by Timothy Egan, a story about the enormous wildfire that burned over 3 million acres of land between Idaho, Montana, and British Columbia in 1910.

Other favorite non-fiction books that inspire me: *In the Heart of the Sea: The Tragedy of the Whaleship Essex* by Nathanial Philbrick and *Empire of the Summer Moon: Quanah Parker and the Rise and Fall of the Comanches, the Most Powerful Indian Tribe in American History* by S.C. Gwynne.

I cannot wait to read the non-fiction book *The Wager: A Tale of Shipwreck, Mutiny and Murder* by David Grann and the novel *The Candy House* by Jennifer Egan.

I also inhaled a scholarly work recently published by UK geographer Dr. Catherine Oliver called, *Veganism, Archives, and Animals: Geographies of a Multispecies World.*

In fiction I recently read *The Rabbit Hutch* by Tess Gunty, winner of the National Book Award, and I'll say—the ending of this novel is absolute perfection. I rejoiced when I finished reading. I was also floored by the speculative epic *Appleseed* by Matt Bell. Stupendous, imaginative, and powerful writing from Matt Bell.

In poetry, I was torn from my roots and replanted in new understanding by Tiana Clark's collection, *I Can't Talk About The Trees Without The Blood.* I found Marisa Silva-Dunbar's treatment of the real life Allison Mack controversy in her poetry collection, *Allison*, absolutely flawless. I admire how Silva-Dunbar artfully remixes non-fiction writing from Mack's blog and online entries from The Frank Report to create something entirely new and profound. I regularly return to the poetry collection *Kind* by Gretchen Primack.

Are you working on any new 'ecofiction' projects?

I completed my second novel manuscript with generous support from Ashland Creek Press after my first novel won the Siskiyou Prize for New Environmental Literature: I received $1000 and two weeks' writing residency at the Sitka Center for Art & Ecology on the Pacific Coast in Otis, Oregon. With paid vacation offered by my then employer Monterey Bay Aquarium, I had the time, energy, and privilege to hide away among the fog-cloaked crags and Sitka spruce and draft 88,000 words of my second novel, which I completed just a few weeks after returning from the Sitka Center residency. This second novel is in need of a permanent home and is yet to be published, so I won't say too much. The novel could be categorized as speculative epic, eco-literature, and takes place through six characters across a few centuries of the American past, present, and near-distant future. An orchard plays a prominent role in each of the character's lives.

Ana Filomena Amaral

Novelist, historian, and translator Ana Filomena Amaral, born in Avintes, Vila Nova de Gaia, holds a Master's degree in Contemporary Economic and Social History from the Faculty of Arts of the University of Coimbra, has a postgraduate course in Documentary Sciences Mental Health/Library Science, and extensive experience as an interpreter and translator of several European languages, keeping particular contact with the German language. She created and coordinates the International Literary Festival of the Interior – Words of Fire, founded in 2018, in honour of the victims of forest fires. She is also an activist of social, cultural, and climate causes. https://pt.wikipedia.org/wiki/Ana_Filomena_Amaral

How do you define your writing? Ecofiction? Solarpunk? Hopepunk? Or something else?

I think is ecofiction, but I don't think is important that definition.

What examples of work have you written that explore environmental issues?

I wrote the world's only climate fiction trilogy called "Our Mother".

Do you decide to write about a particular issue first, or do you start with a character, a scene, an image, etc., and then the environmental issues emerge?

I decide to write a novel about the destruction of the oceans and I entitled it "The Director", when I finished I felt that I had much more to say and I decided to write a trilogy, the second novel is called "Ice" and the third one "Deserts" soon in English, Finnish and Arabic.

Did you need to undertake research on environmental issues for your writing?

Yes a lot because my area is humanistic, history precisely.

Do you think there are 'conflicts of interest' between didactics and aesthetics—between wanting to convey a message and wanting to tell a story—and if so, how do you navigate them as a writer?

In any moment of my writing I felt that conflict, but we need to be very attentive with the link between literature and science, trying to create a continuous narrative what sometimes can be challenging.

Do the arts have a part to play in the Climate Crisis, and if so in what way?

Arts play a central role in the awareness to the climate crisis because through a less scientific speech and more soft and artistic, literary one, we may reach more audience then a dry and sometimes hermetic text.

Who or what inspires you as a writer—people, places, publications, etc.?

As a writer I am inspired by everything that surrounds me, as I am a very curious person I am always asking questions and listen carefully what people say, what is happening in my neighbourhood and farer in the world. Images and feelings are very important for me.

Are you working on any new 'ecofiction' projects?

No, I think I said everything I wanted about this problem, now I am focused on political and social issues that are affecting mankind and obviously the planet too. Always fiction.

Anna M. Holmes

Anna M Holmes enjoys serving up hefty topics as easy-to-read page-turners. World-building on large canvases is her thing. Originally from New Zealand she lives in the U.K. with her Dutch partner. Visit her website to find out more about her books, links to retailers, and suggested topics for book clubs. FFI: https://www.annamholmes.com

How do you define your writing? Ecofiction? Solarpunk? Hopepunk? Or something else?

Ecofiction (Environmental thriller)

What examples of work have you written that explore environmental issues?

Blind Eye, an environmental thriller, raises awareness of the climate crisis—illegal rainforest exploitation in particular. The screenplay version of *Blind Eye* was joint winner of the 2020 Green Stories screenplay competition.

Do you decide to write about a particular issue first, or do you start with a character, a scene, an image, etc., and then the environmental issues emerge?

I started with the topic of illegal logging and protection of ecosystems. My partner is a founder member of Forest Stewardship Council (FSC)—an organisation to promote responsible forest management. I felt I was in a unique position to write this story, and judging from feedback from foresters and activists who have read *Blind Eye* I feel I have done justice to the complexity of the subject.

Did you need to undertake research on environmental issues for your writing?

A lot of research. In this I was assisted by specialists via my partner's network: foresters, environmental activists, partnership organisations. Through my own networks I received advice on UK political scenes.

Do you think there are 'conflicts of interest' between didactics and aesthetics—between wanting to convey a message and wanting to tell a story—and if so, how do you navigate them as a writer?

Some novelists forget they are storytellers and from page one their books bash you with clumsy heavy-handed didactics. Total turn-off! Foremost, I want to tell a story that makes readers engage with characters and situations and want to turn the page.

Do the arts have a part to play in the Climate Crisis, and if so in what way?

Most definitely. I have a background in arts management, and know that creative projects (film, play, book) can play a part in drawing attention to serious issues.

Who or what inspires you as a writer—people, places, publications, etc.?

I admire good writing (Amor Towles, David Mitchell, Annie Proulx amongst others). Each book I've written has been inspired by a wish to explore a topic.

Are you working on any new 'ecofiction' projects?

Since *Blind Eye* I have written a contemporary fiction, and now working on an historical fiction. But in the future…who knows. The subject matter and characters have to grab me.

Anne Morddel

Anne Morddel began as a fifth-generation, northern Californian. She worked in library and information management for over thirty years on four continents. It found expression in her drawings and children's books about the Atlantic Rainforest during her years as a school librarian in Curitiba. She now lives in France, where she has been exploring, writing, and speaking about French genealogy. She is the sole author of The French Genealogy Blog and has published some of the posts in book form as well. Most recently, she has been working on a study of Napoleon's American prisoners of war.

How do you define your writing? Ecofiction? Solarpunk? Hopepunk? Or something else?

Children's picture books.

What examples of work have you written that explore environmental issues?

The Big Field: A Child's Year Under the Southern Cross.

Do you decide to write about a particular issue first, or do you start with a character, a scene, an image, etc., and then the environmental issues emerge?

Initially, my intention was to write a children's picture book about the seasons of the year in the southern hemisphere, specifically in the Atlantic Rainforest of southern Brazil. As I interviewed people about their childhood activities in the region, environmental issues quickly became apparent and a part of the story.

Did you need to undertake research on environmental issues for your writing?

Huge amounts! Dozens of books on biology and botany. Many visits to universities and research stations. I had to properly identify all of the species I was seeing. Tree species, birds, flowers, insects, especially butterflies. As I said above, there also were interviews. I spoke to many people about how they, as children in and near the rainforest, had interacted with the nature there.

Do you think there are 'conflicts of interest' between didactics and aesthetics—between wanting to convey a message and wanting to tell a story—and if so, how do you navigate them as a writer?

For me, the story must always come first.

Do the arts have a part to play in the Climate Crisis, and if so in what way?

Absolutely. Tell the truth; show a way forward.

Who or what inspires you as a writer—people, places, publications, etc.?

Strangely, I am initially inspired by a sense of justice. The children of southern Brazil have a right to books and stories about their own nature, for example, or, that many people have a right for their stories to be heard, or that we all have a right to an unpolluted world. I am old enough to remember when the fight was about something much more tangible and measurable, and therefore less debatable than climate change - pollution, which is what causes climate change.

Are you working on any new 'ecofiction' projects?

No. At the moment, I am writing a work for adults on maritime history.

Anthony Nanson

Anthony Nanson is a writer, storyteller, editor, and the publisher of the small press Awen Publications. His publications include *Exotic Excursions* (2008), *Words of Re-enchantment* (2011) (Storytelling World Award), *Gloucestershire Folk Tales* (2012) (Storytelling World Award), *Deep Time* (2015), *Storytelling and Ecology* (2021) (Storytelling World Award and Association of American Publishers Prose Award), *Storytelling for Nature Connection* (2022) (co-editor), and *Gloucestershire Ghost Tales* (2015) and *Gloucestershire Folk Tales for Children* (2020) (co-author). He taught creative writing at Bath Spa University for 18 years and in 2023 completed a PhD by publication at the University of Gloucestershire. FFI: https://nansondeeptime.wordpress.com/

How do you define your writing? Ecofiction? Solarpunk? Hopepunk? Or something else?

Fiction. My fiction doesn't easily sit inside particular categories of genre or subgenre. There is even an element of blending between fiction and memoir. I describe my general approach to creative work as 'ecobardic'.

What examples of work have you written that explore environmental issues?

The novel *Deep Time*; most of the short stories in my collection *Exotic Excursions*; 'The Dead Are Not Dead' (in *Ariadne's Thread*); 'The Migrant Maid' (in *Ballad Tales*); plus various original stories composed for oral performance and included as scripts or summaries in *Words of Re-enchantment* and *Storytelling and Ecology*.

Do you decide to write about a particular issue first, or do you start with a character, a scene, an image, etc., and then the environmental issues emerge?

My ideas for fiction usually begin with a setting—an environment, if you will—and then characters, plot, and themes emerge from that.

Did you need to undertake research on environmental issues for your writing?

Yes.

Do you think there are 'conflicts of interest' between didactics and aesthetics—between wanting to convey a message and wanting to tell a story—and if so, how do you navigate them as a writer?

Yes. *An Ecobardic Manifesto*, which I co-authored, conveys some of my thinking about this, as do some sections of *Words of Re-enchantment* and *Storytelling and Ecology*. I think that it is possible to write fiction that has 'commitment' without compromising its quality as art. One key principle is to bring to the writing a commitment of concern about the issues but to let go of the wish to control the impact of the writing upon the reader. A deeper conflict of interest is that between aesthetics and commitment, on the one hand, and commercial imperatives that are hostile to both.

Do the arts have a part to play in the Climate Crisis, and if so in what way?

I do not think the climate crisis can be separated from the larger multi-stranded ecological crisis. But, yes, absolutely. *An Ecobardic Manifesto* explains the contribution the arts can make to responding to this crisis.

Who or what inspires you as a writer—people, places, publications, etc.?

Places, other creative people, books, experiences, ideals, spontaneous inspiration, and especially the long-standing myth of earthly paradise.

Are you working on any new 'ecofiction' projects?

Yes. I'm writing a novel with an ecological theme and set in the South Pacific.

April Doyle

April Doyle is a writer, tutor, and editor who lives in rural Kent with her family. She has been teaching creative writing since 2012. April's short stories have been published in women's magazines in the UK and Australia, and her short story *Elsewhere* was published in an anthology *Tales From Elsewhere* in 2016. Her short story *Rise on the Wings* was long-listed for the 2019 Mslexia Short Story competition. *Hive* was shortlisted for the 2019 Exeter Novel Prize.

How do you define your writing? Ecofiction? Solarpunk? Hopepunk? Or something else?

I think of *Hive* as Climate Fiction or Ecofiction—one reader described it as an Eco-Thriller and I'm happy with that too. When I was writing it I didn't know about these definitions and I first thought of it as Speculative Fiction, and the publisher has defined it as Science Fiction.

What examples of work have you written that explore environmental issues?

Apart from *Hive* an earlier (unpublished) novel centres around a group of characters who volunteer to live on the on the island of Skomer in West Wales to support the conservation work there. Several of my short stories circle around environmental issues too.

Do you decide to write about a particular issue first, or do you start with a character, a scene, an image, etc., and then the environmental issues emerge?

In *Hive* the environmental issue of pollinator decline was the driver for my writing. For my earlier work (see above) I think the issues are very much woven into the stories but in a way that is less up front: characters living in a landscape which is affected by climate change and biodiversity loss but it's not as crucial to the plot.

Did you need to undertake research on environmental issues for your writing?

I made a note of what I needed to research as I was writing the first draft of *Hive*, then as I was working on the second draft I sketched in the details I'd discovered during my research. A lot of the groundwork was already covered because I'd been taking an interest in pollinator decline for some time before I started writing the novel.

Do you think there are 'conflicts of interest' between didactics and aesthetics—between wanting to convey a message and wanting to tell a story—and if so, how do you navigate them as a writer?

For me, the subject of pollinator decline had to play a central part in the novel. Some of the feedback I had from early readers indicated that they felt the story was too issue-led and not focused enough on the characters and their stories. I addressed this in subsequent edits, and I'm very happy with the final version, having achieved the best balance I could.

Do the arts have a part to play in the Climate Crisis, and if so in what way?

I think so. The arts have a part to play in exploring all aspects of what it means to be living in these unsettling times.

Who or what inspires you as a writer—people, places, publications, etc.?

Lot of writers. A few months ago I read Barbara Kingsolver's astonishing *Demon Copperhead*, and I'm still thinking about it. I think will live with me for a long time (her books always do). Mary Oliver's poetry. Ursula le Guin's novels and essays. Nora Ephron, an all-round genius. Stephen King's *On Writing*, Anne Lamott's *Bird by Bird*, Elizabeth Gilbert's *Big Magic*. Landscapes inspire me, and all kinds of artworks. More and more these days I'm thinking about noticing small details and how they can inspire a response (which prompts me to add the novels of Ann Tyler to my list. Her little character details have always been an inspiration).

Are you working on any new 'ecofiction' projects?

My current novel in progress is not an ecofiction project, however I'm usually tinkering around with a short story or two, and these often have an ecofiction flavour. Once I've finished my work in progress I'll be going back to revisit the novel I set on Skomer—it's on my mind because of the David Attenborough *Wild Isles* documentary and I'd like to see if I can rework it.

Austin Aslan

Austin Aslan was elected to be Flagstaff Vice Mayor in November 2022. Austin was born and raised in Arizona. He earned a Master's degree in Conservation Biology at the University of Hawaii, after receiving a BS from the University of Arizona in Wildlife Biology and Natural Resource Management. His research on rare Hawaiian plants earned him a National Science Foundation Graduate Research Fellowship. Austin's debut Random House novel, *The Islands at the End of the World*, was named a Best Book of 2014 by Kirkus Reviews. It was ranked by *The Guardian* as a top-ten climate fiction read, and is listed by BookRiot as a top 100 must-read book in the category of young adult science fiction. Austin's environmental adventure series, *The Endangereds*, co-authored with Philippe Cousteau Jr., was long-listed for the Green Earth Book Award.

How do you define your writing? Ecofiction? Solarpunk? Hopepunk? Or something else?

Islands has been widely characterized by others as "eco-fiction" "eco-thriller" and "Cli-Fi". I honestly wasn't so sure about the "eco-thriller" label at first, but I quickly embraced it nonetheless. I had never heard this term when I wrote the novel, so I certainly wasn't writing with this designation in mind. I'm still not 100% sure what the label means, actually, but to the extent that it might entail a plotline that is driven by, or affected by, a problem or crisis involving the natural world, I suppose *Islands* can loosely be defined this way. The Hawaiian Islands are more of a character than they are a set of places in this book. And the islands are innately imbued with such a great natural presence that any crisis involving them will evoke "eco-thriller" sentiments. In many ways this book channels a "Human vs Nature" dynamic, but I balk just a little bit with the "eco" aspect because this story and the disaster that sets the plot in motion aren't caused by, or motivated by, nature per se. (Unless an extra-terrestrial entity akin to a space turtle is considered natural.) Geography and poor human planning are the culprits.

When I set out to write *Islands*, I thought to myself, "Everybody knows what happens at the end of the world in New York and LA, but what would a global disaster mean for Islanders?" 95% of Hawaii's food is imported every day. *Ninety-five percent!* The islands are home to 1.5 million people. If things got tough there, what would they eat? Where would they flee?

I have an even harder time with co-opting the term "Cli-Fi" for this novel. Climate and weather and global warming and climate change have nothing to do with this story. However, at its heart, *Islands* is a cautionary tale about human hubris and too much reliance on technology and globalization to make our world work, and it begs for a new vision for a Hawai'i that is much more self-sustaining and locally operated than it currently is. I think these labels were in their infancy still in 2014, and were being cast widely about so as not to miss anything exciting that might help the cause. ISLANDS benefited from this wide net.

My *Endangereds* series with Philippe Cousteau Jr. was long-listed for the Green Earth Book Award, so is naturally categorized and recognized as some sort of environmentally-aware book, but I'm not familiar with any settled-upon "definition" for the series, other than maybe what the NYTimes called it in their book review: "puts endangered wildlife front and center" and "combines ecological thrills with a simple, vital message: Protect biodiversity and work together."

What examples of work have you written that explore environmental issues?

I think this is pretty well covered above. Though I will add I tried my best to maintain my brand as an "eco author" even with my *Turbo Racer* series, which is more about hi-tech vehicles and high-octane action, if you know what I mean. I focused as much as I could on making my settings "eco-rich" with biodiversity, beautiful landscapes, and an eye toward the balance of nature being important to the health of even the racing industry. My settings are epic and cinematic, and both books are set in places I've visited. Book Two has a particular emphasis on South America and Antarctica. I wanted their ecosystems to focus prominently into the narrative and plot, and worked to do so discreetly lest my editor balk that I was veering too heavily into an arena of awareness that would turn off or bore reluctant readers, which were a focus of ours.

Do you decide to write about a particular issue first, or do you start with a character, a scene, an image, etc., and then the environmental issues emerge?

For *Islands* and its sequel, *Girl at the Center of the World*, the story emerged first, and the environmental themes arose naturally and quickly as I sat down to write. For *The Endangereds* books, the exact opposite.

Did you need to undertake research on environmental issues for your writing?

I'm always looking things up and doing my homework to make sure I'm accurate. But my background in the sciences prepared me to have a general working knowledge of the topics I tackle.

Do you think there are 'conflicts of interest' between didactics and aesthetics—between wanting to convey a message and wanting to tell a story—and if so, how do you navigate them as a writer?

I lived in Hilo (pronounced HEE-lo), on the Big Island, when I was getting my Master's degree in Tropical Conservation Biology. My field sites were high up on the forested slopes of Mauna Loa Volcano. I was coming home from a rainy day of doing pollination experiments with rare Hawaiian flowers and I drove down through the clouds and suddenly had a great, clear view of the ocean surrounding the island. I was struck by how alone and isolated the Hawaiian Islands were (this is something that people in Hawaii think about frequently, and it wasn't a new thought for me, either). The idea popped into my head that it would be really interesting to set a post-apocalyptic story on the isolated Hawaiian Islands, and the story and characters just started flowing out of me like lava! My master's program and my background in science helped me immensely in the writing of my book, mostly in terms of identifying the powerful themes of interdependency and sustainability, which undergird the entire story. While my background helped to steer the book in certain thematic directions, I didn't allow the scientist in me to overpower the story that I was telling. I wanted to keep my training out of the way of the narrative that was unfolding as best I could. The quickest way to kill a good plot and deaden great characters is to start using them as bullhorns for specific agendas. My main character is a 16-year-old girl. It wouldn't make sense for her to feel and sound like a scientist. I was able to use Leilani's father (who is a professor of ecology at UH-Hilo) as my nearest proxy for letting my science background show through. However, I was still intentionally careful not to abuse that conduit. I'm lucky, because I think the general "scientist" can't de-couple their training from their voice, and that's why there are so few successful scientist-novelists. I hope I can be one.

Do the arts have a part to play in the Climate Crisis, and if so in what way?

The brief answer, from my perspective, is that fiction writers have a GINORMOUS role in calling attention to environmental issues.

Here's the deal: most scientists are actually very uncomfortable taking a stand on any issue. Most scientists want to generate data and conduct experiments and solve mysteries and answer questions—and they want to stop right there. The moment they're asked to place a value judgment on a finding, or take sides in a political debate, they get very squeamish. Most scientists (too many, in my view) abdicate their responsibility to call for action when their findings demand attention. They'll leave that work to others, to "boundary organizations" and "advocates" and "non-profits" and "activists." But many of these groups don't have loud enough voices or strong enough followings to gain critical momentum on issues. This is where popular entertainers like novelists or movie directors and their ilk can step in and carry weight that would otherwise be very heavy lifting for grassroots advocates. Stories are POWERFUL. Story telling is how people listen and learn new things. Data and facts and figures go in one ear and right out the other. These days, we're all so hardwired to reinforce things we already "know" and to ignore anyone saying something that contradicts our "knowledge" and our personal experiences. But here's the key: story telling *adds to our personal experiences!* Without knowing it, we absorb and assimilate what other people and characters are going through. So, yeah, we novelists have a disproportionate share of the burden in calling attention to issues, whether they be environmental or social or cultural or whatever. The key is for our ideas to infiltrate critical minds in the smoothest possible way. As I mentioned above, I think that's best done not by proclaiming the facts and the truth as we know them, but by getting out of the way of our own training and allowing our stories to speak for themselves, out of the vast array of experiences that our readers already carry with them when they turn to a story.

Who or what inspires you as a writer—people, places, publications, etc.?

That's always hard to define for me. I love beautiful nature writing, but don't read much of it. I'm influenced by Barbara Kingsolver, Paulo Baccigalupi, Barry Lopez, Cormac McCarthy, Ursula K. Le Guin, and others whose prose always seems most beautiful to me when focused on describing landscapes and people's relationships with them.

I'm even more inspired and influenced by places. I focus my writing on places I've been. Setting descriptions need to be as sensual as possible. Maybe it's my lack of imagination, but I find it extremely advantageous to write about places I've personally visited. A real sense of authenticity comes out of that that readers see and appreciate. I like to think it helps others to experience and value locations they don't already know—and maybe they go on to help protect them even though they haven't been there.

Are you working on any new 'ecofiction' projects?

I have completed a new environmentally themed time-travel story for middle-grade readers. To risk giving it all away, *The Occurrences at Meteor Loop* is set in the beautiful Sonoran Desert outside a fictional, Tucson-like town, and involves stopping a plot by aliens to terraform Earth toward their own designs by using our own polluting ways to their advantage. This book has not yet found a home.

David Barker

David Barker is the author of three Climate Fiction thrillers—*The Gold Trilogy* (Bloodhound Books)—and gives talks on water shortages and climate change. Prior to writing full time, David worked in the city as an economist where his fascination with commodity shortages began. He attended the Faber Academy in 2014 and, more recently, completed a scriptwriting course with the National Writing Centre. A trilogy of children's adventures about a boy caught up in a future Civil War in Britain was published in late 2023. FFI: https://davidbarkerauthor.co.uk

How do you define your writing? Ecofiction? Solarpunk? Hopepunk? Or something else?

Cli-fi (short for climate fiction)

What examples of work have you written that explore environmental issues?

The Gold Trilogy (*Blue Gold, Rose Gold, White Gold*), all thrillers set in the near future during a world war for water.

Do you decide to write about a particular issue first, or do you start with a character, a scene, an image, etc., and then the environmental issues emerge?

I started with a central theme of conflict over the precious resource of freshwater and then built a world around that, before honing in on some characters to show that world to the reader.

Did you need to undertake research on environmental issues for your writing?

Yes, I had done lots of work on the economics of commodity markets during the late noughties and came across several references to potential shortages of, and conflict over, freshwater in future decades due to demographic and climate change pressures. I decided to use that as the setting for my story and did further research into the technologies we might adopt to overcome these shortages of water.

Do you think there are 'conflicts of interest' between didactics and aesthetics—between wanting to convey a message and wanting to tell a story—and if so, how do you navigate them as a writer?

For sure, readers get bored of stories that repeatedly bash them over the head about a message. So, in my stories, the world war for water is a backdrop to the adventure but one that proves crucial to the plot. It drives the central conflict in the story. It acts as a warning to what might happen if we don't look after our freshwater supplies, but doesn't tell anybody what to do about that.

Do the arts have a part to play in the Climate Crisis, and if so in what way?

They can be used to show what the future might look like if we do nothing about the crisis. But they can also (and indeed should) give people hope by showing protagonists and/or technology making a difference. Too much gloom leads people to give up and decide it's not worth trying to change their own behaviour.

Who or what inspires you as a writer—people, places, publications, etc.?

People for sure. Aside from the high-profile names like Greta, there are many examples of people I personally know striving for less plastic pollution, cleaning up beaches, raising awareness of things we can do in our daily lives to contribute to a better future. I also love reading publications like *Circle of Blue* and *MIT Technology Review*, which highlight advancements in technology that might help solve our crisis. And I am a keen supporter of charities such as Water Aid that directly address the issue of a lack of freshwater in the poorest parts of the world.

Are you working on any new 'ecofiction' projects?

Yes, a contemporary fantasy children's story about a girl who joins up with King Arthur to save the world from three buried giants who have been awoken by climate change.

Denise Baden

Denise Baden is a professor of Sustainable Practice at University of Southampton. She is particularly keen in exploring innovative ways to maximise engagement and impact from research. She runs the Green Stories Writing competitions that challenge writers to embed green solutions in their stories. Current research interests include ways to motivate sustainable practices, positive role models and solutions-based approaches, climate change communication, sustainable business models such as the sharing/access economy and comparative approaches via her research in Cuba. Her most recent research explores the use of fiction to promote green behaviours and her eco-themed rom-com *Habitat Man* was published in Autumn 202. In 2022, she compiled an anthology of 24 inspirational short stories called *No More Fairy Tales: Stories to Save Our Planet*.

FFI: www.greenstories.org.uk https://www.dabaden.com/habitat-man/

What's your earliest memory of a natural place or the presence of nature?

I suppose my garden growing up. I was always one who liked to explore. Any little alleyway or behind any shops, I'd find little patches of wildlife and me and my friend would make camp in a tree or under a bush. I came across some frogs as well. We had a pond and, I mean, I look back now with shame, but as a kid you don't think about it. So, I took a couple, and kept them hidden in the house in the bath. And then I put them in a sort of tank in the sideboard. I remember once one of them was perfectly silhouetted, jumping in front of the television going ribbet.

When did you first become aware of environmental issues? Did you have any formative experiences or eco epiphanies that focalize your concern?

OK, so it actually was a novelist. Do you know Ben Elton?... I read *Stark*. There was this bit where he had these little vignettes and the one that got me was Dave, who's the water birth. And shortly after being born, he died, and it turned out Dave was a dolphin caught in this new fishing net.

And I thought, alright, I should get dolphin friendly tuna. And it was my first idea that fiction could be a way to enlighten you about things. You know, I wouldn't have watched a nature documentary, really. I found them a bit violent. I couldn't cope with the red in tooth and claw-ness of nature. So, his first few books had very strong environmental themes, and that really influenced me.

Have you been involved in other forms of activism, for example, campaigning, protest demonstrations, marches, and violent direct action, lobbying, etc.?

Yes. So I teach business sustainable business and one of the things I do is I encourage my students to do some activism. So I'll tell them what Green Wash is and I'll say look at a company with a good sustainability policy. And is there anything they're doing that you think contradicts that? So for example, B&Q, I rate them as a good company, but you know, they've had peat in their compost for the longest time. And yes, they have peat-free compost, but they don't tell people that peat is in their general-purpose compost. So I would encourage them to write and say what they're doing that they think contradicts their policy, what they'd like them to do instead and. And for the record, B&Q changed their policy.

So how do you define your writing? Is it Ecofiction, Solarpunk, Hopepunk, or something else?

I know it's certainly not climate fiction, because I don't actually like much climate fiction. It's too dystopian for me. I'm afraid I'm very frivolous in my reading habits because of what I do for a living, which can be quite scary. I like escapism and I guess I write what I like. So my first novel was a Romcom, with green bits? So, ecofiction probably—more that. Amazon don't have a category for it, neither do Instagram or most of them, which I think is shocking. Or I think I might have coined a term social-science fiction: social-science fiction can take systemic solutions like, say, switching from the GDP to well-being index or adopting personal carbon trading or personal carbon allowances, or switching to having a House of Citizens as opposed to a House of Lords. A citizen assembly, direct, participative democracy. These are the things that I think would be utterly transformative, because they would change what decisions are made and they would change what we look at as success. But how would it look like in practice if everything is geared around the wellbeing index or if that actually carbon is rationed like a carbon currency? Who would win, who would lose? So I like to write these kinds of ideas.

What other examples of work have you written that explore environmental issues?

I edited an anthology called *No More Fairy Tales: Stories to Save Our Planet*. I co-wrote two stories and also contributed three myself and one of them is actually more of a novella called *The Assassin*. It's eight people set in a citizens assembly, debating climate solutions and one of which is an assassin. Actually citizens assemblies are way larger than that. But for whodunnit, you need a small number, so I call it a citizens' jury. I'm now extending it in into a full-length novel. It's a nice opportunity to talk about citizen assemblies and why it's so important that we develop this form of decision-making, and also to talk about some of the climate solutions that are debated in that.

Do you decide to write about a particular issue first, or do you start with a character, a scene, an image, etc., and then the environmental issues emerge?

Well, it depends on the story. I actually was working on something else to do with Cuba, but then I met this green garden consultant that set up in the area to help make gardens wildlife-friendly. He came over, and he helped me put up a water butt to capture water, and a hawthorn hedge and a pond and native plants and so on, and put up a bat box. He'd given up his job, took an early retirement because he wanted to do this. He is so worried about biodiversity loss and said. I want to do the world, but all I can do is a few back gardens. And I thought, well, hang on a minute, what a perfect idea for a book and I added a romance and a body he digs up. In the process of writing the book I learned so much about biodiversity, but also plugged in more general green stuff as well.

And while this connects really, maybe, maybe you already answered this. Could you tell us about the research you undertook on environmental issues for your writing? So, with *Habitat Man*, how did you research the biodiversity?

Dave Goulson is a professor of Biology at Sussex University. He set up the Bumblebee Conservation Trust, and is a lovely guy. He was kind enough to read *Habitat Man* from start to finish and check all the information, and suggest ideas of his own. He was really, really helpful. Also, I did my bulk of writing during the first lockdown. And can you remember what a lovely spring it was? And I had nothing to do but sit on my decking and watch nature and go for long walks. A lot of it was just direct observation—of the spiders weaving a web on my patio, or the birds harassing each other.

Do you think there are conflicts of interest between didactics and aesthetics, between wanting to convey a message and wanting to tell a story, and if so, how do you navigate them as a writer?

That is the hardest thing. I mean, it's hard to write a decent book anyway, even if your only goal is to entertain. If you're also trying to educate, inform, persuade, change behaviour, you just made it really, really difficult. So yeah, I think with every draft I've had to take information out. Because you want to inform and educate and there's so much you've got to say, but you have to remind yourself all the time that they're choosing to read fiction, not nonfiction. Their attention is the primary thing you have to hold on to. So I don't, but I won't ever compromise on truth for entertainment.

Do the arts have a part to play in the climate crisis, and if so, in what way?

Oh yes. When people are focusing on the climate crisis, people tend to look at government, or money or funding, but what we consider normal, what we can aspire to, who we want to be like—that is driven by culture. I'm engaged in a project with BAFTA and Albert at the moment called climate characters and #HotOrNot, where we're trying to start the conversation on that—not in a finger-wagging way, but in a kind of fun way. So we've got Instagram tiles where we've got James Bond with a single-use Aston Martin and takes twenty planets to kill the bad guys, but then you got Jack Reacher also killing bad guys, but he travels by bus and shops and second-hand shops, so it's just a fun way to showcase some of these ideas. Culture is the backdrop to everything because government and politicians aren't leaders, they're followers, really. Culture sets what's normal, what's aspirational.

So who or what inspires you as a writer? People, places, publications, etc.?

I think what inspires me is nature. You look out and think we live in such a beautiful world, and you just want to hold on to it.

Are there any projects you're working on new Ecofiction projects in the pipeline?

I've got this idea for a 'Green Santa' Christmas movie where instead of toys coming from the toy factory, they come from the toy hospital, and it ties into this girl and her brother. They've seen all the documentaries of whales and plastic and then Christmas comes and there's all this stuff and they're like, 'is this still OK?' and the parents don't know how to answer. The little boy ends up in hospital and to make him feel better, they say, well, we're making the toys better too. And then they get the idea of this toy hospital, and it becomes a whole campaign to, you upcycle, repair, reuse and transform Christmas.

So what about other forms of public engagement? Book tours, festivals, talk shows, interviews, obligation, or pleasure? And do you ever use them to discuss environmental issues?

Yes, I've done quite a few. I did a really nice talk at the responsible media summit last October. BBC was there and Netflix and loads of journalism students. And I used that as an opportunity to talk about the role of script writers in the culture of consumerism. So that was really nice. I've spoken to a few book clubs. I talked for the University of the Third Age. I do quite a few talks locally on different aspects. I also do this sustainable hairdressing project which is part of my day job. Now I'm getting into podcasts lately, so I'm going to talk on Manda Scott's. Accidental Gods podcast.

I find because my background is quite mixed, I've studies politics, economics. I've worked in business, I've worked in NGOs, charities and run my own business. I've done quite a PhD in Psychology. So all of that makes me a bad academic in the sense of going deep into one subject, but it gives me a good bird's eye view where I can bring together a lot of stuff and see the big picture. That's quite useful for the podcasts, because it means you could talk off the cuff wherever the conversation goes. You can see how the bits join up, and it is why I quite like doing them so—a popular format which gets a wide audience.

Any advice for budding writers of fiction?

Yes, I would say enjoy the process. And value people who are honest with you, your beta readers. I had a nice mix of people who are nice to me and people who were honest and they weren't the same people. But you need *both* because you don't start off being brilliant. I mean I can write an academic paper easily enough, but I had to learn a whole new technique, writing fiction, so I just think, and if you don't really enjoy the process, you probably won't stick to it. Another thing is just crack on. Don't try to make your first draft brilliant. Get it down and *then* have a look at it. By the time you got to the last chapter, you probably will get rid of the first chapter anyway, or, your characters would have changed as you've written.

Gill Lewis

Gill Lewis a multi award-winning children's writer who writes about wild animals, wild places, and our human relationship to them. Her books are contemporary stories that explore very real threats facing our planet. FFI: https://www.gilllewis.com/web/

How do you define your writing? Ecofiction? Solarpunk? Hopepunk? Or something else?

Ecofiction for 8–12 year olds.

What examples of work have you written that explore environmental issues?

Sky Hawk	—about how a migratory bird (osprey) connects communities.
White Dolphin	—about the destructive dredging of the seabed.
Moon Bear	—about deforestation and bear bile farming.
Gorilla Dawn	—about the illegal mining of coltan, deforestation and gorilla poaching.
Sky Dancer	—about raptor persecution and the destructive practice of driven grouse shooting.
Eagle Warrior	—about raptor persecution and the destructive practice of driven grouse shooting.
Crow Wars	—about the removal of trees and people trying to save them.
Song of the River	—about reintroduction of beavers.
Swan Song	—about mental health and protecting habitats.
Run Wild	—about protecting urban wild habitats.
Willow Wild Thing	series—about protecting urban wild habitats.
Closest thing to Flying	—historical—about the feather trade.

Do you decide to write about a particular issue first, or do you start with a character, a scene, an image, etc., and then the environmental issues emerge?

I start with an issue and then do much research, and out of that research a character emerges to tell the story.

Did you need to undertake research on environmental issues for your writing?

I always do meticulous research about animals, habitats and people and the conflict issues.

Do you think there are 'conflicts of interest' between didactics and aesthetics—between wanting to convey a message and wanting to tell a story—and if so, how do you navigate them as a writer?

No—I always aim to tell a story that could be a reality.

Do the arts have a part to play in the Climate Crisis, and if so in what way?

As humans, our survival strategy is communication through story. Everything is story, and we need to convey the threats facing our planet through story to emotionally connect with each other.

Who or what inspires you as a writer—people, places, publications, etc.?

Others' stories in the real world, animals and wild places.

Are you working on any new 'ecofiction' projects?

n/a

John Yunker

John Yunker writes short stories, plays, and novels focused on the complex and often conflicted relationships between humans and animals. He is author of the novels *The Tourist Trail* and *Where Oceans Hide Their Dead*. And he's co-founder (with Midge Raymond) of Ashland Creek Press, a publisher devoted to environmental and animal literature. FFI: https://johnyunker.com/about.html

How do you define your writing? Ecofiction? Solarpunk? Hopepunk? Or something else?

I first say that I write novels and short stories and plays. Because, sadly, there is no "ecofiction" category in bookstores. But if I had to choose a label for the past two novels I'd say they are environmental thrillers.

What examples of work have you written that explore environmental issues?

The Tourist Trail is my first novel. It's a story of a penguin researcher and an anti-whaling activist on the run from the law. Ultimately, it's a novel about protecting the oceans and their many residents. The second novel, a sequel of sorts, is called *Where Oceans Hide Their Dead*. This novel spends more time on land and focuses on animal agriculture and the tragic interconnectedness of poverty and animal cruelty.

Do you decide to write about a particular issue first, or do you start with a character, a scene, an image, etc., and then the environmental issues emerge?

I began with a character. For *The Tourist Trail*, I was actually volunteering down in Patagonia to assist with counting penguins when the idea came to me. It's safe to say that that brief trip changed my life.

Did you need to undertake research on environmental issues for your writing?

Absolutely. I wish I could spend more time alongside researchers but mostly I spend time reading the books and papers they write.

Do you think there are 'conflicts of interest' between didactics and aesthetics—between wanting to convey a message and wanting to tell a story—and if so, how do you navigate them as a writer?

The old axiom of show don't tell is all too applicable to environmental fiction. It's all too easy to lead with the message. So I try to bury it as well as possible and also include contradictory characters who may be absolutely opposed to whatever message I hope to convey.

Do the arts have a part to play in the Climate Crisis, and if so in what way?

I'll let Camus say it first: "The purpose of a writer is to keep civilization from destroying itself." Also, I believe that novels have a role to play in creating heroes for a new age. When I was growing up the heroic stories were those of exploration and battle. I believe the heroes of our age are those who devote their lives to protecting animals and the planet. Literature does that.

Who or what inspires you as a writer—people, places, publications, etc.?

Activists and scientists inspire me.

Are you working on any new 'ecofiction' projects?

Another novel, the final in the trilogy. Slowly. And short stories.

Julie Carrick Dalton

Julie Carrick Dalton is the Boston-based author of *The Last Beekeeper* and *Waiting for the Night Song*, which was a CNN, *USA Today*, *Newsweek,* and *Parade* Most Anticipated 2021 novel. She is a frequent speaker on the topic of Fiction in the Age of Climate Crisis at universities, museums, and conferences. When she isn't reading, writing, or wrangling her four kids and two dogs, you can probably find her kayaking, skiing, or digging in her garden.

FFI: juliecarrickdalton.com.

How do you define your writing? Ecofiction? Solarpunk? Hopepunk? Or something else?

I usually say ecofiction or climate fiction.

What examples of work have you written that explore environmental issues?

My novels *Waiting for the Night Song* (Forge Books, Macmillan, 2021) and *The Last Beekeeper* (Forge Books, Macmillan, 2023) both engage environmental crises and are grounded in real science, but have a speculative edge. I recently signed another two-book deal with Forge for two additional ecofiction titles.

Do you decide to write about a particular issue first, or do you start with a character, a scene, an image, etc., and then the environmental issues emerge?

My stories and characters always emerge first. Coming from a background in farming and beekeeping, issues of slow-burning changes in my ecosystem are always on my mind. These are the things that keep me awake at night, therefore they bubble up in my writing. I often think that writing these novels is my way of processing my climate anxieties. I can imagine 'what if?' What is the worst thing that could happen? What are the best-case scenarios? Who will rise to challenges? Who will crumble? Who will suffer most? Who has something to gain? Where do inequalities exist? I believe that exploring my climate fears in fiction gives me a bit of emotional control over the things that terrify me. Owning those fears can empower us to take action to seek out the future we hope to see.

Did you need to undertake research on environmental issues for your writing?

I have a background in agriculture and in beekeeping, but I'm in no way an expert. I'm a hobbyist. So I had to do a lot of research for both of my novels. While researching for *The Last Beekeeper*, I connected with a beekeeper from the Cummings School of Veterinary Medicine at Tufts University to advise me on the beekeeping aspects of my book. Although the premise is speculative, I wanted the science to be solid and plausible.

Do you think there are 'conflicts of interest' between didactics and aesthetics—between wanting to convey a message and wanting to tell a story—and if so, how do you navigate them as a writer?

As a fiction writer, I believe the story must come first. If a writer is too didactic and overpowers the story with an agenda, she dilutes the emotional value of her writing. It's fine to want to convey a message, but if readers put the book down because they lose interest or get annoyed at the preaching, they will never hear that message. Make the readers fall into your story and see through the eyes of your characters. If the characters are dimensional and convincing, the reader will care about the world they live in. And in the case of ecofiction, readers might care a little more about the state of the climate crisis impacting that world.

Do the arts have a part to play in the Climate Crisis, and if so in what way?

The arts have a huge role to play in conveying climate narratives. Reading any novel is an act of empathy. A reader is temporarily giving up their own view of the world to see through the eyes of the characters in the story. Perhaps the reader will see the real world differently after inhabiting someone else's life for a while. Maybe they will see the inequalities exacerbated by the climate crisis. Who is being impacted first and worst? Who is not feeling the impacts, and why? People who might not attend a lecture on climate change or read an article about rising ocean levels might pick up a novel. And that novel might be enough to open their eyes to the impacts of a warming climate.

Who or what inspires you as a writer—people, places, publications, etc.?

I'm definitely inspired by the quiet elements of nature. Not the loud, more visible disasters. The extinction of a tiny, barely noticeable songbird. The absence of fireflies that populated my childhood. The changing ecology in the forest near my home. What do these small changes portend?

Are you working on any new 'ecofiction' projects?

I'm currently working on my third book which engages deforestation in New England. After that, I have a fourth novel under contract that deals with species extinction.

Lynn Buckle

Lynn Buckle is a Deaf/hard-of-hearing author and visual artist. She teaches creative writing and fine art. Her novel *What Willow Says,* published by époque press, won the international Barbellion Prize, received Special Mention in the Saboteur Awards, and was a Critics' Pick of The Year in *The Irish Times* and *Irish Independent*. Publications include her debut novel *The Groundsmen*, anthologies *What Meets the Eye: The Deaf Perspective, Infinite Possibilities, Brigid,* and commissions for *Massachusetts Review, Exacting Clam, époque zine, The Irish Times,* and *Books Ireland Magazine*. Awards include John Hewitt Society Bursary, Greywood Arts Carers Residency, Red Line Short Story Competition shortlist, and she represented Ireland as UNESCO City of Literature Writer in Residence at The National Centre for Writing UK. She hosts Ireland's Climate Writers at The Irish Writers' Centre, interviewing international authors, politicians, and NGOs. FFI: https://lynnbuckle.wordpress.com/links/

How do you define your writing? Ecofiction? Solarpunk? Hopepunk? Or something else?

None of the above, as my primary aim is to target a much broader audience with my solution-based approach to climate change which is embedded into my literary fiction. I prefer not to restrict my appeal solely to readers who are already interested in ecofiction because the planet does not have time for us to preach to the converted. I am more interested in reaching those readers who are disinterested in climate change and hopefully disrupt their viewpoints. My publications are therefore defined by the publishing industry as literary fiction. They are solution-based, intersectional, fictional nature writing, within the genre of literary fiction.

What examples of work have you written that explore environmental issues?

What Willow Says (époque press 2021)—solution-based literary fiction novel. Nature writing from a disability perspective. Includes climate solutions. *H is for Plane* in *Exacting Clam* magazine (Sagging Meniscus Press 2023). —short fiction about ableism within environmental writing, written specifically for sign language users. *The Sound of Red in Green* in *Massachusetts Review* (Vol. 63: 4, 2022)—environmental short fiction from a disability perspective. *Ailbhe's Tale* in *What Meets the Eye: The Deaf Perspective* (Arachne Press 2021). *Ailbhe's Tale* was first commissioned by The National Centre for Writing UK. Solution-based environmental short fiction from a disability perspective. I write regular articles and reviews of climate fiction and environmental creative non-fiction for *The Irish Times* Books Section.

Do you decide to write about a particular issue first, or do you start with a character, a scene, an image, etc., and then the environmental issues emerge?

I embed environmental issues and climate solutions into all my writing as a matter of course so it is not a question of when they are added, just a matter of how I will tell my story. Each work begins slightly differently with me.

Did you need to undertake research on environmental issues for your writing?

Yes. All writing needs to be well-researched, whatever the issues being conveyed. One advantage of hosting the Climate Writers' Group at the Irish Writers Centre is that we have over 200 members, many of whom are leading academics or NGOs specialising in conservation and climate change. They are a rich resource, and we share our knowledge freely. The Irish Writers Centre works on various collaborative projects with leaders in the field of climate change, adding to writers' environmental knowledge-base.

Do you think there are 'conflicts of interest' between didactics and aesthetics—between wanting to convey a message and wanting to tell a story—and if so, how do you navigate them as a writer?

Good writers are always able to 'show rather than tell' and know to avoid info-dumping and lecturing. Their skill lies in wearing a cause lightly and in knowing how to entice readers into a story. I do not see this as a conflict, it is just a normal process of learning how to write.

Do the arts have a part to play in the Climate Crisis, and if so in what way?

The arts have always influenced society and vice versa. Besides holding a mirror to humanity by describing the destruction we cause, or simply eulogising nature, or writing disaster-based climate warnings, writers can also affect change for a positive future. Research at the University of Southampton has proven that presenting solutions to the climate crisis in our fiction actually motivates readers to change their behaviours. I would encourage writers who are truly driven by a desire to save the planet to go even further and avoid writing just for the converted. It is quite possible to write in any genre if you want to reach people who are disinterested in climate change, to embed climate crisis issues and solutions into any genre of writing.

Who or what inspires you as a writer—people, places, publications, etc.?

Place and injustice inspire me to write. I draw on what I know, imagine new scenarios, and use emotion to pull the reader in.

Are you working on any new 'ecofiction' projects?

Yes, I have commission to write new pieces and am concentrating on my next novel. I continue to run the Climate Writers Group on behalf of the Irish Writers Centre where I interview international authors, academics and politicians. I also speak at literary festivals on climate fiction from an inclusive viewpoint and run masterclasses on the topic.

Manda Scott

Manda Scott used to be a veterinary surgeon. Now, she is an award-winning novelist, host of the Accidental Gods podcast, and co-creator of the Thrutopia Masterclass that is evolving into a think tank to equip writers with the tools they need to write paths to a future we'd all want. She believes absolutely that we need to tell ourselves new stories of how we created a path to a future we'd be proud to leave behind. FFI: https://mandascott.co.uk/

How do you define your writing? Ecofiction? Solarpunk? Hopepunk? Or something else?

I have defined it as THRUTOPIAN after the 2017 paper in *Huffington Post* by Rupert Read. His definition is not quite mine, but it's close enough. This is not dystopian (we truly don't need to see how bad it could be ever again), nor Utopian—which is lazy because it misses the *crucial steps of how we get to where we need to be to bequeath a functioning, flourishing future to the generations that come after us.* That's my definition of Thrutopian writing.

What examples of work have you written that explore environmental issues?

I have a 181,000 word novel with the editors as we speak. There's a 3-article series in press with *Permaculture Magazine.*

Do you decide to write about a particular issue first, or do you start with a character, a scene, an image, etc., and then the environmental issues emerge?

I was given a vision by my shamanic guides, but I was already running the Accidental Gods podcast, so the idea that we needed a new narrative was part of my life. I just thought novels were too slow a means of exploring ideas. But if we're going to knit them all together into a theory of everything that will inspire people and give them agency, then we need the broader canvas of a novel (or its televisual equivalent)

Did you need to undertake research on environmental issues for your writing?

Yes, but I'm doing it anyway for Accidental Gods podcast. And I ran the Thrutopia Writing Masterclass for 6 months in summer 2022 in order to help create a Future-imagining think-tank.

Do you think there are 'conflicts of interest' between didactics and aesthetics—between wanting to convey a message and wanting to tell a story—and if so, how do you navigate them as a writer?

No. Any novel has a political basis, the only question is whether the author is aware of it or not. Every single story we tell ourselves has a frame. Most current writing is framed in the old paradigm. The difficulty lies in creating a coherent, accessible, engaging narrative that leads the reader/viewer out of the old paradigm (in which they are somewhat comfortable) into the interim space from which a new paradigm can arise.

Do the arts have a part to play in the Climate Crisis, and if so in what way?

The arts are absolutely essential to shifting the greater mass of public awareness away from the old paradigm towards the space I mentioned above. "When a system is far from equilibrium, small islands of coherence can shift the entire system" (Ilya Prigogine). We have a moral, ethical and practical responsibility to do the inner work that lets us abandon the old paradigm and embrace the uncertainty that leads us towards whatever we can grow out of this.

Who or what inspires you as a writer—people, places, publications, etc.?

As a writer, I am deeply impressed with Natasha Pulley and Clare North. Each of these is a superlative writer with a capacity to render complex ideas comprehensible. They are not (yet) writing Thrutopian fiction. In the Thrutopian field, I am deeply inspired by Della Duncan's Upstream podcast, by Daniel Schmachtenberger's thinking and the work of the Consilience Project; by Nate Hagens' 'The Great Simplification' Podcast and by the work of economist Kate Raworth. In more general terms, I have recently been introduced to the work of the Ruby and Christabel Reed in the Advaya project, to Zineb Mouhyi of YouthxYouth and to the Cynefin work of Dave Snowden. Each of these in its own way is inspiring. I could keep listing people, but you could also just look at the guest list of the Accidental Gods podcast.

Are you working on any new 'ecofiction' projects?

Any Human Power is in editing and will be followed by at least one sequel (current working title of book 2 in the series is 'For the World for the Win' I doubt if that'll make it past the publishers, mind you). I'm also planning a non-fiction book called, 'Yes, but wtf can I actually DO?'—and there's a TV series at Narrative Ark (https://narrativeark.net) which we submitted to the BBC's Climate Spring project.

Mary Woodbury

Mary Woodbury (fiction pen name: Clara Hume) is a localisation specialist by day and fiction writer by night. An editorial advisor at Climatelit.org, she curates the popular website Dragonfly.eco and is the author of *Back to the Garden, The Stolen Child,* and *Bird Song: A Novella.* She's also a contributing author to *Wild Tales from the River.* She's part of the core writer team at Artists and Climate Change and has written for *Impakter, Chicago Review of Books,* Ecology Action Centre's magazine, and ClimateCultures.net. Her articles have been translated at Chinese Science Writers Association and *Zest Letteratura Sostenibile.*

How do you define your writing? Ecofiction? Solarpunk? Hopepunk? Or something else?

I usually use the term ecofiction or speculative fiction. I've also dabbled in weird fiction. I am not sure it matters too much about the genre name because we don't want to preach to the choir, rather reach out across the aisle, so sometimes I think more general genres are just fine to describe this literature.

What examples of work have you written that explore environmental issues?

My debut novel was part one of a duology called the Wild Mountain series. I recently published the final part. Book One, *Back to the Garden,* had a pretty broad cast of characters and was about a road trip they took together after economic collapse due to climate change. The second novel, *The Stolen Child,* takes place at the turn of the next century and focuses on the kidnapping of one of the main character's children. I wrote a lot about natural ecology in a climate-changed future world in this series, but in the second novel, I also wanted to tap into how society has both changed and not changed.

I also wrote a novella, *Bird Song,* an experiment in both weird fiction and a reimagining of mythology. Again, ecology is a big part of the story, as is climate change.

Do you decide to write about a particular issue first, or do you start with a character, a scene, an image, etc., and then the environmental issues emerge?

I began writing the Wild Mountains series after a dream about a day in the future where climate change would be more drastic. In my dream, I was at a lake in the mountains, but my throat was parched, the temperatures hotter than usual, and the land drier than usual. I saw a man across the lake, and he seemed gruff toward me and untalkative. So, two main characters and one of the early scenes in the novel were directly from my dream. The other environmental issues emerged via research about climate models, early feedback from a scientist's review, and first draft readers. I was also wondering how other authors were addressing climate and ecological issues in fiction. Outside of science fiction, eco-fiction, and environmental fiction, the others genres came after I began writing that first novel.

Did you need to undertake research on environmental issues for your writing?

Yes, and though I can't say everything about the Wild Mountain series is factual, it's not denialist or too crazy either. I think the hardest part was trying to figure out a major plot line while not having great information about predictions for how future Canadian rivers might change in the future after glaciers melt.

My other title, *Bird Song*, is not factual outside the broad fact that climate change is happening. It's more experimental and involves some genre-blurring of mythological, weird, magical realist, and time-travel fictions, along with paradoxes and mystery. I really liked writing this piece. It's by far my favorite.

Do you think there are 'conflicts of interest' between didactics and aesthetics—between wanting to convey a message and wanting to tell a story—and if so, how do you navigate them as a writer?

I think there are conflicts. I subscribe to the concept of stories being pieces of art over polemics, and know from participating on panels and even conducting a survey that readers just don't want to be preached at. I've learned (and have had the experience) that my favorite stories touch my heart somehow, whether it's an emotional journey with some tears and some laughter or just something that is mind-blowing and stays with me. A lot of times it's marginalised people and unlikely heroes working together to bring about good in times of crisis. Stories where characters fight the good fight inspire fearlessness and courage instead of just passive hope really get to me, in a good way. Navigating that talent of storytelling is the hardest part of being a writer. I know what works for me, but can I have that effect as a writer? I still don't know.

Do the arts have a part to play in the Climate Crisis, and if so in what way?

Short answer, yes. Longer answer, we've always told stories as people. We share experiences about our connections with other people as well as places and things. The climate crisis is our current reality, and it's only natural that artists would create stories about it, whether via novels or other arts. From cave art depicting animals and plants to modern-day stories about how nature around us is evolving, art is so important, as it always has been. When I became interested in the intersection of ecology and fiction—well, it really happened when I was a young child and my favourite stories were about the great outdoors—I wrote my first novel with climate change in mind. I started that in the early 2000s. Then in about 2008, I began to compile a list of novels about climate change. In 2013, that list turned into a curated website (dragonfly.eco) about ecofiction overall, which is broader than novels about climate change. Year after year, novels, anthologies, and other written fiction have continued to rise in number. At the site, I do interviews and spotlights, but also curate a database, with the most notable fiction, and as I write this today, the database has nearly 1,000 books. This project is also a hobby, and I haven't had the time to be more exhaustive. But I've noticed more and more fiction in the past decade about ecological and climate issues. What's more, these novels are increasingly winning literary awards.

Who or what inspires you as a writer—people, places, publications, etc.?

I'm inspired by other stories that I read or watch (film, for instance). Also, when I run or hike, I think a lot, which provokes me to write down some weird thing I want to write about someday. As far as people, that's tough, because I do these interviews in a world ecofiction spotlight, and people from around the world have participated. I think my favourites are interviews that I've done with people living in and writing about places like various African countries, Indigenous authors (such as Waubgeshig Rice), Borneo, and Argentina. I get bored with always reading western literature. I really get inspired being exposed by stories from other places. Also, Jeff VanderMeer turned me onto what I call the ecological weird, because the weird is such an effective way to get me to question things.

Are you working on any new 'ecofiction' projects?

Other than Dragonfly.eco, mentioned above, I have an early work in progress, but I am not sure I'll continue or do something completely different. I have some story ideas, for sure!

Michelle Cook

Michelle Cook writes thrillers and thrutopian fiction and lives in Worcestershire, UK, with her husband and two children. She took her first joyful steps into creative writing when her middle school teacher read out her short story in class. A slapstick tale of two talking kangaroos breaking out of a zoo, the work was sadly lost to history, but Michelle never forgot the buzz of others enjoying her words. More recently, she was long-listed for the Cambridge Prize for flash fiction and placed first in the Writers' Forum competition with her short story The Truth About Cherry House. Her debut novel, *Tipping Point*, was a genre winner in the 2022 Page Turner Awards. FFI: https://www.michellecookauthor.com

How do you define your writing? Ecofiction? Solarpunk? Hopepunk? Or something else?

Until recently, I've called my books ecofiction or eco-thrillers. I moved away from the name dystopia because it seems to be thought of and marketed as sci-fi and my writing is soft sci-fi at most. I'm not interested so much in tech as I am in how contemporary issues like climate change and AI effect human behaviour, society, and our relationship with the environment.

I recently met a wonderful writer, fellow Climate Fiction Writers League member Manda Scott. She calls the kind of stories we write thrutopia and I love that name. It's more optimistic than dystopia. It was coined by Professor Rupert Read to describe fiction that takes us from the mess we're in to a world we'd be proud to leave for future generations. If climate change is a crisis of imagination as Amitav Ghosh said, then we storytellers must imagine something better and explore how we might get there.

The crazy thing is, we are perfectly capable of repairing the damage we've done and living in balance with our environment. Most of the technology, knowledge and skills already exist. It's the systems we have constructed that hold us back: our economic model built on eternal growth and consumption. And electoral systems that leave us vulnerable to tribalism, vested interest, and short-term thinking.

What examples of work have you written that explore environmental issues?

I seem to return to the theme almost without intention. Many if my short stories and flash pieces speculate on how the human race will fare in the future. Climate change is the central theme of my first two novels, *Tipping*

Point and *Counterpoint*. They follow the story of a bereaved teenager who uncovers a corporate conspiracy to suppress planet-saving tech. She must risk everything to expose it and create the prototype before Earth's ecological collapse reaches the point of no return.

Do you decide to write about a particular issue first, or do you start with a character, a scene, an image, etc., and then the environmental issues emerge?

It's strange, because when I started writing *Tipping Point* (erstwhile working title, Resilience), climate change was only one of the things I set out to explore. I wanted most of all to write a page turner; an adventure story with a troubled but unbreakable heroine. As I wrote, climate change became a more important aspect of the story. I discovered I had quite a bit of climate anxiety to work through.

The first book was quite emotional to write—my main character, Essie, goes through a lot. So much so, I wasn't sure I wanted to write another book about her. As time went on, I realised I was only halfway through Essie's story. As much for her sake as my own, I had to go back in and imagine her an optimistic future. The first book ends on a spark of hope and I wanted to turn that into a proper campfire to warm us both. I'm happy I did—writing the second book was great fun as I got to up the action ante as well as expand on the complexity of the characters and points of view. It also gave me room for some satire, which I loved writing.

Did you need to undertake research on environmental issues for your writing?

Loads! The technology in the story is carbon capture and conversion so I did a lot of frowning over scientific papers and articles for that. And there was a whole lot of work on climate forecasts. The story is set 15–20 years in the future, so I researched a lot about likely temperatures, wildfires, floods, storms and coastal erosion. The super fun bit was imagining how that would effect social norms and cohesion as well as things we used to take for granted like food and energy supply. I have scared myself more than once with the accuracy of some of the predictions I came up with. The signs are all there if we care to look.

Do you think there are 'conflicts of interest' between didactics and aesthetics—between wanting to convey a message and wanting to tell a story—and if so, how do you navigate them as a writer?

The key to this will always be putting the story first. For me, this message is a no brainer, but that's not true for everyone. People are in all kinds of different places on climate change and the environment. Some of us are sick with worry, others haven't even started stressing yet. Without a great story no one's going to care about your message, not least because no one's going to read it.

I'm glad my first book evolved the way it did, because the plot and characters preceded the message. I wasn't even aware I *had* a message until much later, when the story had taken me there. As these awful things happened to Essie and her friends, I got madder and madder about the injustice of her world, which is really our world a few steps on. I am aware how weird that sounds, since I was the one making the awful things happen!

The message grew from my love for the main character and my horror at her plight. That's a good place to be in as a writer because that way you serve the story best and the message can take care of itself.

Do the arts have a part to play in the Climate Crisis, and if so in what way?

Absolutely, and so much more than I would have believed just a few years ago. Taking up writing later in life has been an epiphany for me. Things I have ranted about for decades, without hope of changing a mind, make more impact when I write.

The human brain is an odd place. We grow weary of real-life footage of huge-scale suffering and injustice shown nightly on the news. When our politicians lie and cheat, we shrug our shoulders. When thousands are killed in climate disasters, it feels disconnected from our actions. But show us a character we care about being trodden down and we want to fight for them. We can't look away.

I've come to realise what an incredibly powerful tool that is. Not just to convey a message, but to open up human imagination and empathy, which I'd argue is the starting point for solving all of our problems.

Who or what inspires you as a writer—people, places, publications, etc.?

Other writers and passion for ideas. I love exploring issues with thoughtful people. Most of those who have to put up with me in real life are tired of hearing me hold forth. I need a release valve, and that's writing.

More and more I'm motivated to find hope. I recently got involved in Climate Emergency UK's local council audit project. We're assessing all councils in

England, Scotland and Wales against climate action. Researching the work taking place across the country is inspiring. We have so much to do but there are projects out there improving things right now: active travel schemes, clean air campaigns, tree planting, local grants for businesses to decarbonise. And there's widespread support among the public for solutions like wind and solar power. Now it's for world leaders to catch up.

As writers, our job is to help push them past their short-term vested interests into action. And to give our readers hope and a sense of agency. It feels like this change will only happen from the bottom up.

Are you working on any new 'ecofiction' projects?

I've started writing a dark urban fantasy featuring naughty angels, which is morphing into thrutopia as I ruminate. I think I'll always go back to stories that touch on climate. It's the show stopper for me. Not much else will really matter if we don't urgently solve that one. As story stakes go, they don't get any higher.

Midge Raymond

Midge Raymond is the author of the novel *My Last Continent* and the award-winning short-story collection *Forgetting English*. Her writing has appeared in *TriQuarterly, American Literary Review, Bellevue Literary Review,* the *Los Angeles Times* magazine, the *Chicago Tribune, Poets & Writers,* and many other publications. Midge worked in publishing in New York before moving to Boston, where she taught communication writing at Boston University for six years. She has taught creative writing at Boston's Grub Street Writers, Seattle's Richard Hugo House, and San Diego Writers, Ink. Midge lives in the Pacific Northwest, where she is co-founder of the boutique publisher *Ashland Creek Press.* FFI: www.MidgeRaymond.com

How do you define your writing? Ecofiction? Solarpunk? Hopepunk? Or something else?

I'd define my writing as ecofiction. My novel, *My Last Continent*, is about a penguin researcher in Antarctica whose season is disrupted by a shipwreck; her vessel has to go to the aid of the stranded passengers. The book was inspired by not only the fact that penguins are suffering due to climate change but also that Antarctic travel is increasingly popular, and there are concerns about its sustainability. And the shipwreck itself—an all-too-real possibility—shows that nature's wild places cannot be controlled, and that climate chaos is impacting the entire world.

What examples of work have you written that explore environmental issues?

My novel, *My Last Continent*, explores endangered species, sustainable travel, and climate change. I'm working on a new novel that also explores endangered species, invasive species, and fragile habitats.

Do you decide to write about a particular issue first, or do you start with a character, a scene, an image, etc., and then the environmental issues emerge?

My Last Continent was always going to address the environment—it's hard to avoid when writing about Antarctica! The Antarctic peninsula is the fastest-warming region in the world, and the concerns about its melting ice are very relevant; rising seas due to ice melt will affect the entire world.

The novel itself began with a short story ("The Ecstatic Cry," which appears in my collection *Forgetting English*), and the story began with a specific moment: a tourist falling on ice on the Antarctic peninsula, which I witnessed when I was traveling there in 2004. In real life, the man got up; in the story, he did not. And in the novel, this story—of what to do when tragedy strikes at the bottom of the world—was expanded to reveal the dangers and consequences of traveling in a wild, remote, and environmentally fragile region. In 2004, only 20,000 travelers visited Antarctica—during the 2022–2023 season, that number reached 100,000. So there's a lot of concern about how to ensure the continent and its creatures are protected, with so many more travelers.

Did you need to undertake research on environmental issues for your writing?

I was fortunate to have been able to visit Antarctica in 2004, and it was the trip itself that inspired the novel, not the novel that inspired the trip. I wasn't able to return while writing the novel, so I had to undertake a great deal of research. For example, I'd never been to McMurdo, the U.S. research station, and so I had to do a tremendous amount of research about life at the station, from reading books to watching documentaries. I was fortunate to get hands-on penguin research experience as a volunteer for the Center for Ecosystem Sentinels, counting penguins in Argentina; this gave me insight into the life of a penguin scientist.

Do you think there are 'conflicts of interest' between didactics and aesthetics—between wanting to convey a message and wanting to tell a story—and if so, how do you navigate them as a writer?

A writer's job is to engage and entertain—and conflicts arise for us when we attempt to teach (or, worse, preach) in a way that isn't completely and seamlessly woven into the story. To avoid this conflict, I always aim to stay focused on the characters; if the characters are authentic, their beliefs and passions will feel real to the readers. I also try to have characters with different points of view, just as we all do in life. And this is when the story's and characters' conflicts can be entertaining as well as edifying—for example, when characters argue over politics or climate change, just as so many of us experience in real life at holiday dinners. I myself love books with a point of view—but not if I'm being preached to! So, in the end, we writers have to find that balance and aim to tell a great story that also teaches readers a little something in the end.

Do the arts have a part to play in the Climate Crisis, and if so in what way?

Absolutely! Books, art, film—everything is important when it comes to how we can save the environment and the planet. I find that fiction especially has tremendous power to open hearts and minds; we all love to immerse ourselves in great stories. Although someone who doesn't believe in climate change is not likely to read a nonfiction book about it, they may pick up a thriller that happens to deal with climate issues and learn something along the way—and perhaps even change their mind along the way. I review books for EcoLit Books, and I've discovered that even as someone interested in these issues—the climate crisis, animal protection, endangered species—I'd prefer to read fiction, as fiction offers a bit of escape along with the reality.

I believe so strongly in the power of art as activism, I co-founded an environmental press, Ashland Creek Press, with my partner, John Yunker, in part because as writers we noticed that—at the time, back in 2011—very few mainstream publishers were interested in environmental writing. This has changed tremendously over the past decade, which is wonderful—and we're now turning our focus more toward animal protection, because this is an area in which we'd like to see more storytelling. It's hard to get folks to make the connection between animal protection and the environment—whether it's the air and water pollution caused by animal agriculture, the destruction of the rainforests to raise cattle, or the overfishing of our oceans—and we're hoping to see these connections made and to see change for the better in the coming years.

Who or what inspires you as a writer—people, places, publications, etc.?

Environmental and animal activists inspire me, but I especially adore writers who bring these issues to people through their art. Karen Joy Fowler's *We Are All Completely Beside Ourselves* is simply a gorgeous novel, but it's also very much an animal rights novel. Barbara Kingsolver's books always teach me something about the natural world. Ann Pancake's *Strange As This Weather Has Been* is one of the most powerful environmental novels I've read. All of these novels are amazing, beautifully written stories that just happen to have a lot to say about animals, the planet, how we are engaging with them, and how we might do better.

I also love seeing so many great documentaries out in the world, from *Blackfish* to *Cowspiracy* to *Seaspiracy*, that highlight animal protection and the environment—these two issues are so closely connected, and I'm hoping more readers and viewers will see these connections and be inspired to help out the planet a bit.

Are you working on any new 'ecofiction' projects?

I'm working on a new novel, again featuring penguins—but this one is set in the Galápagos Islands, another fragile environment that is well protected but is facing risks from climate change, overfishing, and poaching. The novel follows two women, a hundred years apart—one who was an early settler on Floreana Island, and another who's building nests for Galápagos penguins who are losing their nesting sites due to climate change and erosion. During this island's history, a lot happened on Floreana—the tortoises went extinct, and then they were brought back; invasive species flooded the island, and now they're being eradicated so that native species can thrive again. The two women's stories are told against the backdrop of these mistakes we humans have made, and our attempts to correct them and to try to bring habitats back to how they used to be, if we can.

R.B. Kelly

R.B. Kelly is a science fiction author and film theorist. Her debut novel, *The Edge of Heaven*, was published by NewCon Press and was shortlisted for the Arthur C Clarke Award and the ESFS Award for Best Written Work of Fiction. The sequel, *On The Brink*, was released in May 2022, also from NewCon Press. She has been writing since she was old enough to hold a pen, publishing since 2003, and teaching other writers since 2013.

FFI: www.rbkelly.co.uk

How do you define your writing? Ecofiction? Solarpunk? Hopepunk? Or something else?

Dystopian science fiction, though I've recently been exploring some solarpunk themes.

What examples of work have you written that explore environmental issues?

My two novels, *Edge of Heaven* and *On the Brink*, are set in a climate-changed future and explore the realities of life for ordinary people once Earth's resources have been stretched to their limits and beyond.

Do you decide to write about a particular issue first, or do you start with a character, a scene, an image, etc., and then the environmental issues emerge?

I started writing in the 1990s, as concerns about our impact on the environment were beginning to gather momentum, so it was a natural progression for me to use my novels to explore those issues. *Edge of Heaven* began as an image of a city in two layers, and I knew immediately that it had been constructed as a response to the pressures of climate change. From there, the story coalesced around that initial concept.

Did you need to undertake research on environmental issues for your writing?

Yes, lots! I wanted both novels to flow logically—if speculatively—out of the real environmental catastrophe we're currently brewing, so it was very important to me that I got the climate science right (with possibly a little bit of room for artistic licence). I spent a lot of time researching changing fluvial patterns and other exciting stuff like that.

Do you think there are 'conflicts of interest' between didactics and aesthetics—between wanting to convey a message and wanting to tell a story—and if so, how do you navigate them as a writer?

Yes, of course—my primary responsibility as a storyteller is to the story itself. If the didactic side is allowed to take centre stage, the story will suffer. I want my fiction to explore the human side of climate change so that's one of the ways I navigate the conflict of interest. I keep the story focused on what's happening to the people in my narrative, and let the message play out implicitly in the background: a climate-changed Earth is not going to be a fun place to live, and there's plenty of narrative conflict to be drawn from that fact.

Do the arts have a part to play in the Climate Crisis, and if so in what way?

I believe the arts have a part to play in any crisis, and the climate is the biggest crisis of our generation.

Who or what inspires you as a writer—people, places, publications, etc.?

I was absolutely enthralled by Ben Elton's early 1990s climate fiction—*This Other Eden* was a huge influence on my writing, as—albeit to a lesser extent—was *Stark*. But if I had to list my biggest source of inspiration, it's Terry Pratchett, without question. His Discworld books were where I learned that a speculative fiction writer has an enormous array of tools at their disposal when it comes to discussing huge, important, universal issues. And that if you can make a reader laugh, you can nudge them all the more easily towards the message you want to convey.

Are you working on any new 'ecofiction' projects?

Always! I'm currently putting the final touches to a new solarpunk short story about found family, which imagines a hopeful future where we've learnt to work with our beautiful planet instead of against it.

Somto Ihezue

Somto Ihezue is a Nigerian–Igbo editor, writer, and filmmaker. He is Original Fiction Manager at Escape Artists. He is an editor with Android Press and an associate editor with *Apex Magazine*, and *Cast of Wonders*. He was awarded the 2021 African Youth Network Movement Fiction Prize. A BSFA, Nommo Award-nominee and finalist for the 2022 Afritondo Prize, his works have appeared and are forthcoming in *Tor: Africa Risen Anthology, Fireside Magazine, Podcastle, Escape Pod, Strange Horizons, POETRY Magazine, Cossmass Infinities, Flash Fiction Online, Flame Tree Press, OnSpec Magazine, Omenana,* and others. FFI: https://somtoihezue.wordpress.com

How do you define your writing? Ecofiction? Solarpunk? Hopepunk? Or something else?

Writing is many things for me. Joy, fear, defiance, hope, and everything in between. Existing in a society like Nigeria, rife with bigotry, corruption, bad governance, unending societal crisis, and everything else, my writing has also become escape. An escape into futures that are kinder, spaces where we are allowed to be brave… be afraid. Escape into places that are home. My writing is resistance. It is how I get to be fierce and unbowed. Be a masterpiece, and a work in progress. Or just be.

What examples of work have you written that explore environmental issues?

Like Stars Daring To Shine, published in Fireside and reprinted in Escape Pod. In the September 2022 issue of *Locus Magazine*, Charles Payseur made a comment about this work. He said, "Ihezue captures a sense of imminent danger, everything hanging on a thin thread of community and inequality, while also showing that people, and the natural world, are full of surprises and resilience. The piece challenges what recovery can look like, and through the grim implications of the ravaged Earth and all its coldness, there remains some warmth to find in the story." This statement vividly captures the message I hoped to pass across with this story.

Do you decide to write about a particular issue first, or do you start with a character, a scene, an image, etc., and then the environmental issues emerge?

It's always the theme first; in this case, an environmental issue I intend to shed light on. So I weave a story around it. The story could change along the way, become something entirely different, but the theme remains. Now, building characters, events, and places around that one singular subject takes a great deal of effort. Sometimes I start a story by writing the end. Other times, the first paragraph does not fit into the story in the long run. That's the thing about the first draft; it gives you the freedom to be reckless, imperfect, and incomplete. It's like a window into a world, a guide, a stepping-stone. That in itself has helped form the idea of what a story should be.

Did you need to undertake research on environmental issues for your writing?

Definitely. Definitely. While writing *Like Stars Daring To Shine*, I had to research on volcanic disasters in the past, the possible causes and the aftermath. It's also different when I have to write about things closer to home. The oil spillage and drastic water pollution in oil producing Nigerian states. Those situations are our lived experiences.

Do you think there are 'conflicts of interest' between didactics and aesthetics—between wanting to convey a message and wanting to tell a story—and if so, how do you navigate them as a writer?

I don't think it's been an issue for me. In stories, those I read and those I write, I do not seek perfection, but beauty and truth, in all its many forms.

Do the arts have a part to play in the Climate Crisis, and if so in what way?

I would say yes—simply because fiction in this case portrays an alternative to what we see as the mainstream or what is portrayed in reality. A lot of times people believe that a climate sustainable future may be too hard to picture, but stories specifically envision the shape of our future. It's one thing for people to read policy on our carbon footprints and all; it's another thing to see it established and illustrated within the framework of a story.

Who or what inspires you as a writer—people, places, publications, etc.?

People. Their fight, their drive. It's like a wave, a ripple. Despite all the odds, we see people daring to defy. We witness individuals carving out spaces for themselves, and for others, spaces where we get to thrive, be boundless and infinite.

Are you working on any new 'ecofiction' projects?

Oh yes! Currently working on a story where technology collapses and humankind has to resort to using pigeons as a means of communicate. Then the pigeons revolt.

T.C. Boyle

T. Coraghessan Boyle is the author of thirty-one books of fiction, including, most recently, *The Harder They Come* (2015), *The Terranauts* (2016), *The Relive Box* (2017), *Outside Looking In* (2019), *Talk To Me* (2021), *I Walk Between the Raindrops* (2022), and *Blue Skies* (2023).

He received a Ph.D. degree in Nineteenth Century British Literature from the University of Iowa in 1977, his M.F.A. from the University of Iowa Writers' Workshop in 1974, and his B.A. in English and History from SUNY Potsdam in 1968. He has been a member of the English Department at the University of Southern California since 1978, where he is Distinguished Professor of English.

His work has been translated into more than two dozen foreign languages, including German, French, Italian, Dutch, Portuguese, Spanish, Russian, Hebrew, Korean, Japanese, Danish, Swedish, Norwegian, Lithuanian, Latvian, Polish, Hungarian, Bulgarian, Finnish, Farsi, Croatian, Turkish, Albanian, Vietnamese, Serbian, and Slovene.

His stories have appeared in most of the major American magazines, including *The New Yorker, Harper's, Esquire, The Atlantic Monthly, Playboy, The Paris Review, GQ, Antaeus, Granta,* and *McSweeney's*, and he has been the recipient of a number of literary awards, including the PEN/Faulkner Prise for best novel of the year (*World's End*, 1988); the PEN/Malamud Prize in the short story (*T.C. Boyle Stories*, 1999); and the Prix Médicis Étranger for best foreign novel in France (*The Tortilla Curtain*, 1997). He currently lives near Santa Barbara with his wife and three children. FFI: https://www.tcboyle.com/

What's your earliest memory of a natural place, or the presence of 'nature'?

I grew up in a housing development in Westchester County, circa thirty miles north of Manhattan on the Hudson River. Out back of the development were a couple of square miles of woods. I made those woods my home, both in the presence of other neighborhood kids and alone, and it was during that period that my love of the outdoors—in those thorny, swampy, mosquito-ridden acres—was born. I would follow creeks to see where they went, climb mountains for the pleasure of standing atop them. When the snows arrived each winter, everything became magical, near and far and in the smallest recesses.

When did you first become aware of environmental issues? Did you have any formative experiences, or 'eco-epiphanies' that focalised your concern?

I had no idea that nature wasn't infinite until I was well into my teens. Like most ecologists, I began to resent the presence of others as I started exploring the great tracts of Harriman and Fahnestock Parks. They tossed candy wrappers and beer cans along the trails. They interfered with the peace I was seeking. They were innocent, oblivious hikers, dough-faced and living their lives, but I resented them.

Have you been involved in other forms of activism, for example, campaigning, protests, demonstrations, marches, non-violent direct action, lobbying, etc.?

I'm not a joiner. So, no. My response has been through my fiction, which, from the earliest days, focused largely on ecology and the effects our species has on the environment.

Your 2000 novel, *A Friend of the Earth*, set in a climate-ravaged 2025, seems eerily prescient now. Can you tell us about what fed into its development, and what you set out to do with the book?

What I set out to do with *A Friend of the Earth* is what I set out to do with all my books and short stories: create a work of art that allows me to discover how I feel about a multiplicity of issues, in this case climate change and extinction, among other things. If it seems prescient—we even have a pandemic featured—it's because I read deeply and revolved the issues in my mind at a time when few of us were paying attention.

How do you define your writing? Ecofiction? Solarpunk? Hopepunk? Or something else?

I leave definitions to my readers. When I'm asked (The party full of strangers: "Wow, you write books? What is it, horror, romance, thrillers, or what?"), I reply: "Literature." I am not consciously delivering "messages," but rather exploring the madhouse world we live in as a way of trying to make sense of it for myself.

What other examples of work have you written that explore environmental issues?

None. I only write fiction because, for me, it is magical, a way of singing on the page and translating the images floating in my brain into some coherent—and, I fervently hope, beautiful—form.

Do you decide to write about a particular issue first, or do you start with a character, a scene, an image, etc., and then the environmental issues emerge?

All my work proceeds organically, from the whispering voice of a first line to the complications and the resolution. That said, in novels like *A Friend of the Earth* and *Blue Skies* (which is a sequel of sorts, projecting from now into the future as the previous novel did), I set out to research a subject and hope that in the process of so doing a scenario presents itself to me. What kicked *Blue Skies* into gear were the news reports of the worldwide decline in flying insects and what that might mean for the terrestrial food chain. One of the three principal characters is an entomologist, another an entomophage.

Your novels always seem incredibly well-researched, often drawing upon specialised bodies of knowledge, for example, research into health and wellbeing, psychotropic drugs, animal communication, etc. So, could you tell us about the research you undertook on the environmental issues for your writing?

For *When the Killing's Done*, inspired by the removal of invasive species from the Santa Barbara Channel Islands, in addition to research about island biogeography (see David Quammen's magisterial *Song of the Dodo*, for instance), I was fortunate to get to go out in the field with the biologists tagging and monitoring the population of dwarf island foxes. Ditto with *Blue Skies*, with the exception that the field biologists were entomologists for the most part.

Your writing belies remarkable inter- or trans-disciplinarity, as well as a certain genre-fluidity. Is this just natural curiosity, a wish to be boundary-pushing and transgressive, a refusal to be pigeon-holed, or something else? Can you give us some idea of your ethos and/or modus operandi?

All the above, I suppose. I am an artist, making art. I know no boundaries or labels. I go where my interests take me and so my books and stories often reflect my passion (and worry) for the natural world. See a story like "Hopes Rise," for instance, in which I explore the radical decline in Batrachian populations worldwide.

Do you think there are 'conflicts of interest' between didactics and aesthetics—between wanting to convey a message and wanting to tell a story—and if so, how do you navigate them as a writer?

I abjure all messages in art. Art is for exploration. Period. If you begin with preconceived notions, you should write essays, not fiction. Art is a seduction, not a means of delivering political statements. That said, readers of my work will discover their own meaning and the reflection of my passions in the process of decoding the stories in their minds. All hail literature!

Do the arts have a part to play in the Climate Crisis, and if so in what way?

More and more, it seems to me, the central existential topic of our time—of all time—is the catastrophe we've wrought on the environment that gave rise to us. And, of course, fiction can have ten times the wallop of an essay because it so deeply involves our emotions.

Who or what inspires you as a writer—people, places, publications, etc.?

Being a creature among creatures in a mysterious universe that has no discernible meaning when our brains are hard-wired for meaning and purpose. Ultimately, nothing matters. But here we are, slowly dying, and everything around us is dying too. I'm often asked if there's any good news, and I say, "Yes, of course—in a mere three-and-a-half or four billion years the sun will expand and incinerate this big rock we so precariously ride and everything else on it as well."

Your latest novel, *Blue Skies*, is due out in May [2023]. On your blog you describe it as 'unfolding in the uncertain present and working through several even more uncertain years down the line. It deals with how regular people like you and me will live with the new normal and what it might mean in the larger context of our tenuous animal existence on this big hurtling rock we call home'. It sounds like what the British philosopher Rupert Read has called a 'thrutopia'. Can you talk about its evolution? And how does it differ from *A Friend of the Earth*, written twenty plus years later?

Blue Skies focuses on a single bicoastal family living a daily existence in the teeth of what the climate change foretold in *A Friend of the Earth* has already delivered. One of the ironies I explore lies in the fact that the protagonist, a young woman, has translocated from drought-ravaged California to sea rise-devasted coastal Florida. Oh, yes, and I as mentioned above, the insects are taking a big hit.

Are you working on any new 'ecofiction' projects?

I'm writing short stories at present and three of the six new ones have to do with facets of climate change and extinction. "Sanctuary," published in *Esquire*, has to do with politics and a butterfly sanctuary in Texas, while "Cold Summer" explores what happens when an individual decides to take global warming in his own hands sans reference to the rest of us.

You have an active presence on social media. Do you see this as an expectation of a modern writer? Do you find it enjoyable?

I'd never taken a photo in my life till my publisher put me on Twitter. And now, I never post sans a photo and the photos are often of nature, which sharpens my eye and appreciation too. I like the platform because it gives me a chance to perform for my readers and to learn from and be turned on by them. As for the expectations of a modern writer, to each his own. No expectations of others have any influence whatever on me. I'm going to what I'm going to do.

What about other forms of public engagement—book tours, festivals, talk shows, interviews—obligation or pleasure? And do you ever use them to discuss environmental issues?

I've always loved performing for an audience, so over the years I've done a lot of traveling with my books and have sat for infinite interviews in all media. I enjoy it, but only in season—i.e., in support of a given book. Otherwise I live a solitary life, reading and writing and spending as much time outside as I can.

As a writer you are vocal about the political situation. How important do you feel a certain level of awareness and engagement is for the modern author? Should politics and art be kept separate?

Again, an artist owes nothing to anyone. That said, if I am asked about my political or ecological views, I am pleased to express them.

Any advice for budding writers of ecofiction?

Follow the beat.

Finally, introduce yourself as a writer

For those who haven't read all my thirty-one books of fiction, I should say that you are in for a treat. I've been the grateful recipient of numerous prizes and I've published in most of the major magazines, most frequently in *The New*

Yorker. I earned my MFA and Ph.D. degrees at the Iowa Writers' Workshop, a process that saved me from a life of bar-hopping and distorted rock and roll. For a demonstration of what might have been but for the salvatory influence of literature, go to the Media section of tcboyle.com and listen to me screech out "I Put A Spell on You" with the Ventilators. Yes. And breathe a sigh of relief.

Index

A
Acidification 4, 76, 99
Agenda 45, 68, 91, 97–100, 109, 132, 146, 210, 225
Anglophone 75, 81
Anthropocene 5, 8, 13, 17, 24, 48, 67, 75, 98, 106, 139
Anthropocentric 39, 68, 104, 175, 179, 191
Archives 59, 66, 85, 117
Artificial Intelligence (AI) 24, 129, 146, 177, 235
Atmosphere 4, 43, 48, 57, 86
Author 6, 15, 17, 18, 21, 47, 56, 63–66, 80–82, 86, 87, 90–92, 100, 103, 107, 111, 113, 116, 131, 133, 134, 137, 139–141, 144, 145, 154, 161, 166, 169, 174, 177, 202, 213, 222, 224, 227, 229, 231–234, 239, 243, 247

B
Bard 181
Biocommunities 62, 102
Biodiversity 10, 36, 58, 76, 97, 99, 103, 161, 162, 206, 209, 217
Biome 46, 162, 179
Biosphere 17, 91, 99, 102, 112, 156, 183
Body Writing 50

C
Cartography 20, 21, 47, 58
Censorship 55
Character 20, 23, 36, 44, 45, 58, 63–66, 72, 83, 86, 88, 89, 93, 100–102, 108, 111–114, 116–120, 131, 134, 137, 140, 141, 146, 147, 149, 162, 166, 167, 190, 191, 193–195, 197, 198, 200–202, 204, 206–208, 210, 211, 213, 218–220, 222–225, 228, 230, 232, 233, 236, 237, 239, 240, 245, 249
Cli-Fi/Climate Fiction 18, 23, 65, 90, 137, 189, 190, 195, 206,

208, 213, 216, 224, 228, 229, 244
Climate change 3–6, 18, 25, 75, 76, 103, 106, 109, 112, 138, 165, 167, 168, 203, 206, 208, 213–215, 225, 227, 228, 232–237, 239–244, 248, 250, 251
Climate crisis 4, 6, 8, 18, 24, 40, 48, 49, 76–78, 87, 112, 163, 164, 173, 191, 196, 199–201, 203, 205, 207, 210, 214, 218, 221, 223, 225, 228, 231, 234, 237, 241, 244, 246, 250
Climate Denial 49
Climate emergency 14, 99, 100, 105, 110, 115, 116, 137, 237
Climate justice 76, 79, 80, 92, 99
Coastal 46, 134, 236, 250
Colonialism 76, 80, 87
Community 11, 17, 25, 43, 66, 68, 69, 79, 97, 101, 106, 136, 153, 157, 168, 174, 180, 181, 183, 184, 193, 245
Consciousness 10, 14, 17, 26, 35, 47, 80, 87, 90, 101, 102, 107, 132, 134, 144, 168, 194
Conservation 15, 58, 69, 206, 228
Countryside 22, 114
Creative assemblages 79, 102
Creative writing 40, 55, 57, 60, 92, 116, 176, 180, 206, 227, 235, 239
Creative Writing Courses 213
Creativity 5, 24, 89, 100, 146, 167, 178, 195
Criticism 68, 81, 109, 113, 169, 170, 184, 196
Cultural appropriation 24, 55, 68, 75, 80, 81, 137

D

Decolonising 22, 92

Deep mapping 23, 47, 48, 137
Deep place 23
Deforestation 4, 76, 99, 220, 226
Description 35, 41, 44, 46, 49, 50, 65, 93, 106, 138, 140, 179, 211
Desertification 46, 64, 142, 146, 160, 174, 198
Diachronic 136
Didacticism 24, 97, 161
Docemes 117, 129, 143, 144
Dogma 7, 24, 97, 98, 118
Drafting 134
Dystopia 11, 68, 69, 135, 153, 158–160, 163, 164, 166, 168, 235

E

Earth, planet 5, 10, 65–67, 78, 90, 106, 113, 138, 139, 147, 161, 180, 192, 193, 212, 236, 243–245
Ecobardic 204
Ecocide 8
Ecofiction 6, 7, 9, 11–13, 16–19, 21–23, 25, 35, 36, 40–43, 45, 46, 48, 49, 62, 64, 69, 76, 86, 89–92, 97–99, 102–105, 110, 113, 115, 116, 121, 123, 129, 130, 132, 135, 142, 145, 146, 153, 154, 157, 164, 166, 168, 169, 173, 176, 177, 179, 180, 182, 183, 189, 191, 192, 197–208, 212–214, 216, 218, 220–227, 229–232, 234, 235, 238, 239, 242–246, 248, 251
Ecoliteracy 25
Ecology 17, 58, 62, 156, 163, 184, 210, 225, 232, 234, 248
Ecosystems 4, 13, 14, 17, 22, 25, 35, 39, 40, 57, 106, 138, 161, 173, 174, 182–184, 200, 209, 224

Editing 121, 179, 231
Embodiment 59
Environment 5, 18, 35, 38–40, 48, 65, 67, 89, 101–103, 106, 123, 139, 142, 146, 176, 180, 192, 204, 239, 241, 243, 248, 250
Ergodic 25, 87, 147, 182
Ethics 17, 23, 75, 85, 174
Experiential 23, 46
Extinction Rebellion 24, 99, 110, 115

F

Fake news 146, 148
Feedback 130, 179, 200, 207, 233
Flash fiction 72, 130, 131, 194, 235
Food security 129
Forest 22, 37, 45, 46, 62, 63, 105, 175, 225
Fungi 175

G

Gender bias 22
Glaciation 4, 76, 233
Glacier 46
Global South 5, 22, 38, 75, 114

H

Habitat 4, 17, 37, 38, 40, 50, 76, 100, 108, 162, 221, 239, 242
Hegemonic 9, 13, 14, 23, 38, 90, 146, 160, 176
Holobionts 102

I

Indigenous rights 24, 75
Intersectionality 14, 76, 79, 80, 92, 99
Intertextuality 105, 134

IPCC 5, 49, 162

M

Manuscript 134, 143, 179, 197
Maps 48, 58, 59, 175
Markley, Stephen, 2023. The Deluge. New York: Simon & Schuster 119
Media 100, 110, 111, 117, 129, 168, 177–179
Modernism 108
More-than-human 12, 38, 39, 71, 89, 99, 103, 104, 106, 108, 118, 123, 132, 135, 175, 176, 179, 180, 182
Multimodality 178
Mycelia 23, 175, 177

N

Nature 4, 7–14, 16, 19, 21, 24, 26, 35, 38, 39, 47, 58–62, 78, 88–90, 98, 101–103, 106–109, 123, 129–131, 133, 141–143, 147, 156, 157, 160, 161, 166, 169, 176, 177, 180–182, 202, 203, 208, 209, 211, 215, 217, 218, 225, 228, 234, 239, 247, 248, 251
Nature writing 12–16, 21, 24, 25, 36, 40, 46, 49, 103, 123, 227
Neuronormal 24
New Nature Writing 14–16, 19, 21, 22
Non-anthropocentric 65, 71, 106, 133
Notebook 23, 26, 38, 39, 41, 44–47, 49, 68, 70, 109, 123
Novel 4, 8, 12, 18, 21, 46, 61, 62, 64–70, 72, 76, 77, 82, 86–89, 91, 98–113, 115–119, 121–123, 130, 131, 134, 136, 138–143, 145–147, 149,

153–155, 158, 161, 162, 165, 166, 169, 175, 177, 179, 180, 182, 192–194, 197, 198, 204–208, 216, 217, 222–227, 229–235, 239–243, 247–250
Novelist 36, 42, 60, 81, 86, 98, 100, 106, 112, 130, 131, 138, 164, 198, 200, 210, 211, 215, 230

O

Oceans 4, 46, 76, 99, 112, 135, 140, 193, 198, 210, 222, 225, 241
Ozone layer 99

P

Paratext 117, 142, 144, 145
Perception 23, 39–43, 47, 83, 93, 101, 118, 140
Phenomenology 19, 47, 78, 145
Place writing 16, 25
Plot 10, 45, 58, 65, 70, 77, 100, 105, 107, 111, 116–120, 143, 144, 175, 190, 204, 206, 208–210, 212, 214, 233, 237
Pollution 18, 193, 203, 214, 241, 246
Polycrisis 129, 130, 160
Postcolonial 90
Posthumanism 61, 160
Protest 81, 108, 110, 111, 216, 248
Publishing 22, 81, 100, 103, 145, 146, 177, 227, 239

Q

Qualia 23, 26, 44–46, 48

R

Reading 3, 6, 37, 55, 56, 84, 97, 101–103, 115, 116, 120, 133, 143, 144, 179, 181, 190, 194, 197, 214, 216, 222, 224, 225, 234, 240, 251
Representation 23, 24, 44, 62, 65, 67, 75, 76, 80–84, 92, 101, 149
Review 84, 98, 112, 179, 208, 209, 228, 233, 241
Rhizomatic 25, 45, 48, 174, 176, 183

S

Sea levels 18, 143
Senses 8, 9, 13–16, 18, 20, 23, 35–37, 40, 41, 43, 47–50, 58, 59, 62, 64, 65, 67, 71, 84, 98, 101, 102, 110, 117, 123, 130, 131, 137, 139–143, 145, 148, 155, 157, 168, 169, 176, 195, 196, 203, 210, 211, 219, 238, 245, 248
Sentience 61
Setting 4, 17, 58, 100, 103, 105, 106, 112, 161, 166, 191, 204, 209, 211, 213
Shifting baseline syndrome 129, 138
Short story 40, 42, 72, 90, 112, 130, 166, 206, 207, 235, 239, 244, 247
Situatedness 14, 20, 36, 136, 142
Solastalgia 48, 160, 175, 192
Storytelling 5, 24, 66, 67, 139, 140, 184, 196, 233, 241
Structure 23, 24, 67, 75, 99, 123, 129–133, 135, 136, 140, 141, 147, 149, 177
Synaesthesia 26, 145
Synchronic 136

T

Taproot texts 6, 10

Theme 13, 23, 26, 86, 88, 105, 106, 109, 123, 131, 147, 148, 167, 192, 204, 205, 209, 210, 212, 213, 215, 235, 243, 245
Thrutopia 24, 69, 112, 153, 163, 164, 168, 235, 238, 250
Thunberg, Greta 110, 115, 117
Tone 65, 161, 164–166
Transmedia 24
Trespass 123

U

United Nations 4, 77
Utopia 66, 110, 135, 153–156, 158, 166, 168, 169

V

Voice 14, 15, 22–24, 39, 71, 72, 75–78, 80, 84–86, 91–93, 108, 118, 122, 129, 131–133, 136, 145, 146, 148, 166, 194, 195, 210, 211, 249

W

Walking 16, 36, 109, 140, 180
Writer 6, 9, 13, 14, 20, 22–24, 35, 38–50, 55–59, 61–63, 65, 67, 68, 70, 75, 77, 82, 83, 85, 87, 89, 90, 98, 99, 102, 103, 106, 108, 115–117, 120, 123, 130–132, 134, 135, 138, 142, 143, 147, 153, 154, 158, 159, 161, 164, 165, 168, 173, 176–183, 190–192, 195, 196, 198–201, 203–207, 210, 211, 214, 215, 217–221, 223, 225, 228–238, 240, 241, 243–246, 249–251
Writing workshop 55, 92, 116, 180

Printed and bound by CPI Group (UK) Ltd, Croydon, CR0 4YY
03/12/2024
01799310-0015